Some Pioneer Women Teachers of North Carolina

Some Pioneer Women Teachers of North Carolina

Compiled by

The Delta Kappa Gamma Society
North Carolina State Organization

Committee On Pioneer Women In Education

Cordelia Camp, *Chairman*

Mamie E. Jenkins

Grace Van Dyke More

Hattie S. Parrott

1955

Preface

THESE one hundred and twelve sketches of pioneer women teachers in North Carolina are not all inclusive. The selection represents materials compiled within the past fifteen years by several chapters of Delta Kappa Gamma, in North Carolina. A greatly enlarged membership and a number of vigorous new chapters give promise of abundant material for a second volume.

However, this is the story of women in education in North Carolina throughout a century and a half. Its purposes is to show what has been done for the education of women in North Carolina and to show what has been done by women for education in the State.

It is divided into three parts: a brief history of the education of women in North Carolina, showing their emergence as teachers, supervisors, college instructors and professors, and administrators:; the biographies of more than one hundred women teachers of long and distinguished service; and a fairly complete list of the early schools for women with dates of establishment and their locations.

As to the accuracy of the historical survey, the reader's attention is called to the Bibliography at the end of the book. The biographies are based upon firsthand sources such as interviews, letters, and entries in journals and diaries. They were written by numerous members from the several chapters of Delta Kappa Gamma throughout the State. These human interest stories have been edited for the sake of some degree of uniformity yet the editor has endeavored to keep the general style and language of the writers. Here are the records of courageous, pioneer women who met the educational needs of the changing decades comprising this period of one hundred and fifty years.

The list of schools presents a continuity of the interest manifested in the education of women in North Carolina throughout the period involved in this study. The varied regions in which the schools were located, the discontinuance of many of them, and the consolidation of a few parallel the history of the geography and social development of the State.

It is the hope of those who have engaged in the Preparation of this book that the accomplishments of the biographees who in many instances carried on amid great difficulties and adverse circumstances will inspire many capable young women of the present and the future to enter the teaching profession and become forces of power and influence. Furthermore: "The burden which Western Civilization loads on the backs of education can be borne neither by ignoring the past nor the present. There must be a living union of the two."

The Committee of Delta Kappa Gamma is indebted to the many members of Delta Kappa Gamma in North Carolina who aided in the compilation of this volume. Deep appreciation is due to Miss Mamie Jenkins who gave yeoman service in the early years of the project. Thanks are extended to Dr. Christopher Crittended and his associates in the department of Archives and History for checking and arranging the list of schools, and grateful acknowledgement is made to Dr. A. L. Bramlett of Brevard College for reading the historical survey and offering constructive criticism.

C. C.

CONTENTS

CONTENTS (Continued)

Some Pioneer Women Teachers
of North Carolina

A Brief History of the Education of Women in North Carolina

By Cordelia Camp

G ENERAL indifferences to the education of women prevailed throughout the Colonial era in North Carolina and continued for a considerable portion of the nineteenth century. Although North Carolina developed before 1860 the most creditable system of public schools to be found in any of the states which seceded from the Union, her educational growth was very slow during the Colonial period.

This tardy development was largely due to the geography of the region. The dangerous coasts and poor harbors made the colony difficult of access. Also, for many years, the tendency was toward rural rather than urban communities. This rural character of the country proved a hindrance to education generally and especially to the social and literary development of the women in comparison to conditions in the neighboring colonies. For example, Colonial Records give an account of fashionable boarding schools in the coastal towns of Virginia, South Carolina, and Georgia, whereas no such schools are mentioned in North Carolina prior to the War of the Revolution.

Educational advantages for girls in any of the Southern colonies were restricted to the families of the well-to-do. These girls were either taught in their own homes by private tutors or sent to private schools. Moreover, a small number of girls was sent to England to attend school. For instance, North Carolina records show that Frances, daughter of John Rutherford, was sent with her two brothers to England to be educated after the death of her mother in 1768. However, judging from the activities of such groups of women who attended the Edenton Tea Party or who filed petitions to the authorities in behalf of the wives and children of Tories, it is evident that the better class of women was educated.

Here it is interesting to note that there are records of wills in which fathers provided for the tuition for the instruction of their daughters. A striking illustration is the will of John Baptista Ashe, dated November, 1731. This states: "I will that my daughter be taught to write and read and some feminine accomplishments which may make her agreeable." Yet there is no record that any schools were established to carry out these wills.

The first effort of the Colony itself to foster education began in 1695 when William Read, an orphan boy, was bound to Thomas Harvey to serve him until Read was twenty-one years of age. At this time the general court required that Harvey teach the boy to read and write and also teach him a trade. The same law applied to girls who were apprenticed. A Pasquotank County court in April, 1752, when binding Ann Stewart, ordered that her master "learn her to read and write."

On the other hand, girls were admitted to the elementary schools founded by the different religious denominations. The first denominational group to send teachers to the Colony was the Society for the Propagation of the Gospel in Foreign Parts, a missionary organization of the established Church of England. These missionaries served as lay readers and teachers. The German and Scotch immigrants and Quakers were especially active in founding schools for their children. Then, while the Presbyterians were particularly insistent that all their children learn to read, they were so zealous in securing education for the boys that they sometimes regarded girls "sufficiently learned if they could read the Bible, repeat the catechism and write a legible hand."

And yet despite the fact that the women of the more prosperous families, the girls belonging to the ambitious church groups, and the girls who were apprenticed could read and write, "a large majority of the seventeenth and eighteenth century women were totally illiterate, unable to write their names." This was true in all the Southern colonies.

Although it may be assumed that the mistress of the house aided the master by teaching apprenticed boys and girls to read, there is no record of such activity. The only recorded cases of women's teaching outside of church schools before the nineteenth century are in connection with Dr. Bray's Associates. This was an organization perfected in England "by a decree of chancery" in 1731 for the purpose of providing parochial libraries and the conversion of Negroes in the British plantations. It was closely associated with the Society for the Propagation of the Gospel in Foreign Parts and seemingly took in a broader scope of work than its original purpose provided. For example, Alexander Stewart, a missionary sponsored by the Society for the Propagation of the Gospel, wrote in his report of 1763:

"I accordingly baptized 6 adult Indians, 6 boys, 4 girls and 5 infants and for their further instruction (at the expence of a Society called Dr. Bray's Associates who have done me the Honor of making me Superintendant of their schools in this province) have fixed a school mistress among them to teach 4 Indian and 2 negro boys and 4 Indian girls to read and to work and have supplied them with books for that purpose."

Four years later John Bennett wrote to a Missionary Society in

2

his home town in England that it was his intention to start a school at Brunswick provided he could enroll fifteen pupils. He stated: "I had agreed with a widow woman here of good character . . . to teach the girls to Sew, knit, and Mark, but I cannot make up more than 8 or 9 therefore must for a time drop the design."

The women of the Moravian settlement were the first to take up teaching in a formal way. The Moravian records state that in 1778 "Sister Osterlain had charge of the school for several years until she married." And a little later: "The teacher of the girls' school has been getting three shillings a week and it is recommended that she be paid an additional shilling from the congregation." The school for little girls which was established at Salem in 1772 developed into Salem Academy and finally into Salem College.

The first organized movement by women themselves toward an educational cause came in the first decade of the 1800's. At that time groups of women in various towns began to organize Societies for the education of "poor female children." The first of these groups was the Newbern Female Charitable Society which was incorporated in 1812. This was soon followed by similar Societies in Fayetteville, Raleigh, and Wilmington. These groups usually rented a house which they turned over to a woman teacher. While this movement took place at the beginning of the nineteenth century, the work characteristically belongs in the eighteenth.

It is evident thus far that provision for the education of women came slowly in North Carolina and that their participation in teaching and other educational activities was in keeping with their opportunities for training. Educational opportunities for women and their contribution to the cause of education have gone hand in hand. The history of women in education in the State falls roughly into three periods: 1800-1860, 1860-1900, and 1900-1950.

1800-1860

From the standpoint of public education, the nineteenth century opened without emphasis being placed on the education of girls. Of the 177 academies chartered by the State before 1825 only thirteen were for women. The State provided a small sum for the chartered academies which enabled these to admit pupils who were unable to pay tuition. However, educational opportunities for girls were left largely to private schools.

In the period between the establishment of the Raleigh Female Academy in 1800 and 1840 no less than seventy-five schools for women were started in North Carolina. Many of these private schools flourished for only a few years yet others continued for quite a period of time or even became permanent institutions. A striking example of one of these private schools which became permanent is Salem College whose development has been previously mentioned. Among those estab-

3

lished during this period and which continued for a considerable length of time were Warrenton Academy, Hillsboro Female Academy, Louisburg Academy, and Charlotte Female School.

Since North Carolina had provided no facilities for educating women for teachers, many of the women who taught in these early schools came from the North, having been trained in Emma Willard's famous Female Seminary at Troy, New York. However, several other states were represented. A few specific names and teaching positions will serve as illustrations.

Among the teachers from New York were: Miss Beze at Newbern in 1809; Miss Nye at the Raleigh Female Academy in 1810; Miss Haskins who opened a female school at Wadesboro; Misses Elizabeth Slater and Mitchell who assisted the principal of Liberty Hall Academy at Salisbury in 1818; Miss Salmon at Smithfield Academy in 1827; Mrs. Harriet J. Allen, principal of Warrenton Female Academy about 1830; and Miss Harriet A. Dellay, assistant in the school at Jackson in Northhampton County in 1837.

From Connecticut came Mrs. Terrell to take charge of the Warrenton Female Academy in the 1820's. Miss Eliza Rea of Boston taught in the Asheboro Female Academy in 1839. Miss Abigail Mason of Pennsylvania came to Lincolnton to take charge of the girls' school. In fact, the phrase "from the North" is used frequently in the reports of the period. Miss Martha R. Richardson, "a young lady from the North," taught at Pleasant Grove Academy in Wake County; Miss Louise Moar, "a lady from the North," was conducting a school in Northhampton County in 1838. And Miss M. C. Street served in the Raleigh Academy in the late 1820's as "an experienced preceptress from the North."

Also, there are records of English women who taught in the State at this time. For instance, Mrs. Sarah Faulkner accompanied her husband to Warrenton and here she set up a school in 1802 and ran it continuously until her death in 1819.

Charles L. Coon lists the names of ninety-five women teachers in the period 1790-1840.

In the records of these schools there may be found an account of the everyday school life. For example, Jacob Mordecai who conducted a school for girls in Warrenton was assisted by his daughters Rachel and Ellen. Each girl was required to go to the well every morning with her tin basin and towel and bathe her hands, face, and neck, even though the weather might be so cold that the water would freeze as she bathed. Each girl reported daily to a Negro mammy for a hair dressing. She carried with her a comb and brush. After her hair was dressed, she dropped her name into a box. The names were checked by Miss Ellen and any delinquents were called to task. There were ninety girls enrolled in this school.

Frances Ormond Gaither gives in *Little Miss Cappo* an authentic description of life at Salem Academy about the first quarter of the nineteenth century. She tells that the girl arrives at the school riding horseback, is met by a man whose specific duty is to place her saddle in the saddle room for safe keeping until the time from two to four years hence when she will need it to ride home. He sells her horse and deposits the money for the purchase of another horse when needed. The author gives a picture of the rooms in the dormitory, tells how the girls adapt their clothes to their physical growth over a period of time, and gives the strict rules by which they must abide.

In 1836, the State was able to add directly to the Literary Fund, which had been established in 1825, the sum of $500,000 from the total sum received from the Federal Government's distribution of surplus revenue. Therefore since the Literary Fund now amounted to nearly $683,000 and was receiving considerable annual revenue, the Literary Board recommended to the Legislature a plan for beginning a system of elementary schools. The report was accepted and the Legislature of 1838-39 provided for an election to be held whereby the counties might vote on a plan of furnishing $20 for each school district within their respective borders and thus receive $40 from the Literary Fund. Accordingly public or common schools were established in the State, and in 1840 the State reported 141 academies and grammar schools and 623 elementary or common schools. The State had now provided a foundation in education for both sexes.

After 1840 a number of the leading schools for women began to adopt the name of college although their courses of study were little more than those offered in the female academies and boarding schools prior to that date.

In the decades 1840-60, the churches were very active in the education of women. A group of Methodists founded Greensboro Female College, now Greensboro College for Women in 1846. St. Mary's School in Raleigh was opened in 1842 by the Episcopal Church. Chowan Baptist Female Institute was founded in 1848 and closely following this were: Oxford Female College, sponsored by the Baptists, in 1851; Statesville Female College, now Mitchell College, established by the Presbyterians, in 1857; Davenport College, founded by the Methodists in 1858; and Peace Female Institute founded by the Presbyterians in 1857. In 1860, Governor John W. Ellis stated that there were thirteen female colleges in the State. These denominational schools supplemented the public schools of that era and served to bridge a gap until a system of secondary and higher education was developed.

A few parents sent their daughters to school outside of the State. For example, in 1841, Judge John Bryan sent his oldest daughter, Mary, to Miss Breshard's School in Washington, D. C. Later, the second daughter, Isabel, went to school in Reirstown, Maryland, whereas Charlotte, the third daughter, attended Miss Carpenter's School in Philadelphia.

5

However, the number of women who taught upon leaving school was a small one. These few who were interested in teaching went into the private schools to teach. There were two reasons for this. First, women teachers were looked upon with disfavor by the general public since it was thought that they could not discipline; and, in the second place, the public schools were not socially favored. The State report of the public schools in 1846 showed only nineteen women in a total of 1,487 teachers. Yet, on the other hand, Calvin H. Wiley who became State Superintendent of Public Schools in 1853 believed that women were in every sense equal to men teachers and that they were even better than men in controlling and teaching small children. He favored employing them whenever they were available. He encouraged poor girls from small farms and from factories to educate themselves through the common schools and by self help to take the examinations and become teachers. However, women came slowly into the public schools prior to 1860.

Such was the picture of women in education in 1860 when the War between the States, followed by the Reconstruction Period, disrupted the entire school system of the State.

1860-1900

The War between the States caused an increase of women in the public schools. Superintendent Wiley's report for 1863 showed that within four years the number of women teachers had increased from $7\frac{1}{2}$ percent of the total number in 1859 to 40 percent of the total number. The leaders in education were now beginning to realize the importance of women teachers in the schools. They saw, also, that instead of depending upon the North, the State must provide her own teachers. In 1862, the Reverend Dr. Kilpatrick, president of Davidson College, addressed the young ladies of Concord Female College on "The Duty of Females to the Future Education Interests of Our Country." In his address he asked the question: "Who is to teach the children when the bloody war shall close?" He answered this by saying that "for the first generation and possibly for more than one the work of teaching must be done by our educated women."

Through the help of women teachers, Wiley was able to report to Governor Jonathan Worth on January 18, 1865, that "the common schools had lived and discharged their useful mission through all the gloom and trials of the conflict; and when the last gun was fired the doors were still open and the teachers numbered their pupils by the thousands."

During the period of the War between the States and Reconstruction, many academies and private schools and those sponsored by churches were opened in various communities for both elementary and high school education. Private schools taught by women sprang up in many towns. Then, in the late 70's, graded schools were provided.

Thus women soon dominated the elementary field. The Summer Normal and Institute for teachers during the 80's and 90's gave women an opportunity to prepare for the teaching profession. The private high schools were generally coeducational. And tax supported high schools in many towns offered opportunities for those women who were not financially able to enter the newly established State Normal and Industrial School, church colleges, and the like.

In the last decades of the nineteenth century and in the first decade of the twentieth century, the female academies, institutes, and colleges for women which had been established before the middle of the 80's began to make their influence felt in teaching circles. At least seventy of the 112 women whose biographies are included in this book were born prior to 1860 and were educated in one of these institutions. These women generally made a contribution to education by teaching in private schools in the years following Reconstruction and many of them transferred to the public schools as soon as these were reestablished. A striking example is Miss Margaret Hearn who was educated in private schools, at the age of eighteen founded her own private school which she conducted for eleven years, then in 1881 began teaching in the public schools of Wilson and continued here for fifty-three years.

It was in 1860-80 that women began to play a part in higher education. An illustration is Mary Mendenhall who joined the faculty of Guilford College in 1878 and through her teaching, writing, and lectures promoted the cause of higher education for women.

Yet while women were teaching on all levels in these decades, private and church schools furnished the only facilities for higher education of their sex in North Carolina. Twenty-four such schools were reported at this time.

The State made a beginning of the professional training of women as teachers in 1877 when women were admitted to the Normal Summer School held on the campus of the University. That women were eager for this work was shown by the fact that 107 attended the six weeks' session. The number of men enrolled was 128. At this time over 600 women were teaching in the public schools of the State.

While the entrance of women to the University marks the beginning of large numbers to come, North Carolina as a state, made no general provision for the higher education of its women before the establishment of the State Normal and Industrial School in Greensboro in 1892. The State Normal numbered among the charter members or early members of its faculty a number of women who had received their basic education at private or church schools in the state and their advanced education out of the state. Among these were Gertrude Mendenhall, a graduate of Guilford College with a B. S. Degree from Wellesley; and Viola Boddie, a graduate of Littleton College with a degree from the Normal School at Nashville, Tennessee, now Peabody College. The second year came Mary Petty, a graduate of Guilford College, with a

7

B. S. Degree from Wellesley. The Misses Mendenhall, Boddie, and Petty remained on the faculty during the rest of their teaching careers. Other names listed in the faculty of early years were; Annie Petty, a graduate of Guilford College; Mary Settle Sharp from St. Mary's; Bertha Marvin Lee from Greensboro College; Sue Mae Kirkland, the first Lady Principal, a product of Nash and Kollocks' Select School for Young Ladies at Hillsboro; and Laura Hill Coit, a graduate of the Statesville Female College, (now Mitchell College) who remained on the faculty more than forty years.

The 1890's were outstanding in the establishment of institutions of higher learning for women. In 1891, the Baptists founded Meredith College in Raleigh and one year later the Presbyterian Church in the United States of America opened a normal school for girls in Asheville.

While the Asheville Normal expanded little in size or numbers of students it could accommodate, its academic standard was revised to keep pace with the demands of the State. In 1925, the institution was authorized to confer the degree of Bachelor of Education upon its graduates, and in 1929 it became a member of the North Carolina Conference. In 1933, it was placed on the list of accredited American Teachers Colleges. This institution trained hundreds of teachers for the western part of the State in a period when they were most needed. It was discontinued in 1944.

By 1920, the State Normal and Industrial School which had opened its doors in October, 1892, with an enrollment of 176 had become a standard four year college and its name had been changed to the North Carolina College for Women. Throughout these years the institution had enrolled over 10,000 women, 565 of whom had graduated. Numbers left without graduation yet went into the rural schools and small towns to teach. Later, the college was made a part of the Greater University of North Carolina and was given the name *Womans College of the University of North Carolina*. It has granted 10,070 degrees, and a large per cent of these graduates have entered the teaching profession.

In the same decade that Womans College was established at Greensboro, two State Normal Schools had their beginning: the State Normal School at Cullowhee and the Appalachian Normal at Boone. Both of these schools are coeducational and both have become accredited teachers colleges. In 1907, a third Normal School was established at Greenville. This is now an accredited teachers college.

As to the State University: the trustees first made women eligible to the regular session in 1897. The statement was to the effect that women should be admitted for graduate work. Edwin A. Alderman, president at that time, interpreted the ruling to mean that a woman who had finished any kind of college including junior colleges, was eligible. In the fall of 1898, six women were admitted: Sallie Stockard, Dixie Lee Bryant, Mary L. McRae, Alice Jones, Martha Latham, and Susan Williams Moses. Sallie Stockard was the first woman to register and the first woman to graduate. An interview with Alice Jones in 1951 has given a glimpse into the life of these early "coeds":

"We dressed just as if we were going to church—hat, gloves, and the like. We pulled off one glove to take notes in class. It was wonderful in Chapel Hill in those days. We were invited to many social functions and the girls who danced had a wonderful time dancing with the boys. The boys resented our being there, but in the evenings and during off-school hours we were very popular socially. Some of us felt a great responsibility in that we realized that we were making history. The professors were hard on us and we studied diligently."

1900-1950

This is a period of rewards and fulfillment. Women have become leaders in significant movements and have achieved success in many fields of education.

About the turn of the century the number of women teachers in the public schools increased rapidly. In 1910, Dr. J. Y. Joyner, State Superintendent of Public Instruction, reported a total of 11,156 white teachers of which 6,431 or 55 per cent were women. As this number increased and as advantages for higher education expanded, women gradually entered supervisory and administrative positions, served in the Department of Public Instruction, or became instructors in the various colleges and universities. They were admitted as students in practically all of the institutions of higher learning in the State.

The attitude of the professors at the University of North Carolina toward the capabilities of women for learning has changed to a marked degree. Despite the statement of Dr. Cain, head of the Department of Mathematics, that the entrance of women into the University would not trouble him since they could not learn mathematics, Marcia Latham in connection with her A. B. degree in 1900 was awarded the Cain prize for the best work in mathematics.

In the fall of 1917, the University opened its doors to freshmen women who were living with their parents or with relatives in Chapel Hill. The School of Pharmacy was opened to women regardless of where they lived. In the academic year 1917-18, the number of women exceeded any previous enrollment. In 1924, Anna Forbes Liddell of Charlotte and Irene Dillard of Clinton, South Carolina, had the distinction of receiving the first earned doctors degrees granted to women at the University. Mrs. Marvin Stacy was officially made the first Dean of Women in the spring of 1919 and began her duties that fall. Spencer Hall, the first dormitory for women on the campus was opened in 1923. Women continued to enroll in all departments. By 1945 the University had granted 742 graduate degrees to women, and by 1950 the enrollment of women had reached 944. These were housed in six dormitories

9

erected especially for women. Three national sororities are maintained by women on the campus.

In the closing days of 1924, a second university for North Carolina was suddenly announced to the people. In 1838, the Methodists and Quakers of Randolph County established a school to which the Reverend Brantly York, leader of the movement, gave the name Union Institute. Four years later it was chartered as Normal College, and in 1859 with its named changed to Trinity College it passed into the service of the Methodist Church. In 1892, the College was moved to Durham where it at once entered upon a new life. In December, 1924, James B. Duke offered to the trustees a building fund of $6,000,000 with the stipulation that the name be changed to Duke University. Later he added $2,000,000 to the building fund for the creation of the Duke Foundation carrying a trust fund of $40,000,000. Within a few years the new Duke University was built about a mile west of the Trinity campus and the latter was developed into a great coordinate college for women. These women students share all the advantages of the entire university on equal basis with men, and a goodly percent of the faculty are women.

Since the opening of the century the entrance of women to the faculties of the colleges in the State has been phenomenal. An examination of the catalogs of 1952 for thirty-two accredited junior and senior colleges shows an approximate total of 660 women on the faculties, and about 100 of these hold the Doctor's Degree.

Women have entered the area of urban and county supervision on a large scale. This work began in 1910 under the stimulation of L. C. Brogden, State Agent for Rural Elementary Schools. At first the work was on an elementary basis financed by a grant from the Peabody Fund. In 1920, the State made a substantial allotment for rural supervision and the work began in earnest. In that year thirty counties employed supervisors all of whom were women. While supervision experienced a hard struggle during the depression of the 1930's and during World War II, the work has continued in the State exclusive of those in specific subjects.

In chronological order, L. H. Jobe, Director of Division of Publication in the State Department of Education, has made a survey of *First's* among women in service of a State-wide nature and through State government commission and boards whose work was in the field of education, particularly in educational administration. His report is as follows:

1915. Miss Mary O. Graham of Charlotte was elected first woman president of the North Carolina Education Association. She was followed by Miss Elizabeth Kelly of Franklin who served in 1924 and Miss Annie M. Cherry of Enfield who served in 1930.

1916. Miss Hattie S. Parrott of Kinston was appointed by the Governor to serve for five years on the State Textbook Commission, the

10

first woman to serve on this Commission. Members of the Commission took the oath of office as administered by the Chief Justice of the Supreme Court of North Carolina. The record shows that Hattie S. Parrott was the first woman to take the oath of office to serve on an educational commission in the State.

1917. Miss Elizabeth Kelly of Franklin was the first State Director of School for Adult Illiterates in North Carolina.

1917. Miss Hattie S. Parrott was appointed and elected first chairman of the North Carolina State Board of Examiners and Institute Conductors. Other members of this Board to serve for four years with Miss Parrott, 1917-21, were two women also pioneering in State educational programs: Miss Susan Fulghum of Goldsboro and Mrs. T. E. Johnston of Salisbury.

1921. Miss Ethel Terrell of Asheville, now Mrs. Guy Weaver of Asheville, was Superintendent of Buncombe County Schools, the first woman to be elected to that office in North Carolina. During the same year, Miss Mable Evans of Manteo, now Mrs. O. Jones of Manteo, was elected Superintendent of Dare County Schools.

1921. Miss Mary Arrington of Rocky Mount was the first woman to serve on the North Carolina State Board of Vocational Education.

1929. Miss Elizabeth Kelly of Franklin was the first woman to serve on the State Equalization Board.

Looking in retrospect over the years one may conclude that women may justly feel proud of the contribution they have made to the cause of education in North Carolina and of the advancement they have made. Now that all avenues in the profession are open to them and the State has provided opportunities for women equal to those for men, the next half century will doubtless be marked by great professional advancement on the part of women. Quite likely they will produce additional textbooks, a greater number of books of a professional nature, and hold a greater number of administrative positions. Above all: women are in a position to do a higher quality of teaching on whatever level they may choose to work.

11

BIBLIOGRAPHY

Spruill, Julia Cherry, *Women's Life and Work in the Southern Colonies*, Chapter. IX and Pp. 109, 193, 205; Chapel Hill, 1938.

Grimes, M. C., *North Carolina Wills and Inventories, Pp.* 16, 21, Raleigh, N. C., Edwards and Broughton, 1912.

Knight, Edgar W., *Documentary History of Education in the South, before 1860*, Vol. I, pp. 91, 93, 176, Chapel Hill, Univ. N. Carolina Press, 1949.

Foote, William Henry, *Sketches of North Carolina*, p. 518, New York, R. Carter, 1846.

Smith, Charles Lee, *History of Education in North Carolina*, P. 176, Washington, Govt. Printing Office, 1888.

Gaither, Frances Ormond, *Little Miss Cappo*, New York, Mac-Millan, 1937.

Johnson, Guion, *Ante Bellum North Carolina*, P. 306, Chapel Hill, University North Carolina Press, 1937.

Henderson, Archibald, *North Carolina*, Vol. II, P. 366, Chicago, Lewis Publishing Co., 1941.

Noble, M. C. S., *History Public Schools in North Carolina*, Pp. 241-249, Chapel Hill, University N. C. Press, 1930.

Battle, Kemp Plummer, *History of the University*, Raleigh, Edwards and Broughton, 1907.

Records of the Womans College of the University of North Carolina.

Catalogues of the University of North Carolina, 1917-1920, Inc.

Catalogues of thirty-two North Carolina Colleges, 1949-1950.

Beiennial Report of L. C. Brogden, 1910-1912.

Educational Directory of North Carolina, 1950-51.

JULIETTE GRAVES ADAMS

1858-1951

WHENEVER modern musical education is discussed, the name of Mrs. Crosby Adams emerges as that of a musical pioneer. She had sound principles upon which the musical ideas of today are based. After a long and busy career devoted to artistic ideals, Mrs. Adams still maintained all her youthful interests, especially in her contacts with the young, and in her training of teachers who planned to work with children. Ernest Hutcheson pronounced her "the foremost composer of music for children in America."

Although her special field was creating music for young people, her compositions cover a wide range. She was also a crusader for better church music, and, at the age of eighty, wrote a book entitled, "Studies in Hymnology," which was enthusiastically welcomed by musicians, ministers, and laymen, alike, as filling a great need in promoting good church music.

Mrs. Crosby Adams, Dean of North Carolina Composers, was born Juliette Aurelia Graves at Niagara Falls, New York, March 25, 1858. By the time she was fourteen she was teaching piano and playing the organ in her home town. At twenty-one she began teaching in Ingram University, LeRoy, New York, working under the musical guidance of Claude Crittendon, who had been a pupil of Liszt.

On September 18, 1883, she married Crosby Adams whom she had known since childhood. They were born in the same town, attended the same schools and church, and they sang in the same choir. They moved to Buffalo where Mrs. Adams became a successful teacher, a capable organist, and a concert pianist. Because of Mr. Adams' ill health, they moved from Buffalo to Kansas City, Missouri, where they lived for four years. They left Kansas City and moved to Chicago, where in 1892 they organized the Crosby Adams School of Music. Their classes in public school music had the distinction of being the first two-year course in public school music in America. In 1904 they held their first Summer Class for Teachers. For forty summers music teachers came from everywhere to listen and absorb the ideas of the Adamses.

In May, 1908, Mrs. Adams held her first Dolls Music Festival which she was to continue for many years. One day she was struck by the fancy that a small doll in a nearby cabinet was enjoying the

13

music. From this idea grew the festivals—annual affairs at which the girls brought their dolls to be the audience for the recitals. Before long, the idea grew to include children who could not attend—ones who had little of the pleasant things of life—and Mrs. Adams asked each little girl to bring a doll to "go away," as well as one of her own favorites, so that other children could share their pleasures. Later the time was changed to December, when it became a Christmas festival for the dolls.

After twenty-one years of teaching and creative work in Chicago, Mr. and Mrs. Adams came to Montreat, North Carolina, in 1913. Here, in the mountains, they built their picturesque home, "House-in-the-Woods." The world which they left behind soon found its way to their remote retreat, where they spent the remaining years of their lives. Here Mrs. Adams was known and loved not only as a student, educator, concert pianist, composer, penwoman, collector, lover of all things beautiful, home-maker, but also to all, as a rare friend. It is said that as a homemaker she never bought a loaf of baker's bread in sixty-four years.

North Carolina, the adopted state of Mrs. Adams, paid tribute to her in many ways. The State Federation of Women's Clubs voted her the outstanding woman musician in 1926. Later her name was presented at the Sesquicentennial in Philadelphia as the woman who had done most for the progress of music in North Carolina. She was the recipient of two honorary degrees—Doctor of Music. The first was conferred on her by Converse College, Spartanburg, South Carolina, in 1932; and the second, by the Woman's College of the University of North Carolina, Greensboro, North Carolina, in 1945, when she was at the age of eighty-eight.

From the time of her very first composition, "The Dance of the Marionettes," and of the publication in 1896 of "Opus 1, Five Tone Sketches," recognition came to her. Understandably, innumerable honors were conferred on Mrs. Adams during her ninety-three years. Among them were a Life Membership in the National Federation of Music Clubs in 1923 and in the Music Teachers' National Association in 1936. She was a member of the National Association of American Composers, Conductors, and Poets; Hymn Society of New York City; Friends of Music, Washington, D. C.; and honorary member of Mu Phi Epsilon and Pi Kappa Lambda—Music Fraternity, and Delta Kappa Gamma—Honorary Teachers Society. She was founder and first president of the Asheville Branch of the national League of American Penwomen and later the State President.

In 1948, when Mr. and Mrs. Adams were both ninety, the Chicagoland Music Festival paid them the highest tribute in the world of music. They were the guests of honor on this occasion and she played a number of her compositions in a stadium seating 100,000, during which 600 Girl Scouts, costumed as dolls, lined the pathway along which Mr. and

Mrs. Adams rode, as a tribute to her Dolls' Festival. To commemorate their endeavors and accomplishments, the Crosby Adams Fine Arts Building at Montreat has been dedicated to them, in which is housed their famous collection of rare shells, their collection of baskets, her pianos, and, her priceless collection of music.

Mrs. Adams gave an annual concert on her birthday at Anderson College, Anderson, South Carolina, until her ninety-third year, when illness and failing strength prevented it. Death came to her on November 9, 1951, only a few months after the death of Mr. Adams, February 27, 1951. It is impossible to separate Mr. and Mrs. Adams in one's thinking either in life or death. She often said, "I owe to Mr. Adams much of the inspiration of both teaching and composing. Together, we have walked down life's highway with a harmony of purpose and a complete understanding and appreciation of each other." It has been said of her that "she made her life a pattern of symphonic understanding." She had the power to be, to think, to create, and to inspire.

KATE ALBERTSON
1867-

Miss KATE ALBERTSON, who served the State of North Carolina in every teaching position except that of college president, was retired in 1934 after more than forty years of service.

Her long career took her from a tiny Pasquotank County country school to the deanship at Saint Mary's School and Junior College, Raleigh, and her students can be found in every town and hamlet of the State. And during those forty years, Miss Albertson became well-known as a writer of Albemarle history, as a poet, and as a great booster in the State's school system.

The history of Miss Albertson's career uncovers a graphic picture of the advancement of the educational system in North Carolina.

Teaching as a profession came to Miss Kate quite by accident. Her sister, Miss Marcie Albertson, had accepted a position at Salem School in Pasquotank County, but, when the time came for her to take up her duties, poor health prevented her from doing so. Thus, in the fall of 1894, Miss Kate presented herself at the school door. Principal, teachers, and students were greatly surprised yet she was cordially accepted. Here, at a salary of $30 a month, with $15 deducted for board and lodging, she began her teaching career.

The following year Miss Kate went to the Shawboro School in Currituck County, then in 1898 she returned to Elizabeth City to teach in the Atlantic Collegiate Institute, which was under the guidance of one of Albemarle's greatest educators, S. L. Sheep. Later, when the

Institute became a public school, she was made principal and remained there in that capacity until 1919.

At that time Miss Albertson had an offer from Laurel Springs, near Sparta, in Alleghany County, which would, according to letters from the school board, pay $90 a month. This salary was an almost unheard of figure for school teachers at that time. An added attraction to this position was the announcement that Music, Latin, and French would be taught. It was supposed that these courses would greatly enlarge the school's enrollment since they were rarely found in one school at that time. Therefore, with such allurements, Miss Kate accepted the position.

In making the journey to Laurel Springs, she was forced to make the last part of her trip in a buggy drawn by mules. To her astonishment, when she reached there, she found that the place was hardly more than a settlement.

Her first night in the mountains was one she never forgot. She spent it in the home of the principal. Her room had no glass in the windows, a dirt floor, and cracks in the ceiling that were so large she was able to look up at the stars.

Nevertheless, upon rising the next morning, she was happy at the thought of her new work. But she soon found that "All that glistens is not gold." While the principal was ambitious in his quest for a teacher of "French, Latin, and Music" in order to have, what he termed, "a select and cultured school," only two students enrolled for Music. The price was twenty-five cents a lesson, and the lessons were given on the church organ because the school did not possess a piano. Also, instead of receiving $90 a month for her teaching, Miss Kate discovered that the school could only afford to pay her $5 a month which was what she was paying for board and lodging.

However, Miss Kate liked the mountains in spite of all the disappointments and the fact that she could not get lodging any nearer the school than eight miles. Every day she walked this distance through fields, meadows, and woods.

After teaching for three weeks and seeing no prospects of receiving a salary, she went to the principal and asked him for her pay. He thrust his hand into his pocket and drew out a 50-cent piece which he gave her for the three weeks' teaching. Immediately, Miss Kate decided she had better go home since her "salary" was not providing for actual expenses.

Next, she worked as a reporter for *The Daily Advance* in Elizabeth City and served as correspondent for *The News and Observer* and other State papers. Later she became superintendent of schools at China Grove and remained there for three years. Following that, she served two years as Extension Field Secretary for Parent-Teacher Associations at North Carolina College for Women. She was the first field agent for the Parent-Teacher Association and was instrumental in the organization of groups in fifty-seven counties.

In 1925, Miss Kate joined the staff of Saint Mary's, acting as Dean of Women. It was here that she and her sisters had attended school in former years when the campus was always referred to as a "Grove." She considered her seven years at Saint Mary's the happiest of her teaching career. During the depression, the deanship was abolished and she returned to Elizabeth City to teach in the public schools.

Miss Albertson was a writer as well as a teacher. Her shorter writings are: "In the Ancient Albemarle," "Roanoke Island in History and Legend," and "Legends of the Dunes of Dare." She, also, collaborated in the writing of the book, *The Romantic Record of Peter Francisco*. Francisco was one of her ancestors and a soldier in the Revolutionary War.

MARY LOVE ALDERMAN
1857-1934

"MISS MAMIE" ALDERMAN was indeed an educator in the true sense of the word. If, in her day, there had been the now popular "First Citizen" or "Teacher of the Year" awards, she would have undoubtedly qualified for first place in Wilmington.

Mary Love Alderman, daughter of Archie and Laura Love Alderman, was born June 6, 1857, in Wilmington, North Carolina. Here she grew up, acquired an education, lived, worked, and died. For fifty-three years, she operated her own private school in her home town.

She was a graduate of the old Tileston Normal School of which Miss Amy Bradley, another prominent educator, was principal. After graduation in 1875, Miss Alderman was employed to teach in her alma mater.

When the Tileston Normal School "folded up" in 1881, she opened a private school in her own home and ran it continuously for fifty-three years. This continuous success, even while the expanding public school system was gradually bringing the era of small private schools to an end, is testimony to the need it filled. Miss Alderman was one of those rare educational leaders who was in advance of her time in her methods of teaching. Many were the "misfits" in the public schools who were successfully adjusted in her school and who bless her name today. She possessed a brilliant mind which emphasized thoroughness and an understanding of the practical and the cultural branches of learning. She was also tactful and skilful in imparting knowledge to pupils.

Miss Alderman's teaching career was ended by her death on October 5, 1934. The stately old residence on North Fifth Avenue, in which the school was conducted, she bequeathed to her niece and co-teacher, Miss Laura Carpenter, who with her father and sisters still occupies it.

17

MARY DAVIS ALLEN
1862-

IT has been said: "To understand Louisburg College, one must recapture the spirit which prevailed in 1896 when Mary Davis Allen first became connected with the institution, the condition which existed at her departure in 1920, and know the College of 1953." Indeed, the life story of Mary Davis Allen is that of a woman equipped with personality, talent, common sense, enthusiasm, and also a willingness to put these to work for the benefit of mankind. And all of these assets were in full play throughout her connection with Louisburg College.

She was the daughter of Matthew S. Davis and Louise Hill Davis and came from a stock of distinguished leaders and educators. Her ancestors include: Green Hill, prominent in the days of Francis Asbury and early Methodism; Dr. John King, active in the same cause; Nicholas Long, officer of the Revolution; Charles Applewhite Hill, many years a teacher in Franklin and Warren Counties; and Charles A. Hill, author of the Literary Fund law of 1825 which was really the beginning of public education in North Carolina. Her father, Matthew S. Davis, was Principal of Louisburg Academy for a quarter of a century, then became President of Louisburg College.

Mary Davis attended school in Louisburg and in Franklin County, and received careful instruction under her father. At the age of sixteen, she began her teaching career at Arcola, a rural school in Warren County, where she taught nine years. Then she was asked to teach in Littleton College. At the end of one year at Littleton, Miss Davis was offered a position at Louisburg Junior College which she accepted.

Thus, in 1896, Mary Davis began a career in an institution with which for the twenty-four succeeding years her name, work, and influence were to be closely intertwined.

When she went to Louisburg there was no money in sight, the College property was in the hands of Mr. Washington Duke of Durham, and it looked as if the institution would be compelled to close its doors. A delegation of Louisburg citizens went to Miss Davis and requested her to take over. She consulted with her father, and they decided to make an attempt to carry on the work. It was agreed that Matthew S. Davis would become President of the College and that his daughter, Mary, would serve as Lady Manager.

For about a decade all went according to plan. Then, on February 26, 1906, Matthew S. Davis died; and, since Louisburg was still a privately owned institution, no one wanted the presidency. Finally, Mary Davis, who had now become Mrs. Ivey Allen, agreed to become president, thus succeeding her father. By degrees she gathered around her a faculty of scholarship and ability, well fitted to carry on the work

18

of the College. In 1910, upon her solicitation, the College property was given to the North Carolina Conference of the Methodist Church South by Mr. Benjamin N. Duke who had inherited it as a legacy from his father. Following this change, the College plant was enlarged. The M. S. Davis Memorial Building was erected in 1913, and in that same year a central heating plant was installed.

In 1920, Mrs. Allen with characteristic broad view felt that the further expansion of the institution required the services of a man especially trained for that sort of task. Therefore she resigned. Here it is interesting to note that upon her resignation she was tendered by the people of the town and county a farewell dinner, held on the campus of the College. Speeches of appreciation and praise of her work were made by leading citizens.

From Louisburg, Mr. and Mrs. Allen went to the Oxford Orphanage. Here Mr. Allen became treasurer of the Orphanage, and Mrs. Allen became a teacher in the Orphanage high school. Mrs. Allen's services in that capacity lasted for a period of twenty-five years.

Mr. and Mrs. Allen retired from active work in 1946 and went to Warrenton to make their home. Mr. Allen died a few years afterward. In 1953, Mrs. Allen celebrated her ninety-first birthday.

MRS. J. M. BARBEE
1854-1947

"JOHN, rise and shine!" Jennie Jones Barbee was wont to challenge, her chin high, her voice deep and dynamic, her eyes humorous, yet compelling.

Seventy-one of her ninety-three years Mrs. J. M. Barbee spent in the classroom, teaching boys and girls, sixty-three of those years in her native North Carolina and thirty-four in its capital city, Raleigh. During her last two years of service she wrote a *History of the Raleigh Public Schools, 1876-1942*. In 1941, she received from the Woman's College of the University of North Carolina the degree of Doctor of Education. In those last years the Barbee Association was organized in her honor by her former pupils, now leading citizens of Raleigh, to celebrate her birthday annually and to help needy students the year around. In 1936, she, as an honorary member, received the Delta Kappa Gamma key. In 1934, on her eightieth birthday, the State of North Carolina granted her, unsolicited, an *A* grade certificate as she held no standard degree. And an elementary school of Raleigh was named for her.

19

But honors meant little to this great teacher who spent her life helping boys and girls to grow in favor with God and man.

Jennie Jones was born on February 22, 1854, in Burke County, the daughter of consecrated Christian parents, the Reverend and Mrs. Robert Jones. Her early training took place in private schools. In 1867, she entered Chowan College and in 1871 was graduated at the age of seventeen. The same year launched her on her long teaching career. For ten years she taught in Shelby, Kernersville, and in Wake County. During her stay in Wake County, she married J. M. Barbee. In 1881, she entered the Raleigh school system where she remained until 1916 at which time she resigned to teach in Florida. Again in 1923, she and her husband returned to Raleigh, and she resumed her duties in the Raleigh schools where she remained until her retirement in the spring of 1942. Her last years were spent in Greensboro with her son and daughter-in-law. Enfeebled somewhat by age, but alert in mind and heart, she was to the end "elect lady and beloved teacher" until her death on June 20, 1947.

Mrs. Barbee's early life, both before and after the War between the States, was spent during the time that the South was undergoing its most trying ordeal. Educational advantages were poor; living was restricted; and there were few schools for the training of teachers. Yet Mrs. Barbee made her own opportunities: she was always learning and growing, reading professional books, taking correspondence courses, attending summer schools.

Through the years, she taught in all grades; but her finest teaching was done, perhaps, with high school students in mathematics. Here she took pride in using illustrations and various objects that might be at hand. Few pupils failed, and this is easily understood.

Her tools were text books and the wisdom that they held; her business was the training of boys and girls, physically, mentally, spiritually. How she did it is hard to explain; but she was so honest, so hard working, so ambitious for each pupil, so anxious to help, that she impressed and inspired them. If there were anything to be brought out in a student, Mrs. Barbee developed that possibility. She knew the psychology of the adolescent; she made it her business to know also the background of the individual, his handicaps, his advantages. Boys, she said, were perhaps drawn to her more than girls. Boys understood her langauge; her vigor; her quick, abrupt way of talking; her flashes of humor that delighted the boys but sometimes left the girls a little puzzled.

She had a quick, emphatic way of saying: "John, rise and shine!" John arose, even if he did not always shine. He grinned when she would tersely say, "Sit down." Mary would have blushed and been confused. Mrs. Barbee was tall and commanding, full of quaint sayings and wit. Her keen eyes were kindness itself, but she could be stern enough when she was displeased. There were times when the adolescent youngster, feeling his importance, would swagger in, seeming to dare her. She would flash those piercing eyes upon him, silent for the moment; then, "Young man!" That was all. The swagger left him, and he was but a little boy again, blushing, repentant, meek. Then the flashing eyes were loving, forgiving eyes; and the boy understood full well that it was not he but the deed that was condemned.

Then, Mrs. Barbee's technique was her own. Her manner in the school room was enthusiastic, happy, sympathetic. Knowing her students so well, she made little personal jokes, kept up her interest in sports, in school, in all community affairs. She found in each activity some approach to her subject matter of mathematics; also, she never missed a chance to stress the lessons of good citizenship. She ever sought to arouse the ambition of each boy and each girl. She was an indefatigable worker, going to school early, coming home late, with her satchel full of papers to be corrected before the next day. She described herself as an "old time teacher." Her pupils felt free to go to her with their problems; and during out-of-school hours she taught many a lesson in fine living, through helpful guidance, given as friend to friend.

Though she spent most of the time in the schoolroom, she found time to be a good neighbor, visiting parents and sick children. Where there was sorrow, there was Jennie Barbee; where there was good fortune, she was there, also, rejoicing with the family. She even helped her less fortunate pupils to procure food and clothing that they might attend school, doing this in so tactful a manner that none of the underprivileged students ever knew it.

When asked for a note of appraisal of Mrs. Barbee's work, John A. Park, editor of *The Raleigh Times* and a member of the Barbee Association, wrote:

"My evaluation of Mrs. Barbee as a teacher includes also the appraisal as a citizen that would probably transcend the rating which she has enjoyed for many years in educational circles.

"As one of "her boys," I am proud of the inspiration that came to me from her unsolicited, an inspiration that included not only her love of mathematics, but also an experience that I have prized even more highly in later years in which the fundamentals of citizenship were more artfully injected.

"Another reason for my appreciation for Mrs. Barbee is the fact that her accomplishments were not confined to a small group of her students. They were for all who were fortunate enough to have personal association with her."

For all her modesty, her self abnegation, such a life as hers could not be hidden; and business men, professional men, judges, men and women of all classes who have come under her influence have risen up to call her blessed.

GRACE BEARD BATES
(1861-1950)

and

MRS. MARY B. SHERWOOD

HIGH on hill on the outskirts of Raleigh is an elementary school that bears the name—Sherwood-Bates. The selection of this name met with the enthusiastic approval of the citizens of Raleigh.

Some of the young women who taught in this school the year it opened in 1950 and many of the parents of the children attending had fallen under the influence of the two sisters for whom the school was named—Miss Grace Bates and Mrs. Mary Bates Sherwood.

Both of these teachers grew up in Raleigh and for half a century both taught in the Public Schools and saw the system expand from one building at the foot of Fayetteville Street where the Memorial Auditorium now stands to ten elementary schools scattered throughout the city and two high schools.

Both maintained an active interest in such community organizations as the Womans Club, the Literary and Historical Association and the Daughters of the Revolution.

They were faithful members of the First Presbyterian Church and for years taught the young people of this church.

Those who came in contact with them in church, community and school felt the quiet strength of their Christian faith, enjoyed their delightful sense of humor and were inspired and helped through their teaching.

Mrs. Sherwood was born in Raleigh on October 11, 1866—the year after "the surrender."

The first school she attended was taught by Mrs. W. C. Kerr, the wife of Dr. W. C. Kerr, the State geologist. When about eleven years of age she entered the Raleigh Public school then held in the old Governors Mansion at the foot of Fayetteville Street. The year that she was sixteen there were so few pupils in the seventh grade this grade was closed and she went to Peace Institute, now Peace Junior College, and in 1885 she graduated.

The next January she took the county examination and taught at Cedar Fork in Wake County for two months. For this work she received seventy-five dollars. In the fall of 1886 she began teaching in the Centennial school which had replaced the Old Governors Mansion.

In 1888 she married Mr. Frank Sherwood and two sons were born to them—Dr. Frank Sherwood who now teaches at North Carolina State College and Fleming Sherwood who died of tuberculosis contracted during his service in World War One.

After the death of her husband in 1894 Mrs. Sherwood returned

22

to teaching and until her retirement at the age of seventy-five she taught in the grades and later served as principal of the Wiley School.

Miss Grace Bates was born in Raleigh on November 28, 1861 and was educated first in a private school and then in the public school. She graduated from Peace Institute and at the age of sixteen began a teaching career that lasted for over forty years. Always her work was in Raleigh and always it was with beginning children.

Miss "Gracie" as she was called lost her sight and for ten years was totally blind. During her years of blindness she seemed not merely resigned but she was radiant and happy—always busy crotcheting mats for friends, listening to recording of music and stories, keeping up with radio programs and above all chatting with friends—old and young. Her living room was a place where a visitor would always find good conversation and would always leave with a better feeling toward life in general—when Miss Bates underwent an operation and recovered her sight her reaction was typical of her outlook on life—thankfulness that she was permitted to see again with no thought of bitterness for the years spent in darkness. She was far too busy catching up on her reading and getting accustomed to such changes as short skirts on middle aged women!

Mrs. Sherwood and Miss Grace Bates were unusually close to each other throughout their lives and they were not separated by death. Mrs. Sherwood was stricken while attending a church meeting and was taken to the hospital where she died on October 13, 1950. On October 5 while Mrs. Sherwood was still unconscious Miss Bates died.

In Raleigh today and scattered throughout the country are men and women who have been influenced by these two Christian women who devoted their lives to working with young people. Teachers are today passing on to another generation of children many of the ideas and ideals that they received from contact with Miss Grace Bates and Mrs. Sherwood either as children in the classroom or as fellow teachers in the same building.

In an effort to find why these two quiet, unassuming women had such a lasting influence on so many people some of their ex-pupils were questioned. Some mentioned the love for different types of literature instilled in them; others remembered the emphasis always on the best not only in literature but in art, music and human behavior. Their serenity, their optimism and their sense of humor had impressed many. All felt that both Mrs. Sherwood and Miss Grace had taught out of the overflow of rich lives—lives dedicated to truth, and goodness and beauty.

MOLLIE LUCAS BEAM
1867-1951

To become the first woman to hold the office of County Superintendent of Public Instruction in North Carolina was a distinction and honor that came to Mrs. Mollie Lucas Beam when she was appointed to that post in Person County in 1923. At the time of her appointment she was serving as principal of the Bethel High School, and her husband the Reverend J. A. Beam was County Superintendent. However, his health failed and she was appointed to succeed him. For two years she served in this executive position ably and well, yet, as she expressed it at the time: "I prefer the role of just 'plain teacher' as I miss the direct contact with the boys and girls I love."

On June 17, 1867, in Bleinheim, South Carolina, Mary Susan Elizabeth was born to Huger and Sarah McIntyre Lucas. Since she had been christened with a rather long name, the family soon shortened it to "Mollie."

At an early age, Mollie showed an intensive interest in books and in learning of the things around her. At the age of six, she entered a private school in Bleinheim and two years later began the study of music. In addition to the course prescribed by her teacher, she picked up, on the side, a repertoire of jigs, ballads, and love songs of the day. Whenever "company" came to the Lucas home, Mollie was asked to play and sing for their entertainment. Years later she surprised the members of the Research Literary Club of Roxboro, for the most part a very sedate group, by sitting down at the piano and singing to her own accompaniment these rollicking songs she had learned in her youth. She was asked to repeat this performance many times.

At the age of fourteen, she weighed about two hundred pounds and was athletic to a marked degree. With her older brother, J. M. Lucas, she ran races, climbed trees, walked bridge railings over deep water, and rode horseback. In looking back over her youth, she once said: "I realize now I must have enjoyed life tremendously—and I still do."

Mollie's formal education was received at Oxford College, Oxford, North Carolina. When her schooling was interrupted by her mother's illness, she secured a teaching position at Toby's Creek in Marion County, South Carolina. Here she received $30.00 a month, but she supplemented this salary by giving private lessons in piano. In 1885, she returned to Oxford and graduated at the age of seventeen. She taught in Apex, Morven, and Leaksville schools. The term was usually six months at that time.

To tell solely of Mrs. Beam's work in the field of education without including that of her husband, J. A. Beam, would be difficult for

24

after joining Mr. Beam at Bethel Hill Institute in Person County, their work was a joint undertaking.

Bethel Hill Institute was founded in 1887 by the Reverend J. A. Beam, a young Baptist minister who had graduated from Wake Forest College in 1885. His primary objective was to educate and train young men for the ministry. However, it was not long before the doors of the Institute were opened to both boys and girls desiring an education. It is said that Mr. Beam advertised his school in various newspapers in these terse words: "If you want an education, come to Bethel Hill; if you have no money, come anyway." He helped many a worthy boy to work his way through school, and more than one hundred Baptist ministers were educated at Bethel Hill.

Mollie Lucas joined the faculty of Bethel Hill Institute in 1888. Then a year later she married her principal and together they continued their work here until the Institute was destroyed by fire in 1905.

Following this disaster, Mr. and Mrs. Beam taught in Leaksville and later in Danville, Virginia, where Mr. Beam was business manager of what is now Averett College and Mrs. Beam was instructor of History and Mathematics at the same institution.

When the new Bethel Hill High School was erected on the same site as the old Institute, the Beams returned to Person County. Mrs. Beam became principal of the high school and Mr. Beam was made County Superintendent of Person County.

After sixteen years of service as County Superintendent, Mr. Beam retired because of ill health, and Mrs. Beam was appointed as his successor.

After two years in this office and the subsequent death of her husband, Mrs. Beam resumed the role of teacher; and she continued to teach until she retired in 1942 at the age of seventy-five. As a token of appreciation she was presented a silver plaque on which was inscribed: "For a life of loving service to the Bethel Hill community."

Mrs. Beam was once questioned concerning her philosophy of life. Her reply was: "I tried to do well that which had to be done; and I was convinced that if I could not have what I liked, I would like what I had."

After her retirement from school work in Person County, Mrs. Beam went to Louisburg, North Carolina, to live with her daughter, Mrs. Raymond G. Bailey, a teacher in the Louisburg High School. Here she passed away in 1951.

Mrs. Beam was a loyal member of the Baptist church and was always interested in civic projects. She was an honorary member of Delta Kappa Gamma. One of her achievements was the organizing of the first PTA in Person County. She was one of thirteen teachers on whom the NCEA in 1939 bestowed special honor for having taught for more than fifty years. As a regularly employed teacher and school official, Mrs. Beam held a record of fifty-eight years; and if eight years of substitute teaching is added this would make a record of sixty-six years of service in public education. But to measure the work of Mollie Lucas Beam by number of years alone would be an inadequate appraisement. Her influence and guidance are exemplified in the lives of those who were fortunate enough to have been her pupils.

NETTIE NICHOLS BEMIS
1859-1938

NETTIE NICHOLS BEMIS, a native of New England, had a long and highly useful career (1893-1929) as a teacher and institutional supervisor in North Carolina. Her earliest "pioneering" venture in the State was the introduction, probably in 1893, of drawing and manual training into the public school curriculum in Durham. This is believed to have been the first appearance of such courses in the public schools of North Carolina.

Nettie Bemis, daughter of George H. and Minerva Nichols Bemis, 'of the best stock of Massachusetts," was born November 6, 1859, in Haverhill, Massachusetts. Her secondary education was in the Haverhill High School and her first specialized training was in the old Haverhill Teachers' Training School, where she studied drawing and manual training. After teaching for ten years in the Winter Street School in Haverhill, she again studied manual arts in Pratt Institute in Brooklyn. Later, she attended summer schools in Hyannis Normal School, working in reed and raffia, and also took a course in woodwork at Cottage City.

It was in September, 1893, that Nettie went South to teach in the one public school then existent in Durham. After four years there, through the influence of B. N. Duke and C. W. Toms of Durham, she was offered the position of Lady Supervisor in the Oxford Orphanage (Masonic) in Oxford, North Carolina, which had received its first children in 1873. Years afterward, the late Dr. R. L. Flowers of Duke University stated: "If Mr. Duke had done nothing more for the Orphanage than being instrumental in placing Miss Bemis here as Lady Supervisor, he would have been a benefactor to this institution."

The Oxford Orphanage, covering a territory of more than three hundred acres and caring now for more than three hundred children, with its commodious cottage-homes and industrial buildings, its fine chapel, hospital, school, and recreational facilities, does indeed owe much to the wisdom and devotion of its lady supervisor of earlier years. Not only did Miss Bemis introduce classes in various manual arts; not only did she serve as adviser and exemplar to teachers and cottage "mothers" alike; not only did she effectively cooperate with successive superintendents in special projects; but she kept a place in her mind and heart for every child in the institution.

One of the former Orphanage boys said in a letter to Miss Bemis: "You were a Mother to all of us, and our days were brightened always by your kindness and understanding." Another wrote to her: "Miss Bemis taught us character. She was severe sometimes but we all loved her."

What was the secret of this modest little woman's power? Nettie Bemis had the stamina and the good hard sense to put into daily action her glowing personal vision of service. She had been a member of the Riverside Memorial Church. In North Carolina—in Durham and Oxford—she showed herself a true Christian; her whole personality was attuned to truth—and to duty. A more deeply sincere person, a more faithful and unselfish friend, a more dedicated worker, would be hard to find. Her days brimmed over with labors of love and duty, but her greatest service was an "intangible"; it was the profound impress of her strong character upon the plastic minds and hearts of the Orphanage boys and girls.

Life at Oxford, written by Miss Bemis after she had left the Orphanage, was published by the Herald Press of Charlotte in December, 1937, only a few months before her death. In her "Introduction" to this book, Mrs. Edward A. Hunt (née Linnie Ward) of Greensboro, a former Orphanage teacher, comments thus on Miss Bemis's place in the history of the institution: "Miss Bemis with her keen intellect, with her firmness for the right, with her natural bent toward discipline, with her high standard of living, and with clear-cut ideals for education, mingled with a deep loyalty for the Orphanage in all of its aspects, served as connecting link to unite the different epochs of its history." It is notable that Nettie Bemis served under three superintendents: Colonel William J. Hicks, Mr. Richmond L. Brown, and the Reverend Creasy K. Proctor.

When in 1929 Miss Bemis gave up her Orphanage duties, workers and children knew the institution had suffered a grievous loss. Friends outside the Orphanage also felt this, especially the women of the Saturday Book Club of Oxford, of which she had been a valued member for years; and, in all parts of the State, Masons who had intimately known her worth, felt in like manner. One of these, Grand Master R. C. Dunn, in his report to the Grand Lodge of 1929, paid a special tribute to:

" . . . . that splendid lady, Miss Nettie N. Bemis . . . . Her patience, her even temperament, her sympathetic attitude towards the children, her love for them and their reciprocal affection for her—all make for a condition that is well-nigh ideal. The Masons of North Carolina owe a debt of gratitude to Miss Bemis which only a greater and continuing interest in Oxford Orphanage can repay."

The last years of Miss Bemis's life were spent in the home of a niece, Mrs. Helen West Haberbush, in Verona, New Jersey. Her three sisters had passed away; but nieces, nephews, and cousins left her little time for loneliness. On March 16, 1938, five weeks after she had suffered a stroke, Miss Bemis died in a nursing home in Verona, and two days later was buried in the family lot in Walnut Cemetery, East Parish, Haverhill.

Nettie Bemis will long be remembered. For those who knew her not, the likeness of the former Lady Supervisor hangs on the wall of the Children's Reception Room in the Main Building of the Orphanage, in the form of a beautiful Pompeian bronze relief, which was presented to the Orphanage by the Oxford Orphanage Alumni Association at its eleventh annual meeting on June 23, 1934. The Alumni had received this as a gift from the artist, a cousin of Miss Bemis, Jessie Van Brunt of Brooklyn, distinguished for the numerous stained-glass windows she designed and presented to churches in various parts of the world.

For those who knew Miss Bemis no bronze relief or other likeness is needed for remembrance. Long will live in the most cherished memories of many "old" Orphanage girls and boys, the name of Nettie N. Bemis; for this name comes very close to the revered name of "Mother."

LUCY J. MORGAN BEARD
1853-1917

LUCY MORGAN is numbered among the women who made a contribution to education during the transition period following the War between the States and the reopening of the public schools in North Carolina. She was advanced in her ideas of education and somewhat of an individualist in her thinking, dress, and manner. She was a native Virginian, the daughter of Samuel Morgan who lived in Petersburg when Lucy was born on November 28, 1853. The family moved to Warrenton, North Carolina, near the close of the War.

She received her elementary education under the tutelage of her mother and older sisters. Later she attended Warrenton Academy.

Her first work was in the capacity of governess in the home of her sister, Mrs. Joe Person of Kittrell in Franklin County. Next, she taught Music in the town of Franklin in Macon County for some time. In the year 1883, she went to Weaverville to teach Music. Following this, she taught at Mills River. It was here that she met James Beard to whom she was married in 1889.

Soon after their marriage, Mr. and Mrs. Beard moved to Hickory where he set up a mercantile business and she established a school for little girls in her own home. The school soon became famous throughout the Piedmont region of North Carolina. It provided for both day and boarding pupils.

Mrs. Beard's ideas of education found expression in various ways. She was a great believer in fresh air, consequently many classes were held in her lovely boxwood garden. She insisted that character building was the most important phase of education, thus she endeavored to arouse in each pupil the desire to live a useful life. And while she charged tuition, she did not let the lack of ability to pay keep a studious child from her school.

The reputation that Mrs. Beard made for herself in her private school led to her being chosen as one of the earliest teachers for the public schools of Hickory when the system was established there about 1903. Being a woman of sturdy character and absolute fearlessness in the face of whatever adverse criticism might be brought against the newly established public schools, Mrs. Beard rendered great service for a number of years. Her marked devotion and untiring service to children endeared her to the community. She was a stern disciplinarian, demanding and bringing out the best in her pupils.

After teaching in the public schools for a number of years, Mrs. Beard joined the staff of Lenoir College (now Lenoir Rhyne College) where her last teaching was done.

She widened her own knowledge and that of her pupils and friends through extensive travel in the United States and in Europe. Little incidents connected with her European travels reveal her peculiar trait of positive opinions and her willingness to change her mode of thinking when convinced she was in the wrong. For example: Since several of her formative years were lived under the Confederate flag, she would never honor the American flag until she went on a European trip. While aboard ship, the Captain gave a special dinner for her on her birthday and used the American flag in her honor. She was so deeply appreciative of this courtesy that she changed her entire attitude toward the flag.

Another incident illustrates her appreciation of honesty and fair play: When in London, she was desirous of seeing a section of the city noted for its rough element, pickpockets, and the like. She was warned to be very cautious with money or valuables while going through this section. Therefore she tucked her pocketbook in her stocking. As she was walking along the street, a man stepped up behind her and said: "Lady, you dropped this." Being wary, she told him in no uncertain terms to keep his distance. There was a little insistence on his part and as she turned and looked at him she recognized the pocketbook she had so carefully concealed. She was so grateful to him and so chagrined that she had been rude to him that she sent him money every month as long as she lived and left a small sum to him when she died.

In addition to her work in the schoolroom, Mrs. Beard was active in some of the leading clubs in her town. The following excerpt from the *Memoriam* written by the Wednesday Afternoon Book Club of Hickory shows the esteem in which she was held:

"Mrs. Lucy Morgan Beard, the President of this Club and the beloved friend of each member, died January 2, 1917. As true and brave a heart as ever beat ceased when on that noontide she fell on sleep. In tender affection the Club records its love for her in this Memorial.

"Mrs. Beard was a charter member of this Club. Always full of initiative, always vigorously original, she was one of its most valued members. Her books, her meetings, were always unusual, piquant, and full of charm. . . . One might not always agree with Mrs. Beard, but one always had the most profound respect for her; and while considerate of the feelings of others, she maintained her opinions firmly. While gentleness itself, she held her position unflinchingly on any given subject and without variableness or shadow of turning."

SALLIE BETHUNE
1851-1928

SALLIE BETHUNE was a pioneer teacher and educational leader in Charlotte for forty-six years.

She was born in that town on February 2, 1851, the daughter of Alexander Bethune, a native of Robeson County, and Amanda Bolton Bethune whose family moved from Philadelphia to Charlotte in 1838. Both parents were of Scotch descent. Miss Bethune's family lived for awhile in Columbia, South Carolina, and later in Spartanburg. Here she attended the Columbia Female College and the Spartanburg Female College. When the family returned to Charlotte, she continued her studies in the Methodist College of that city. It was from this institution, located near the old D. H. Hill School Building, that she received her diploma.

Miss Bethune's teaching career began in the 1870's when she opened a private school in her own home on East Ninth Street. To this school came small boys and girls who were later to become leaders in the business and social life of Charlotte. Play as well as study was valued, and the broad open spaces were used to advantage. Following the work in her private school, she taught in a school in Charlotte which was headed by a Mr. Boone where she was assigned to teach a class of eighty-seven pupils.

In 1882 the public school system was established in Charlotte with T. J. Mitchell as superintendent. "Miss Sallie," as she was always affectionately known, was assigned to teach the first grade in what was later the D. H. Hill School. Thereafter her work and life were closely woven with the development of the public school system of Charlotte. As the system expanded, she moved in 1900 to the First Ward School, and in 1908 she became principal of the newly organized Fourth Ward School. This school was opened in a wooden building, later replaced by a brick building. In 1920 she relinquished the principalship of the Fourth Ward School. For a year she served as first grade teacher, and in 1921 was made supervisor of the primary grades in the same school, which position she held for the remainder of her life.

In 1928 an addition was made to the Fourth Ward School; and, when the enlarged school was opened in the spring, its name was formally changed to the Bethune School.

Though her life was dedicated to the teaching of young children, and it was in this field that she made her invaluable contribution, she made an unofficial contribution to the guiding and training of young teachers. She was advisor to primary teachers in Charlotte and the surrounding towns; and her attractive first grade classroom was rarely without a visiting teacher with whom she generously shared the results of her own rich experience. In local groups of teachers, at summer schools, teachers' institutes, and assemblies, she was a leader. Her personality was one of quiet force and charm. In later years her wavy hair added to the distinction of her personal appearance.

Long a member of the Tryon Street Methodist Church, later the First Methodist, she carried responsibilities in many of its activities. For many years she was director of the primary department of the Sunday School. In appreciation of her service, the congregation of her church enrolled her name in the Book of Remembrance of the Methodist Church at Scarrett College, Nashville, Tennessee.

Until shortly before her death on June 10, 1928, Miss Bethune was active in her school duties.

FANNIE CARR BIVINS

1875-1920

DURING her life Fannie Carr Bivins was more closely associated with Trinity College than any other woman of her time. From early childhood until the day of her death, February 10, 1920, the tie was never really severed. She grew up in the atmosphere of Trinity College, living on or near the campus, and few years went by when she was not taking some course in the college, or working in the library and laboratories.

Fannie Carr was born in Randolph County, North Carolina, September 1, 1875. Her father was Titus Carr of Greene County, North

Carolina, and her mother was Eliza White of Old Trinity Village, North Carolina. When Fannie was five months old the family moved to Texas, where they lived only a few years. Mrs. Carr returned to North Carolina with her two daughters, Fannie and Ida, after the death of her husband. The college was the center of life in Trinity Village, so it was naturally the center of Fannie's world as a child.

She went to small private schools in Trinity Village, where she evidently had good teaching, for she developed good habits of study. When she reached high school age she was among a group of girls and boys coached by Trinity College Professors, and in 1890, with her sister and two other girls, Fannie entered the freshman class of Trinity. When the college was moved to Durham, North Carolina, in 1891, the Carrs did not move there at once. Instead the two sisters attended Littleton College for the term, remaining there until the Christmas holidays.

Fannie then re-entered Trinity, making up the work and completing the sophomore year with her class. She dropped out for one year and taught in Weldon, then re-entered with the Class of 1896 with her sister. In the meantime two other girls had joined this class, thus making four girls in the Class of 1896 for the junior and senior years. These were the first four girls to take the full course at Trinity College, receiving diplomas on the same conditions as the men. Fannie Carr was really the pioneer of these pioneers; she was not only one of the first girls to graduate from Trinity, but she was in the first group of girls to enter a regular class, and she could have graduated a year earlier than the other three.

While in college she made a brilliant record in scholarship, easily leading her class in all her subjects. She had a cosmopolitan mind. Professor Herbert Merritt of Trinity College once said that if there were such a thing as having a talent for standing examinations, Fannie Carr had it; she could put down accurately just what was wanted on an examination, writing it out swiftly. She was never a grind, nor cloistered student, and there was never a suggestion of the "blue stocking" about her. She was a swift and accurate thinker, going straight to the heart of a lesson, as later in life she knew how to go to the heart of affairs. She came within a small fraction of winning the valedictory of her class, making a brilliant record during the entire five years of her college work, from her entrance into the freshman class to the end of the year when she obtained the A. M. degree. Joseph Bivins, the man she later married, was a shade ahead of her in the three-year's race for scholarship honors.

The year following her graduation she taught in Houma, Louisiana. Returning to North Carolina, she became principal of the school at Aberdeen, a position which she held for two years. From 1899 until 1920, with the exception of one year when she taught in Richmond College, Richmond, Virginia, she was associated with educational work in Durham.

On September 1, 1904, she was married to Joseph Francis Bivins, a classmate, then headmaster of Trinity Park High School. Three days later he met a tragic death.

Fannie continued to live with her mother, first in the Inn on Trinity College Campus, which Mrs. Carr was operating at that time, and then in their home near the campus. She conducted a school for beginners for the children of the members of the faculty and in the college community. During this time she also taught special classes in French and in English Literature at the Southern Conservatory of Music, located in Durham.

Mrs. Bivins became especially interested in French and German, and took advanced work in these subjects at Trinity. In 1909 she spent the summer in France studying at the University of Caen, going alone and boarding in a French pension so that she would have a better opportunity for acquiring a good French accent. After this she taught one year in Richmond College, 1909-1910, teaching the courses in Modern Languages. Then she returned to Durham in the fall of 1911 and began to teach Modern Languages in the Durham High School. Later she changed to Science, becoming head of the Science Department, which position she held at the time of her death. Her interest in science had been increasing for years and she had been studying biology and kindred subjects purely for her own pleasure. She had spent several summers studying, one at Columbia University, and one other at George Peabody College for Teachers. Those who knew her well, knew her versatility, and the quality of her mind, and could see constant growth in her powers.

Mrs. Bivins was a great teacher, with a sympathetic understanding of boys and girls, inspiring them to do their best and arousing their interest in the subject she was teaching. She loved her church and had charge of the Beginners Department of Memorial Methodist Church for many years. She was one of the organizers of the Epworth League in this same church, and had much influence in bringing together the boys who were attending Trinity College and the people of the town. She took active interest in the Woman's Society of the Church, leading mission study classes and doing various other work when called upon.

She was one of the organizers of the Durham Chapter of the Southern Association of College Women. She was its first president, and was again president at the time of her death. She was the first president of the Trinity Alumnae Association, organized in 1912. Under her leadership the movement for better accommodations for women at Trinity was started. This led to the coordinate Woman's College of Duke University. Mrs. Bivins worked continuously for this cause. She always remained active in the Trinity Alumnae Association, serving on various committees. She served as Chairman of the local committee on Trinity Alumnae War Work, later changed to Reconstruction Work in Devastated France. If the original plan for sending a reconstruction worker to France had not been changed, she would very probably have been the one chosen to go. It was largely due to her efforts that the alumnae Association supported a kindergarten in devastated France.

Thoroughly alive, filled with the joys of living, and interested in the people around her, Mrs. Bivins displayed a spiritual poise that was an inspiration to others.

While holding the position of Head of the Science Department of the Durham High School, she became ill with influenza-pneumonia. She died on February 10, 1920.

DORA ESTHER FISHER BLACKWELDER
1867-1947

DORA ESTHER FISHER, affectionately known as "Miss Essie," was a born teacher. One of "her girls," now the wife of an ex-college president, describes Miss Essie as a "perfect teacher." Another "girl," now the widow of a banker, declares it paid dividends to study for Miss Essie as she could bring out what a student knew. A third "girl," now the grandmother of a large family, frankly admits that Miss Essie was strict but that she could make a student want to learn.

Dora Esther Fisher was born January 10, 1867, at the old Fisher homestead in Cabarrus County, five miles due west of Concord. She was the youngest child of Ephraim Lewis Fisher and Martha Elizabeth Rendleman Nussman and Adolphus Nussman, who was educated at Gottingen University and was the first Lutheran preacher in North Carolina.

Essie always played with her older brother. As a child, she never cared to help with housework but instead followed her father over the plantation and never saw a horse she was afraid to ride. Her mother was relieved when an exceptionally spirited colt died, for she feared the colt would bring mishap to her youngest child.

Essie's first formal education was secured in a subscription school in her neighborhood. Not satisfied with what she learned in that school, she became a boarding student at the Mt. Pleasant Female Seminary. Later she studied for two years at Lutherville Female Seminary in Lutherville, Maryland, and was graduated with distinction in 1889. She was an especially fine Latin scholar and had a deep appreciation of Greek and Roman culture.

Miss Essie's formal teaching covered a period of seven years. She taught in the Cannon Elementary School in Number 4 Township of Cabarrus County; also at Enochville with Professor Peter Wright;

and with Professor C. L. T. Fisher and Professor J. H. C. Fisher at Mont Amoena Seminary, which had earlier been known as Mt. Pleasant Female Seminary. She watched with pride as her students lived useful lives in rural and urban communities. Some of her students became teachers; some of her girls married ministers; others served in varied walks of life. Mrs. T. E. Johnston of Salisbury and Constance Cline of Concord are among those who became teachers; in the group who married ministers are Mrs. P. E. Monroe, Mrs. J. L. Morgan, and Mrs. Edward Fulenwider.

When a teaching position at Elizabeth College in Charlotte was offered to Miss Essie, she declined as she was about to become the bride of John Alexander Blackwelder. For sixteen years after their marriage on January 5, 1897, the Blackwelders made their home in Newberry, South Carolina. Here Miss Essie did not stop teaching, however. Instead, she instructed her children in the home. She taught her first child, Oscar Fisher Blackwelder (at present the pastor of the Lutheran Church of the Reformation in Washington, D. C.), for three years. Her second child was seriously ill during her sixth year therefore Miss Essie was her first grade teacher. This daughter, Ruth, is associate professor of history at Lenoir Rhyne College. Mrs. Blackwelder's third child showed her talent for music at an early age. Miss Essie, who was an excellent organist, supervised Mary Elizabeth's practice. This youngest child, Mrs. E. Ray King, is organist and choir director at St. James Lutheran Church of Concord.

Mrs. Blackwelder made her home in Concord from 1913 until her death. Her many associates there knew her as a devoted mother, a sincere friend, an active member of St. James Lutheran Church and a master gardener. During the growing season, she always had flowers to share with her friends, and many shut-ins were cheered by blossoms from her garden. When she died on March 3, 1947, a young man said to one of her children: "Your mother was my Sunday School teacher when I was twelve years old and I will always remember her." She was sixty years of age when she taught his class but no one ever thought of her as old. Her soft silky hair never lost its auburn color; her grey-blue eyes never lost their warmth and sparkle; her steps were always sure and qnick. After she celebrated her eightieth birthday, her youngest grandson said, "My grandmother's not old." At her death the little five-year-old boy was told that his grandmother was with Jesus. He asked if there are flowers in heaven. His aunt assured him that the flowers in heaven are beautiful and the little fellow's reply was, "Grandmother's growing flowers for God."

Miss Essie's students are still teaching and are teaching others how to teach; and, what is more important, are following her example by teaching the greatest lesson of all: how to live.

35

VIOLA BODDIE
1864-1940

MISS VIOLA BODDIE brought high ideals, thorough scholarship, a love of the classics, culture, charm, and beauty to the charter membership of the faculty of the State Normal and Industrial School when it opened in the fall of 1892. A member of the first student body recalls that Miss Boddie was "young, pretty, and wearing such fashionable clothes that the student's attention often wandered from the Latin which she had at her finger tips."

Miss Boddie, a native of Nash County, where she was born on October 2, 1864, was well prepared for her position by experience and training as well as by aptitude and ability. Her experience included that of governess, teacher in a co-educational academy, work in a one-room rural school, teaching seventy-two primary children in a graded school, and a brief period in each of two denominational colleges for girls.

Her education at Littleton College only whetted her appetite, and after resigning her position as a member of the faculty of Henderson College in 1889, by competitive examination she won a two-year scholarship to the Normal School, Nashville, Tennessee (now Peabody College). It is indicative of her ability, ambition, and courage that she won among forty applicants, and under a ruling that if there were two papers judged to be of equal merit and one that of a man, he should be given the preference.

At Nashville she made a brilliant record, receiving the degree of L. I. (Licentiate in Instruction) in 1891. Her professor of Latin wrote: "Her standing in the College, as a student and as a woman, is of the highest. . . . But it is not in Latin alone that her scholarship is of the best."

Miss Boddie, like other members of that first faculty of the Normal School in Greensboro, did many chores, being listed in the catalogue of 1892 as assistant to Dr. McIver in the Department of Pedagogy, as head of the Department of Ancient and Modern Languages, and as teacher of both Latin and French. In subsequent catalogues for a period of forty-three years she is designated as teacher and head of the Department of Latin.

Throughout her long career Miss Boddie upheld the highest ideals and standards for her students and herself. She was a capable and conscientious instructor, and had the reputation for being a member of the faculty under whom the indolent found no comfort.

Miss Boddie's interests were those of a cultured woman. Along with her teaching of the classics she stimulated her students' interests in world affairs, music, art, and literature.

She loved flowers, especially roses, and she celebrated every Mother's Day by wearing a rose and presenting one to each of her students. Daily in her classroom there was an artistic arrangement of blossoms in season, which after class she shared with other faculty down the hall. She loved beauty in all its forms; and, a devotee of nature, she often admonished her students before examinations, instead of cramming, to take a long walk in the woods.

Possessing a brilliant intellect herself, she fought with Dr. McIver and that early faculty to prove that women do have the brains, the health, and the stamina for higher education as well as men. True to her life plan in later years she gave stalwart assistance in the long struggle to raise the standards of the Normal School to that of the Woman's College of the University of North Carolina.

Still beautiful and mellowed by the years, Miss Boddie, after her retirement in 1935, for five years made her home near the college. She was a frequent visitor on campus, always attending college and alumnae social events, where her upright posture, beautiful white hair, handsome apparel, still beautiful face, bright eyes, grace and charm of manner lent prestige to any gathering.

Death came to Miss Boddie on March 20, 1940, in Greensboro. Her burial was at her old home in Nash County.

A fitting tribute is expressed in the words of one of her "girls":

"Those who took her courses were held to the work. There were no evasions—no question about your ability to learn Latin—you learned it. If she had the keen, incisive mind, quick at repartee, qualities which would have made her a brilliant lawyer or a successful business woman, it was the same quality which contributed to her recognition of women as individuals, with the power and the right to the highest self realization. From the bottom of our hearts we say, 'Thank you'."

EMMA INGOLD BOST

1859-1942

THE name of Emma Ingold Bost is linked with the earliest public schools of Hickory. She served as principal of the town's first public school. Coming to Hickory as a child of ten, her life was closely interwoven with the development not only of the schools but of the church and community as well. She sang in the choir of her church for sixty years.

She was born in Lincoln County, October 14, 1859, the daughter of a pioneer minister, the Reverend Jeremith Ingold and his wife, Margaret Ramseur Ingold. Her father organized the Corinth Reformed

37

Church of Hickory in 1869, and in 1872 the family moved to that struggling little village. While he was pastor of the church, Mr. Ingold founded and taught a private school assisted by his older daughters. Young Emma received her education from her father and her sisters. She early imbibed the culture and religion of her environment which influenced her whole life.

For several years prior to becoming principal of a school in Hickory, Emma Ingold taught in the schools of Catawba County. Then in the early 1880's she became principal of the first public school in Hickory. This was before the organization of the present graded school system. Her school building was only a rude log house, but her educational practice was firm. Here many of Hickory's successful teachers and business men received their early education.

On November 14, 1888, Emma Ingold was married to Charles Carroll Bost, a native of Catawba County. Her wedding was the first one performed in the second building of the Corinth Reformed Church, the first building having been destroyed by fire. Her father was assisted in performing the ceremony by the Reverend Lewis Meiter. The bride wore white nun's veiling trimmed with white moire, a small poke bonnet of white lace, long white kid gloves. She carried Malmaison roses. In 1938, this couple celebrated their golden wedding with a reception.

After her marriage, Mrs. Bost devoted her time to writing and to club and church work.

At an early age, she had shown signs of literary ability. When ten years' old, she wrote a story, "Love's Chiding," which was published under the name of "Olive Ormond" in the *Carolina Eagle* edited by Dr. J. R. Ellis. "October Seventeenth" was written to commemorate the death of her friend, John Charles McNeill, which occurred October 17, 1907. Before and during World War I, she wrote many poems which were published in *The Charlotte Observer*, *The Hickory Daily Record*, and *The Reformed Church Messenger*. In 1921, her poems were published in book form under the title, *Songs in Many Keys*. Critics thought her work compared favorably with that of McNeil who had advised and encouraged her in her writing.

One of Mrs. Bost's red letter days was a reception given by her Book Club in January, 1906, in her home. At this time the organization was honored with the presence of her distinguished friend, John Charles McNeill. During the evening he delighted the one hundred and fifty guests by reading a number of his own poems.

Mrs. Bost was instrumental in organizing the Round Dozen Book Club and the Thursday Study Club, two of Hickory's leading literary clubs. She was president of the Study Club for twenty-two consecutive years.

In church work, she served as follows: president of the Womans Missionary Society of the Corinth Reformed Church of Hickory for thirty-five years; president of the Womans Missionary Society of the

Reformed Churches of North Carolina for twelve years; and corresponding secretary of the Womans Missionary Society of her synod. Mrs. Bost died on January 6, 1942, at the age of eighty-three.

AMY MORRIS BRADLEY

1823-1904

"SO closely and intimately was the work of Miss Amy Morris Bradley woven with the public schools of North Carolina that her labors should always receive the public recognition which is justly due," wrote James Sprunt in his *Chronicles of the Cape Fear*. Miss Bradley was an educational leader in Wilmington for twenty-five years immediately following the close of the War between the States when lines were not tightly drawn between public and private funds for educational purposes. Then the same writer goes on to say: "There was never any conflict between her private interests and the community's public interests." Coming from the state of Maine where she was born of New England stock into a war torn state, Miss Bradley recognized the educational needs of the people and determined to do something about it.

Amy was the youngest of nine children. Six years after her birth, her mother died leaving Amy, a somewhat delicate child, to be reared by her father, brothers, and sisters. Amy attended the district school where teachers were ever changing, books were few, and terms were short. Yet she was so studious that she obtained a fair education.

At seventeen, she began teaching in the rural schools of her native state. She longed for better educational advantages and for contacts with educated and cultured people which this rural school environment did not afford. She attended the writing schools and the singing schools characteristic of that day with the hope of self-improvement. Once when she had taught during the summer she took the money she had earned and entered an academy in the fall. The facts concerning her higher education are somewhat obscure. That she had literary tastes and ambitions is evident from the poems written in her dairy which she faithfully kept after the age of twenty.

In the spring of 1844, Miss Bradley started to Massachusetts to teach because the teachers' salaries were higher there than in her own state. She soon became ill and had to return home. When she had regained her health, she taught a rural school in her home community for Three Dollars a week.

Never a strong woman, she suffered from colds and severe coughs. Therefore, she came South in the fall of 1850 and spent the winter with friends in Charleston in the hope of improving her health. She returned

39

to the North and taught there until the beginning of the War between the States. At the close of the War, she decided to go South again.

On December 30, 1866, Miss Bradley arrived in Wilmington as a missionary, then in January, 1867, she started a school and a Sunday School for poor white children. It seems that her work was financed by some organization or individual in Boston. The school soon attracted the attention of some of the prominent people of Wilmington and they gave her encouragement and some financial aid. Also, according to *Chronicles of the Cape Fear* she received in 1870 State funds to the amount of $1,266.71.

About 1870, the public schools in New Hanover County and in Wilmington were showing signs of growth. Thus, Miss Bradley recognized the need of an institution where teachers might be trained. And it was through her interests and efforts along this line that Mary Hemenway of Boston financed the building and the maintenance of the Tileston Normal School in 1871. She continued to finance the school for twenty years with Miss Bradley as its head. Referring to Miss Bradley's work in this institution, Sprunt says: "The trained and skilful teachers whom she gathered around her in turn trained others, who incorporated into the public schools the best and the most modern methods of instruction." Miss Bradley continued as head of the school until it closed in 1891.

She spent her last years in a cozy cottage which stood in the Tileston School yard facing Ann Street. Here she died in January, 1904.

It was through Miss Bradley's influence and suggestion that at the close of the school Miss Hemenway donated the property of the Tileston Normal School to the Wilmington public schools. As a tribute a bronze tablet over the door bears the following inscription:

Tileston Memorial School
Built by
Mary Hemenway of Boston

who established herein a school for the White People of this community in the year eighteen hundred and seventy-one and maintained the same at her own cost for twenty years under the devoted administration of

Amy Morris Bradley
Given to
The city of Wilmington
in the year nineteen hundred and one,
Mary Hemenway

DIXIE LEE BRYANT

1862-1949

DR. DIXIE LEE BRYANT, scientist, scholar, pioneer teacher, and gentlewoman in her rich, full life of eighty-seven years accomplished many things to which she was entitled to point with pride. In
her autobiographical sketch, she chose two: first, that she was a pioneer
among women in getting a college education; second, that she was
privileged to put all of her preparation and efforts, for the first nine
years of its existence, into helping to form a real college for Southern
girls at the State Normal and Industrial School in Greensboro.

Dixie Lee Bryant was born January 7, 1862 at Louisville, Kentucky.
In 1868 she moved with her family to Columbia, Tennessee, where from
age six to sixteen she received her preparatory education at a girls'
finishing school, the Columbia Female Institute.

Miss Bryant's early teaching experience included one year in an
ungraded school in Culleoka, Tennessee, a year in the first public school
of Columbia, followed by work at Hamilton College, a girls' finishing
school, at Lexington, Kentucky. Teaching only whetted her appetite
for more education for herself.

Finding that a university education was not available for a woman
in the South, Miss Bryant in October, 1887, matriculated at the Massachusetts Institute of Technology, where there was available the best in
scientific education of the day. From the "hardest school in New England," she was graduated with honors and received the B. S. degree in
1891.

The year following her graduation she taught Science in the State
Normal College of New Hampshire. In October, 1892, when the North
Carolina State Normal and Industrial School opened its doors, Miss
Bryant became a charter member of the faculty.

For nine years Miss Bryant did pioneering work in setting up a
four year college curriculum in Science. Beginning with little equipment
and meager facilities, she established laboratories in Biology, Chemistry,
and Physics with standard equipment. In Miss Bryant's own words,
"I also put in a curriculum of the simplest four year college courses
such as women's colleges of the North had."

To the sturdy scholarship and high standards of Dixie Lee Bryant
the State Normal owed its early emphasis upon Science in the college
education of young women. However, the longer she taught the greater
became her ambition for more education for herself.

This desire for further study led to her resignation in 1901. The
same year she sailed for Europe, where she studied in Heidelberg, Ger-
many and later in Erlangen, Bavaria, where in 1904 she earned the
doctorate from Erlangen University.

Returning to America in the fall of 1904, Dr. Bryant entered the public school system of Chicago, and there taught Science in the high schools for twenty-nine years.

In 1931 she retired and moved to Asheville, North Carolina, where she spent the remainder of her life. Although retired, Dr. Bryant never lost interest in education. Her keen alert mind made constant contribution through book clubs and research to the enrichment of life around her. Her physical fortitude was almost unbelievable, and her interest in her church, the Trinity Episcopal Church of Asheville, and all worthwhile civic projects was outstanding.

Her major contributions were made through the American Association of University Women, of which she had been a member for fifty-eight years. It was a source of pride to her that she was elected to membership in this organization in 1891 when it bore the name, Collegiate Alumnae.

Many honors came to Dr. Bryant. On November 8, 1947, she was initiated as an honorary member of Gamma Chapter of Delta Kappa Gamma. At the South Atlantic Regional Conference of the American Association of University Women, held in Asheville in 1948, a tribute was paid to her. In February, 1950, the local members of the organization voted to name a five hundred dollar Study Grant—the Dixie Lee Bryant Fellowship, thus honoring both her long membership in A.A.U.W. and her love of research.

Even as death approached, Dr. Bryant was concerned for matters of education as she planned the gift of her books and pictures to the Asheville-Biltmore College Library. Her death occurred in Asheville on November 18, 1949.

When asked for a brief biographical sketch giving the bare facts of her life, Dr. Bryant had written: "Personally, I like the more intimate record of the pioneer movement and the wonderful women in it." She was one of the "wonderful women in it."

MARGARET ANNA BURWELL
1810-1871

FOR more than thirty years, Mrs. Margaret Anna Burwell was connected with the education of women in North Carolina and left her impress on the students of two schools of that period. For about nineteen years, Mrs. Burwell was in charge of an academy for girls in Hillsboro and for fourteen years she was a member of the faculty at Charlotte Female Institute, now Queens College.

Born in Richmond, Virginia, October 3, 1810, Margaret Anna Robertson was the daughter of William Robertson and Anne Spotswood

Robertson. She inherited the energy and strength of purpose of a Scotch father and the organizing ability of her mother's family. In 1831, she married the Reverend Robert Burwell and went to live in Hillsboro, North Carolina, where Mr. Burwell had accepted a call to the Presbyterian Church of that town. In 1838, assisted by her husband, she opened a boarding and a day school for young ladies which she ran successfully for about fourteen years. The school was noted for the thorough scholarship of the teachers and for their inspirational teaching.

In 1857, Mr. and Mrs. Burwell were called to take charge of the newly established Charlotte Female Institute, later the Presbyterian College for Women, now Queens College.

Many and varied were the experiences of Mrs. Burwell in this institution where she spent the remaining years of her life. In addition to the usual work of a preceptress of that period—disciplinarian, direct teacher of manners and morals, and the like—she taught English, the Bible, and related subjects. She was an enthusiastic teacher. Not only did she have the ability to impart knowledge, but to a marked degree she possessed the faculty of leading pupils to think. Not only in the school room but also in domestic affairs and in social circles, she impressed upon her pupils ineffaceable lessons in culture, morals, and elegance. She was a woman of commanding personality, majestic in size, with fine features and exquisite complexion. She wore her hair in curls around her temples, and, in later years when it was gray, the style added to her dignity. Her dress, always black, was made on simple lines and fitted perfectly.

After the War between the States, Mr. and Mrs. Burwell were assisted at the Charlotte Female Institute by their son, Captain John Burwell.

When the trustees of Peace Institute were ready to open this school in Raleigh in about 1871, they offered the leadership to Mr. and Mrs. Burwell. But before they had made a final decision, Mrs. Burwell suddenly passed away on June 21, 1871, while on a visit in Raleigh. She thus left her husband and son to take up the new work which was really the outgrowth of the school they had managed so well in Charlotte.

The following from the *Presbyterian Standard,* published in Charlotte, March 5, 1902, on the occasion of the unveiling of a tablet to her memory, pays a fitting tribute to this "Pioneer Woman in Education" in North Carolina:

"Wife, Mother, Educator." In letters of gold on a tablet of white marble these great words of our mother tongue are engraved, to describe the life and work of the woman who, perhaps more than any other woman who lived and wrought in North Carolina, left an undying impression upon the life of the State itself— Mrs. Margaret Anna Burwell. The words themselves will have their influence in denoting woman's sphere upon the generation of college girls who shall sit in the auditorium of the Presbyterian College for Women, of this city, the college itself being a monument to her years of service here.

She was the inspiration of her husband in his work as preacher and educator; left her impress for refinement of manner and literary culture upon this community; left her impress on the hundreds of young women whom she trained for the duties of life—and through the pupils' homes and the schools that some of them founded—left her impress upon the life of this State, and other states, that will be real, even though invisible, down to the last syllable of recorded time.

RACHEL CALDWELL

1742-1825

IT can be truthfully said that the work of David Caldwell, preacher, teacher, physician, and Revolutionary hero, would have fallen short, had it not been for his wife, Rachel, a woman of intelligence, zeal, religious piety, tactful manners, and beneficial influence. Rachel Caldwell is prominent in early North Carolina history, not because she herself was a great teacher, but because she was a partner of a great teacher. It was said: "David made the scholars, but Rachel the preachers."

Alexander Craighead, Rachel's father, came to America from Ireland when only nine years old. He was educated entirely by his father, but was ready for a license to preach when a very young man. He grew up in Pennsylvania and served his first pastorate there; moved to Virginia, seeking greater freedom; then, being much troubled by the Indians, moved again—this time to North Carolina. Rachel's mother was outstanding for her happy disposition. To Rachel she bequeathed this fortunate quality and also the training of a good homekeeper, even though under crude, pioneer conditions.

At the age of twenty-four, Rachel married David Caldwell, whose ancestors were also from Ireland. Rachel and David played together as children when both families were living in Pennsylvania, and their marriage was the culmination of a long friendship. Their first home was on Caldwell Farm, a tract of land originally owned by Lord Granville. After settling here, David became a preacher for two Presbyterian churches: Buffalo and Alamance.

In 1767, David began teaching some boys in his home on the farm. The small school grew until it became a classical school for boys, to which pupils came from all over the South: boys from wealthy homes and boys from poor homes. None were turned away. The school became known as David Caldwell's Log Cabin College. Rachel Caldwell's real contribution to education began then. Here was needed the frugality

44

and careful management of Rachel. Her husband's salary was $200.00 per year. And with this she managed the home beautifully and helped everyone who called upon her. She became nurse, counselor, and mother to the boys of the school. They came to her not only when ill but when bothered with problems of all kinds. Her gentle personality invited their confidence, and her faith and ideals inspired them.

The personal bravery and fortitude of Rachel Caldwell in difficult and dangerous situations proved her a fearless heroine during the Revolutionary War. Just before the Battle of Guilford Courthouse, Cornwallis and his army were camped near the Caldwell home. Officers and soldiers came to take over the plantation and the house; but when they entered, Rachel excused herself to look after her baby. This was only a pretext to make it possible to warn two neighbors who were in the house, thus giving them a chance to escape.

Shortly after this, Rachel and her children were locked in the smoke-house for a day with only a few dried apples to eat. In the late afternoon, they were discovered by a physician, who managed to provide them with a bed and some food. However, they were kept prisoners for two more days. When insulted by a soldier who called her people "rebels" and "cowards," she replied: "Wait and see what the Lord will do for us." Such was her faith. At another time, she gave food to a messenger who was carrying an important paper from General Washington to General Greene; and a little later, she helped the messenger to escape from the British soldiers by engaging those soldiers in conversation while the messenger climbed down from the locust tree in which he had been hiding, and got away. In addition to these and other dangerous experiences, many of her possessions, including valuable papers and records, were burned.

Through the War and the years that followed, while always the invaluable helper and comrade of her husband, Rachel bore a family of twelve children, nine of whom grew to adulthood. A son, John, became one of the early legislators of North Carolina, while others made enviable places for themselves in the world in various fields. It is interesting to note that a great grand-daughter of Rachel Caldwell became the first woman physician in North Carolina.

In 1825, just one year after the death of her husband, this great woman passed away. Her death brought grief to many, but her deeds have been remembered and honored in sincere gratitude for her life and achievements.

On an important anniversary of Buffalo Church, where David Caldwell was the first minister, Rachel Caldwell was honored as the organizer of the women's work in the church. Also, on June 12, 1935, a marker of native stone was erected to her memory on the old Caldwell Farm by the Daughters of the American Revolution; and a great grand-daughter, Mrs. Mary Caldwell Jones, made the presentation. This marker was placed beside a companion stone, erected by the Colonial Dames to the memory of her illustrious husband, David Caldwell. The women of North Carolina do well to honor Rachel Caldwell for her unselfish services to early educational efforts and her valiant promotion of rich living in family and in neighborhood, through good management, hard work, high ideals, and an unquenchable faith in God.

DAPHNE KING CARRAWAY

1881-1953

PIONEERING in education in the broadest sense of the term was the ruling passion of the adult life of Daphne Carraway, as well as the main theme of her entire span of life's activities. The records prove this and are substantiated by the personal lives of those whom she influenced. State Superintendent A. T. Allen said of her: "I regard her as one of the most gifted teachers who ever worked in North Carolina." She is equally remembered for her work in the Story-tellers League and on the Chautauqua platform.

To Daphne Carraway teaching was a high calling, and she was always to be found in the lead in progressive and forward-looking plans and programs of educational service whether these had to do with new types of buildings, new methods of teaching or the instruction of teachers.

Miss Carraway was born in Wilson, North Carolina, October 23, 1881. She completed elementary school in her home town. About the time that she was ready for high school, the family moved to Greensboro where her mother became the first matron of the State Normal and Industrial School, later known as the State Normal and today as Womans College of the University of North Carolina. Daphne lived in the institution with her mother and completed high school and college on the campus. She was a pupil in the first training school of the Normal. From the training school she entered the State Normal College, as the institution was then called (now the Womans College of the University of North Carolina) and graduated in the class of 1902. In addition to the diploma, she received a certificate for speed and accuracy in shorthand and typewriting.

Miss Carraway's first teaching experience was in the Primary Department of the Presbyterian Church at Barium Springs, North Carolina. She remained here for one year. In the fall of 1903, she accepted a position in the Primary Department of the Wilson public schools where she stayed until 1914 at which time she became Elementary Supervisor of Wake County Schools. In addition to her supervisory duties, Miss Carraway organized numbers of Betterment Associations throughout the county and assisted in carrying them on.

During these years, Miss Carraway spent the summer months in study. In 1904, she attended the University of Tennessee. In 1905 and 1906, she studied Speech and Dramatic Arts at Atlantic Christian College and received a diploma in the subject. The summer of 1908 was spent at the University of North Carolina. For several successive summers, she taught at East Carolina Teachers College, State College, and at the Normal College in Greensboro. Then, for the following six summers (1912-18), Miss Carraway was Assistant Conductor of State Teachers Institutes in North Carolina.

Her experience in the classroom led her to cultivate the art of story-telling. As time went on, she became so keenly interested in this art that she took special courses in Speech and Dramatic Art in Washington, D. C., and in Boston where she spent a year of study at the Whitney Studio of Platform Art. In 1923-24, she was employed in Washington, D. C., as instructor of short courses in story-telling for professional groups and church workers. During this time, she served as president of the Story-Tellers League of Washington. The Washington correspondent of *The Raleigh News and Observer* wrote of her work:

"Miss Carraway has made an enviable reputation in Chautauqua work, in which she does story-telling, and does this in an engaging and clever way. Since her arrival in Washington, D. C., she has been heard at a number of entertainments given by the Y. M. C. A., the Y. W. C. A., and last night she made a big hit at *The Little Play House* where the Arts Club gave a delightful program. Miss Carraway is making a marked success in her chosen field."

She was employed as lecturer and story-teller on the Radcliffe Chautauqua circuits during the summers from 1919 to 1931. In connection with her work she organized the *Young America Club* and served as organizer of story leagues and as representative of the *Story Tellers National Magazine*. She appeared as guest speaker on local, district, state, and national organizations and on radio networks.

Throughout the years that she spent her summers on the Chautauqua platform, Miss Carraway served during the academic year as the Educational Secretary for the Wilson County, North Carolina, Health Department, at the same time holding the chairmanship of the Junior Red Cross.

Miss Carraway's unexcelled ability as an artist in story-telling was recognized when she was elected president of the National Story-Tellers League of America; and it was then that the charm of her presentations from the platform won for her the title of "The Dixie Story Lady." Here she carried many an audience of children and adults away into a land of pure delight. She held this office four years, 1928-1932, and in her official capacity filled numerous speaking engagements throughout the country.

47

Her work with Chautauqua, Story-Telling League, and the like had taken Miss Carraway away from her native state for several years, and she found herself eager to return. In a letter written from Boston in June, 1930, to the Alumnae office of Woman's College of the University of North Carolina, she said: "I am eager to get back to the dear old North State, and just as soon as I can find a job here I am coming home to stay." The job came as teacher in the Wakelon School at Zebulon, and she began teaching there in September, 1933. However, it seems that through the irony of fate she was not permitted to live and continue her activities. She was on her way home to Wilson on the afternoon of December 18, 1933, after having attended in Raleigh a class in Children's Literature, when she met instant death in an automobile accident.

The life calendar of Miss Carraway is marked by laudatory expressions from numerous newspapers of the nation. Her friends and admirers represent various sections of North Carolina and the United States. And amid such acclaim deep and marvelous were the love and devotion she held for her home in Wilson and her loved ones there—her sister Irma and her Aunt Louisa M. Daniel, and a host of kinspeople, neighbors, and friends.

As a most fitting tribute, commemorating her passion for living and her zest for sharing, *A Teacher's Book of Stories* was compiled and published by Irma Carraway in 1940. The contents of the bulletin were selected from the hundreds of stories which her sister had adapted for story-telling and are representative of her finest contribution to the story-telling art. This bulletin has been widely distributed and used by teacher groups, by schools of education in colleges and universities, and libraries. The following is from the foreword:

"There is always an occasion for a good story. Many of us would use the occasion more often if we had ready-adapted for story-telling selections of intrinsic value and literary significance . . .The stories in this bulletin are selections from the great store of adaptations of some of the best in literature and current writings of human interest by a gifted story-teller—Daphne Carraway.

"As one of the classroom arts, story-telling is more popular than ever before, as all children love stories told by others. Teachers everywhere really crave the gift of the story-teller as they are aware of its usefulness, not only in winning the love and admiration of children but as educational leaders among adults, they know the power of the story-teller's art.

"Through the conversational style of the 'adapted' story as found in this bulletin, Miss Carraway shares with teachers a type of material which is a ready help in becoming a good story-teller. Also, the variety of selections offers an interesting and simple repertoire of stories for use in different situations and as the occasion demands."

QUEEN CARSON
1865-1947

FOR nearly half a century, Queen Carson served in one district of Asheville, North Carolina, as teacher and principal.

Although she had many opportunities to take higher positions, she preferred to stay in this one section in which there were many under-privileged children. For three generations Miss Carson made her school a home, a playground, a nursery, a relief agency, a health center, a library, and a forum for her pupils. She thus acted on her guiding principle: that the individual child is the center of the school and the school is the center of horizons ever to be widened, even for the poorest child, to the unlimited possibilities of the American dream.

Miss Carson was born at Port Deposit, Maryland, February 9, 1865, and came from a long line of leaders and educators. Her father was Samuel Rowland Carson and her mother was Virginia Edwards Randolph. Peyton Randolph, a prominent figure in the First Continental Congress, was one of her ancestors; and her grandfather, John Randolph, was founder of the public school system of Baltimore, Maryland.

She attended the public schools in Baltimore, the Springfield Private School and Darlington Seminary in Westchester, Pennsylvania. Then later she attended summer sessions at the University of North Carolina and Columbia University. The degree of Doctor of Education was awarded her in 1941 by Womans College of the University of North Carolina. This was the only college degree Miss Carson held.

The family moved to Asheville in 1894 and three years later Miss Carson began to teach in what was then known as the West End School in Asheville. This two-room school was conducted in a house loaned for the purpose by the Asheville Cotton Mills. When Park Avenue School replaced the West End School in 1902, Miss Carson was made principal which position she held until her retirement in June, 1945. In May, 1936, the School Board changed the name of the Park Avenue School to the Queen Carson School.

Throughout these years that Miss Carson served as principal, she carried a teaching load as well as her administrative duties.

Her Park Avenue School was the first in the city system to corporate into its regular curriculum the kindergarten which had been established earlier in Asheville by private groups. When many widely known educators of the county were discussing a system of segregation of children according to their mental capabilities for progress, Miss Carson was successfully practicing the plan in Asheville.

In 1937, during the anniversary observance marking her completion of forty years' service to the city schools, the Asheville School Board adopted resolutions which contain the following:

"The City of Asheville owes you a debt which it can never pay. The thousands of school children who have come under your teaching and guidance during the past forty years are better citizens because of their association with you during their school days. Throughout this community are men and women who delight to call themselves Miss Carson's boys and girls. They think of you as their inspiring teacher and they love you as their friend. There can be no higher praise than that. Like the Master Teacher, you have gone about doing good."

At the time of Miss Carson's death, March 2, 1947, an editorial in *The Asheville Times* of March 3, paid this tribute:

"Under other conditions, such a woman leader in education might have been a United States Commissioner of Education. Yet Miss Carson from deliberate choice always declined opportunities for promotion in the local school system because of the need in her own school district. It was a need which she met first of all by the solvent power of love for humanity, for children many of whom sorely needed both love and practical help; and added to these factors was Miss Carson's large vision of an ever-growing educational system in Asheville."

EDWINA SHEARN CHADWICK
1920

"THE most outstanding factor in the promotion of fine arts appreciation in Hickory was Mrs. Edwina Shearn Chadwick, a graduate of Wellesley College, and the first teacher of Claremont College, Hickory, North Carolina. As a result of her untiring efforts Hickory has taken pride in its many cultural achievements."

Thus reads the inscription accompanying the picture of Edwina Shearn Chadwick in the Hickory High School Log of 1939.

Mrs. Chadwick was born in New Orleans, Louisiana; and, while only a baby, was left an orphan when an epidemic of yellow fever took her parents. The tiny one was adopted by Judge Shearn of Houston, Texas, and given his name. No clues were ever found as to her real identity and the Shearns bestowed upon her the love of a true daughter and had her educated in the best schools of the day.

She completed her education at Wellesley College about 1880 and soon after her graduation she went to Hickory to teach in the newly organized Claremont College. Dr. A. S. Vaughn, the first president of the college, soon recognized Miss Shearn's ability and with her assistance he planned the college to be run as the "Wellesley of the South." Edwina Shearn was an excellent musician, and her classes grew with the college.

After teaching here a number of years, she resigned in order to marry a Mr. Chadwick, and the couple went to live in Omaha, Nebraska.

Then, following the death of her husband, she returned to Hickory to make her home. For many years she conducted a private music school, teaching voice in classes. Here she was a pioneer as these class music lessons were forerunners of the present day Public School Music classes. Meanwhile she taught many who were unable to pay for lessons, her only requirement being that the pupil possess talent. She organized the well-known St. Cecelia Music Club of Hickory. Many of her pupils made careers for themselves in the field of music; others became prominent teachers of Public School music.

Mrs. Chadwick was a member of the Episcopal Church of Hickory and was active as soloist and choir director. She was an esteemed member of the town's leading clubs: the Traveler's Club, the Hickory Book Club, and several civic clubs.

On June 17, 1920, Mrs. Chadwick was killed by a Southern passenger train as she was crossing the railroad track near Hotel Hickory.

LAURA HILL COIT
1875-1944

OF the thousands of students who have been graduated from the Woman's College of the University of North Carolina from its initial christening as the State Normal and Industrial School in 1892, none has served the college, the students, and the alumnae longer or more devotedly and efficiently than Laura Hill Coit. Of her it might truly be said, "Many daughters have done virtuously, but thou excellest them all."

Laura Hill Coit, a native of Salisbury, where she was born October 7, 1875, daughter of Julius and Dovie Knox Coit, was a descendant of two prominent Rowan County families. Steeped in the Bible, the Presbyterian faith, and the tenets of the Shorter Catechism, Miss Coit was preeminently a woman of character and good works.

A graduate of Statesville Female College, she entered the State Normal and Industrial School in 1894, became a student assistant in Science in 1895, was graduated in 1896, returned the following year as a teacher of Physical Education, and until 1901 was variously listed as assistant in Mathematics, Physical Education, and English. In 1901, Miss Coit became secretary of the college and administrative assistant to the president, a position she held for nearly forty years.

Miss Coit held a year long job, taking only a month's vacation after the opening of college each fall. Twice only during the forty-three

51

years of her active service was Miss Coit on leave of absence: in 1897-1898 to spend a year at home and teach in the Salisbury public schools; and again in 1919-1920 to visit her brother, Dr. Robert Coit, a missionary to Korea. The latter visit was more or less her farewell to the idea of becoming a foreign missionary, which she had planned to do when the death of President Charles Duncan McIver in 1906 caused her to realize the great need of the college for the continuation of her services. Her interest in missions represented a life long devotion.

In her capacity of secretary of the college the duties that developed upon Miss Coit accumulated with the years until her load of work was staggering to contemplate. A member of the faculty said of her, "Miss Laura Coit, under whose able direction so many wheels move frictionless."

Hers was a marvelously disciplined mind, which executed with accuracy, speed and smoothness. Her sound judgment played upon the many concerns of institutional life as she went about the manifold duties of: secretary of admissions; assemblying the materials for campaigns for appropriations from the Legislature; settling knotty problems of campus and dormitory routine; meeting thousands of parents, speakers and visitors; keeping a minute diary of college affairs in the absence of the president; being for a period of time chief adviser of religious activities; teaching Bible classes on campus, and holding a college girls' class every Sunday at the First Presbyterian Church; conferring with girls on academic and personal problems, before the office of dean of women was established; acting as faculty head of Mid Way dormitory; directing activities for raising the student loan fund, and administering that fund and all scholarships; having charge of the self-help work of students, and the placement bureau; keeping important records of the college, including minutes of the faculty meetings and the college scrapbook of invaluable historic worth.

In all of these capacities Miss Coit came to know the students better than anyone else, and on their return to the campus after years of absence was able to greet them by name. Chancellor W. C. Jackson said of her:

"Miss Coit was the best loved person who ever served on our faculty. More certainly, perhaps, than anyone else she translated the reality of college into the lives of the students. She had a phenominal memory for names and faces. Her devotion to the college was matched only by the devotion of the students to her."

The Alumnae Association was another avenue of service for Miss Coit. Here was a long service of love and devotion to the alumnae on boards, important committees, as secretary-treasurer, twice as president, and as honorary president from 1922 to her death. To the alumnae as to the students she was an anchor, safe and dependable. They trusted her utterly.

It was as a person that Miss Coit was preeminent. An alumnae wrote of her: "Sweet and gentle of heart, a dear, understanding person, keen of intellect, sturdy and fine of character, grounded in the faith of her fathers, Christlike she moved among us."

An alumna and faculty member said of her:

"Forthright, intolerant of sham or inferiority of effort, with a religious faith, saintlike in its intensity and sweetly compelling. Nor can any record tell of the characteristic expression of Miss Coit's rare spirit —the look on her face. It was that look which those who knew her best will remember longest—the radiant light in the eye, the glow of joy, the confidence and delight just ready to break into a smile, which brought a benediction to thousands who came to her office. This look was the seal of her trust in faculty, students, alumnae, and friends, and the symbol of her vision of goodness, beauty, and truth which she confidently expected to be realized on this campus and throughout the world."

According to the wishes of the alumnae, in 1939, the College Board of Trustees changed the name of East Dormitory to Laura Coit Hall.

In time there always comes a breaking point when human endurance ceases. That point came to Miss Coit in 1937, when burdened with her manifold college duties, together with grievous sorrow over the tragic death of a beloved brother, her health became so impaired that she was forced to take a long-needed rest. From that time she made her home with her family at Montreat, where she died February 24, 1944.

Dean of the College, Dr. W. C. Smith once said of Miss Coit: "We are wondering if it is ever vouchsafed to Miss Coit to get a Pisgah view of her service-ableness to this college and to the world."

God grant her that Pisgah view.

ELIZABETH AVERY COLTON
1872-1924

ELIZABETH AVERY COLTON (a pioneer leader for the higher education of women in the South) worked untiringly for nearly twenty years for the standardization of Southern schools and colleges. In one of the earliest of her many pamphlets, she gave as her aim: "To bring about such sentiment as will demand college work for college degrees." *The History of the American Association of University Women* rightfully comments on the significance of her series of pamphlets as the beginning of a new era for the education of women in the South.

Miss Colton lived to see only the first fruits of her labors as the colleges and schools were forced to fall into their places as junior or senior colleges or to close.

53

Her background fitted her peculiarly for her life work and her heritage and environment strengthened the magnificent courage that was hers. Her paternal grandfather, Simeon Baldwin Colton, and her father, James Hooper Colton, were educators and ministers, both having been college presidents. Her mother was Eloise Avery, of a family distinguished in the history of Burke County, North Carolina; one of her ancestors was the first Attorney General of North Carolina. Her parents went to Indian Territory from Morganton, Burke County, as Presbyterian missionaries and it was in Indian Territory, on December 20, 1872, that Elizabeth Avery Colton, the eldest of eight children, was born.

As Elizabeth's family had moved back to Morganton when she was a child, she received her early education in that town. Later she was given an A. B. degree from Statesville Female College (now Mitchell), a typical female college of the day. Yet she found that this degree was tragically inadequate for admission to Mount Holyoke where she later wished to continue her studies. Therefore she had to spend another year in preparation for entering the freshman class. She spent two years (1891-93) at Mount Holyoke, here alternating study with teaching so as to support herself and to aid her family. After six years of teaching in Queens College, Charlotte, she spent two years at Columbia University, getting her B. S. degree from Teachers College in 1903 and her A. M. in 1905. For the following three years, she taught English at Wellesley.

In 1908, she came to Raleigh, North Carolina, as head of the Department of English in Meredith College, then handicapped by the name of "Baptist University for Women," first known as "The Baptist Female University." Meredith was less than ten years old, hence not set in the old pattern. The president candidly told her that his institution was a good high school called a university, and he encouraged her to go ahead and write whatever she chose. She spent the remainder of her active life at Meredith; and the year after she left, 1921, Meredith was fully accredited as a standard college.

Miss Colton's point of view, clarified and broadened by study and teaching in both southern and northern institutions, enabled her to see with sympathetic and dispassionate understanding the problems of colleges in general and also those peculiar to the institutions of this section.

First of all, Miss Colton was a teacher. Her aim, in teaching, was that every student who passed under her tutelage be able to write reasonably clear and correct English and to read with a certain degree of understanding. She was no fosterer of genius, teaching for a select few, cherishing an inner circle. She gave ungrudgingly of her time to the honest plodder. She opened to her students the beauty and the power of the best in literature.

In the South, the educational chaos at the turn of the century included difficulty in adequate support of public high schools and extravagant claims of certain schools as colleges whereas they were only high

54

schools. However, some constructive efforts towards improvement had been made. In 1898, the Association of Colleges and Preparatory Schools (later Secondary Schools) was organized with a three-fold purpose: (1) to organize southern schools and colleges for cooperation and mutual assistance; (2) to elevate the standard of scholarship and to effect uniformity of entrance requirements; and (3) to develop preparatory schools and cut off this work from colleges.

In 1903, Elizabeth Colton was one of a group who met in Knoxville and effected an organization of college women of the South. With a different approach to the problem, in a field limited to the education of women, the aims of this group were almost identical with those of the Association of Southern Colleges. Elizabeth Avery Colton's work was a distinctive part of this whole movement. In 1910, she was appointed chairman of the Committee on College Standards of the Southern Association of College Women; in 1912, she was elected secretary; and, in 1914, she was made president and continued as such until her health failed. In 1915, she became a member of the Executive Committee of the Association of Southern Colleges. The chief work of both associations was the encouragement of those institutions in the South attempting to do work of a college grade and the elimination of those whose quality of work made the name of college fraudulent. Leaders in both associations hoped to aid and hasten this slow work by legislation.

In 1914, when the Southern Association of College Women urged the passing of legislation in each state regulating the conditions under which degree-conferring institutions should be granted, this met with only slight success. However, the Association did not relax its efforts; and, in 1918, a joint committee from both associations drew up a bill to be presented to each state legislature providing for certain minimum requirements which such an institution must meet to be chartered. The bill passed in some states, among them North Carolina, but with modifications that lessened its effectiveness. Yet the education of public opinion in the fight for integrity of college standards was far more important than legislation. Although other persons and organizations had enlightened the public concerning the difference between the real and the sham in education, the application of these principles was Miss Colton's distinctive work.

Years before the attempts at legislation, she had begun a painstaking, detailed survey covering all the colleges for women in the South. She studied the entrance requirements of each college, the courses offered, degrees, diplomas, and certificates and the proportion of students working toward each, the organization, the library, the equipment, and the income of each college on the list. As she worked single-handed, the investigation and her voluminous correspondence involved an incredible amount of work. She had met, however, the hearty cooperation of the state high school inspectors, the United States Specialist in Higher

Education, the investigators for the Carnegie Foundation, and the officials of the better colleges.

The results of her studies appeared in half a dozen pamphlets and articles, giving different stages of her study. These, together with her presidential addresses and illuminating reports as committee chairman and as secretary to the Southern Association of College Women, show one intense desire: "That many sham colleges may within the next ten or twelve years be induced to stop conferring degrees and become good preparatory or industrial schools; that others may die from lack of patronage; and that the righteous remnant may thus be encouraged to strive after ever enlarging fields of service."

Exaggerated claims to excellence and amazing statements culled from catalogues were checked by the facts which it took courage to publish. When the United States Commissioner of Education had made ratings based on actual records made up by graduates of institutions, cautiously prepared, such clamor followed that the President stopped distribution. But what the President dared not let the Commissioner do, Elizabeth Avery Colton did, and the Southern Association of College Women stood back of her. They sent 4,000 copies of *The Various Types of Southern Colleges for Women* to girls graduating from accredited high schools. And what Chancellor Kirkland of Vanderbilt University called the latest of Miss Colton's "highly explosive pamphlets" brought forth floods of protests from outraged alumnae, trustees, and, most of all, from presidents, and also threats of law suits. However, the officials of the better colleges welcomed her criticisms and profited thereby.

Blustering, indignant college presidents who insisted on interviewing her were sometimes disarmed by the appearance of Elizabeth Colton, dainty, slender, distinctly feminine, and by her gracious charm of manner. They perhaps expected a cross between Carrie Nation and the devil.

The influence of her work is incalculable. Dr. B. E. Young, of Vanderbilt University, called her publications an "epoch-making series," as did Dr. E. K. Graham, then president of the University of North Carolina. Dr. Young, in his presidential address to the Association of Southern Colleges, paid the following tribute to her work:

"The Work of Miss Colton has become known throughout the country, wherever there are committees on graduate instruction or committees on admission to advanced standing; in short, wherever education is made a science, she is known as one of the South's leading writers on Education. And it may even be said that the high rating of the members of this association in the educational counsels of other sections of the country is due largely to her willingness to vouch for our educational honesty."

Miss Colton gave the best years of her life to this work of standardization. From 1920 until her death, she was a hopeless invalid. She passed away in Clifton Springs, New York, August 26, 1924.

A figurine of Miss Colton which was presented by the North Carolina State organization of Delta Kappa Gamma to the national organization at the convention in 1939 was returned to the State. In the fall of 1953, this was one of the fine figurines which was placed in the Hall of History in Raleigh.

IDA HEDRICK CONRAD
1867-

W HEN the school bell rings in the fall, I want to go back to my classroom," said Mrs. Ida Hedrick Conrad. "Even after fifty years of teaching, I'd like to be at it again." "Miss Ida," as Mrs. Conrad is called throughout Davidson County, retired from teaching in 1942. She was the first Lexington teacher to claim retirement benefits under the teacher retirement act of 1941.

"Children's lives have been pitched on a higher level; teachers have been inspired by her philosophy of life; and parents have known the feeling of confidence in her ability to guide and teach. Many homes have been influenced by her Christian ideals." These are the words of L. E. Andrews, the Superintendent of Schools, at the time of her retirement.

Ida Hedrick was born in the Pilgrim section of Davidson County, August 12, 1867. She was the daughter of Adam and Mary Hedrick. Her father, a veteran of the War between the States, was a farmer and teacher.

Her basic academic and professional training was done at the Southern Normal School in Lexington. This school was outstanding at the time and attracted students from a wide area. The course of study included work from the primary department to the college level. It offered a teacher-training course also, which Miss Hedrick completed. She continued her studies at Claremont College in Hickory from which she received a diploma.

After she received her diploma, she taught at Mount Hope in Guilford County, at Ebenezer in Davidson, and two years in Burlington. In 1903, she began teaching at Lexington and after a short break came back in 1907 and taught here continuously until her retirement in 1942.

In the meantime, Miss Hedrick married H. J. Conrad, childhood schoolmate of her home community. Mr. Conrad lived only three years after their marriage.

Throughout her teaching career, Mrs. Conrad manifested an interest in new teaching methods. She attended summer schools regularly, thus keeping up-to-date in the teaching profession. One summer she went to Russellville, Indiana, and studied Music under Miss Lucy Leonard.

That she maintained the confidence and respect of her early students was attested by the remarks made by a number of them who had become parents. "Miss Ida taught me and I want her to teach my children" was frequently heard when parents brought their children to school.

In later years, Mrs. Conrad has found great comfort and pleasure in writing poetry and articles. Most of these are of a religious nature and have been published in her church papers, "The Reformed Messenger" and "The Reformed Church Standard."

The life of this splendid woman has extended beyond the schoolroom to her community. Since her early teens she has been a teacher in the Sunday School at Pilgrim Church and has served as president of the State Missionary Society of the Evangelical and Reformed Church for many years.

MARY ELLEN COOK
1853-1934

ON that fine day in the year 1872, when Miss Nellie Cook walked into the one-story frame building on Sixth Street between Church and Nun Streets, that constituted the Wilmington Union School, she had no idea that nearly half a century would roll by before she would relinquish her position as principal of this school.

Education and school systems have taken enormous strides since Miss Nellie journeyed down from Fayetteville, her former home and birthplace, to enter Mrs. Ransom's Select School for Girls, located at Fifth and Dock Streets. She was an outstanding pupil, excelling in rhetoric and mathematics. Upon finishing there with honor, in 1869, at the age of sixteen, she returned to teach a year. She then taught for a season at the old Presbyterian School at Sixth and Dock Streets.

In that day public schools were few and were attended largely by children of the rougher elements of town. However, citizens of the Wilmington area and elsewhere were becoming aware of the vital need of public education. Community leaders therefore conceived the idea of a Union School, the name Union then being applied to any school in which private and public interest were united in accordance with an Act of the General Assembly. This was commenced in 1857.

Then, in 1872, Miss Cook was persuaded by Mr. James H. Chadbourn, Sr., then head of what might now be termed a board of education, to accept the principalship of the old Union School, a bare and barren institution, whose faculty consisted of the principal and one teacher. In all probability, people did not attach any great importance to this appointment as compared with the very progressive private schools of the city, but Miss Cook possessed a vision and felt that a great work was before her. In her forty-eight years as principal, she saw the bare little shack with its two teachers and one hundred pupils evolve into a vastly more modern building on Sixth and Ann Streets that reached an enrollment of eleven hundred pupils and a staff of twenty-four teachers.

Miss Cook faithfully and earnestly guided the youth who came into her school, never forgetting that the training for Christian citizenship was her great responsibility. Many of her students remember the portions of scripture that were memorized to be repeated in chapel on Friday morning.

As the student body of the school increased, Miss Cook was relieved of her classroom work, thus executive duties occupied her time. Later, when the schools had grown, she was appointed supervisor of instruction in all the city schools, both white and colored.

To Miss Cook there was no abrupt change in the public school system during her many years of school work since she grew with the system, discarding old ideas to adopt new ones which she acquired through study and attendance at the most approved summer schools of the north and west.

She labored with the help of her loyal teachers to give Union School a large library. To raise funds for that purpose, entertainments with splendid dramatics and music were given. And these demonstrated the cultural training her pupils were receiving.

Miss Cook served as principal under Superintendent M. C. S. Noble, afterward a member of the faculty of the University of North Carolina, also under the beloved John Jay Blair. In 1921, she was retired after a life of faithful service to the city. Hers was the first pension granted a teacher in Wilmington.

The fragile little lady with iron gray hair and kind blue eyes would rock quietly in her chair and say: "Fifty years of continued teaching in Wilmington seems a long time when you look back, but I loved teaching."

Not only did she serve the public schools, but during the greater part of her life she was a teacher in the First Presbyterian Sunday School and in missions in the vicinity of Wilmington.

Certain of her friends and members of her faculty have honored her memory by placing in Tileston School library a silver scholarship cup. Each year at the commencement exercises a tribute is paid to the memory of Miss Cook and the cup is presented to the eighth grade pupil receiving the highest average for the year. After the pupil's name is engraved on the cup, it is again placed in the library.

After an extended illness, Miss Cook passed away in 1934 at the age of eighty-one. She was laid to rest in beautiful Oakdale in the city where her life was spent in service to others.

Later, Mr. Noble expressed his appreciation of this splendid teacher as follows:

"I knew Miss M. E. Cook, teacher and Principal of the Union School for sixteen years, during which time I was Superintendent of the Public School System of Wilmington. She was a model teacher and Principal and always equal to the discharge of any duty in that dual position. She had the loving respect and confidence of the children, the parents, and the community.

"As teacher, she was kind, patient, and successful; and as Principal, she was firm, careful, and tactful. The City of Wilmington, in my opinion, never had a more enthusiastic, progressive or successful school-woman.

"When I first met Miss Cook, the Union School had less than one hundred pupils and when I left the city in 1898 to come to the University, it had more than six hundred.

"Miss Cook was a born teacher and leader and she taught and led successfully.

"I shall ever remember her with thanks for her loyal service."

CARRIE L. SPARGER COON
1882-

FOUR centuries ago Roger Ascham described the ideal teacher as one in whom "goodness of nature be joined to wisdom." Among those teachers in North Carolina who have embodied this high conception is Mrs. Charles L. Coon. Mrs. Coon, born Carrie Louisa Sparger, in Mt. Airy, October 4, 1882, devoted twenty-eight inspired and inspiring years to the public schools of this State.

Mrs. Coon attended private and public schools in Mt. Airy until 1889 when she entered the North Carolina State Normal and Industrial College in Greensboro. As a student, she attained many honors and demonstrated those qualities of leadership which later were to make her a distinguished teacher. She was a member of the College Glee Club; president of her junior class; class poet in her senior year; marshall in the Adelphian Society; and an editor of *The Decennial,* a history of the first ten years of the college, published in 1902. An additional honor came to her with the winning of the Whitsett prize, offered each year to the senior writing the best essay. Early dedicated to the task of improving education in North Carolina, she was charter-member of the Women's Association for the Betterment of Public School-houses in North Carolina.

In 1902, Mrs. Coon's teaching career began in the Salisbury High School where she was teacher of Latin. It was in Salisbury where she met, and later married, Charles L. Coon whose name has long been honored among educators and laymen in North Carolina. At the time of their marriage, Mr. Coon was engaged in pioneering efforts to bring about consolidation of rural schools. In this capacity he was acting as Secretary of the Southern Education Board which was made up of Southern educators and Northern philanthropists, a group initiating experiments in consolidation in Tennessee. Thus, after living in Tennessee awhile, Mr. and Mrs. Coon returned to North Carolina where Mr. Coon became connected with the State Department of Education. In 1907, they went to Wilson where they were to remain and make their profound imprint upon the life of the city and county. Mr. Coon was responsible for the combining of city and county schools into one unit in 1913, and he was superintendent of both until his death in 1927. The high school in Wilson fittingly bears his name.

Mrs. Coon, meanwhile, taught in the Wilson Graded School from 1917 until 1923. Then, from 1923 to 1935, she taught English in the high school. During three of these years she was Dean of Girls.

Mrs. J. Shepard Bryan who was principal of the Charles L. Coon High School for a part of the time that Mrs. Coon was there, says of her:

"I recall with everlasting gratitude Mrs. Coon's unfailing helpfulness to me during my six years as Principal of the Wilson High School. Although the wife of the Superintendent of Schools and a teacher in the school at the same time, she never tried to assume any administrative authority, but was an ever-present help in times of trouble. At all times she was a constant source of inspiration to me."

In 1935, Mrs. Coon became principal of the Winstead Elementary School; and in the following year, she went to the Margaret A. Hearne Elementary School as principal, a post which she held until her retirement in June, 1945. Miss Bess Sanders, friend and colleague at the Hearne School, has said of Mrs. Coon: "By her steady guiding spirit she led her teachers to a greater appreciation of their profession and encouraged them to grow and to believe in a better and more democratic philosophy of education."

Mrs. Coon's life has had an influence upon varied aspects of community life. She has been a devoted member of the Methodist Episcopal Church. Here she has been a teacher in Sunday School, president of the Woman's Missionary Society, superintendent of the Primary Department of the Sunday School, and superintendent of the Junior Department of the Sunday School. She is a member of the oldest book club in Wilson, organized in 1898; and she was one of the founders and the first president of the Wilson Woman's Club.

Mrs. Coon is the mother of three children: Mrs. John Thomas Baxter of Burlington; Mrs. Thomas Sellman Hall of Wilson; and Charles Lee Coon of Tampa, Florida.

At the time of her retirement in 1945, the teachers, pupils, and citizens of Wilson were saddened by her departure from active service. Yet they were partially consoled by the fact that she continued to live in their midst, thus continuing her gifts of counsel and inspiration.

MARTHA USSERY COOPER
1849-1920

MARTHA USSERY COOPER was born May 19, 1849, and died January 11, 1920. She was one of the outstanding teachers of Rockingham, Richmond County, North Carolina.

She was the second wife of Stephen T. Cooper and was fortunate in that she, as a young bride, entered a well established and organized home with servants. Being physically and mentally strong, she began teaching in the early years of her married life.

The few still living who attended her school, looking back, are amazed at her advanced methods of teaching. "School' always opened with Bible reading and singing. "Miss Martha," as she was affectionately called by her pupils, was far ahead of her times as a teacher. Many of the prominent citizens of Rockingham, in later years, were happy to recall the days spent under her guidance and influence.

The "school" was located on the ground floor of her residence. The speeches made and the poetry recited on Friday afternoons furnished food for thought and developed the memory of many lawyers, politicians, and leaders of the community.

During Miss Martha's day there were no State supervisors of Public School Music or of Physical Education; each teacher made out her own program of studies, or planned her own curriculum. Her pupils were well grounded in the three R's. Then, too, she taught them to sing in the style of Public School Music today. This group she took upstairs to her parlor and here she played the piano for the songs. At such classes, many future choir members received their first music lessons.

Miss Martha believed in developing the bodies as well as the minds therefore periods were scheduled for learning folk dances and for taking calisthenics, or "setting-up" exercises as they would be called today. This was the forerunner of the Physical Education program which is now required in all public schools in all grades from one to twelve.

Martha Ussery Cooper, teaching in her own home, was truly a pioneer and outstanding teacher of her day.

EVELYN ROYAL COWARD
1880-

THE contribution of Evelyn Royall Coward to education in North Carolina has been doubly important. In addition to teaching hundreds of children she has trained scores of teachers on both the in-service and the college levels. A born teacher, she began teaching at an early age and continued in the work for many years.

Coming from a family of teachers, she naturally entered the profession. Evelyn was the youngest of eleven children born to Isham and Rachel Carroll Royall of Sampson County. Evelyn's mother was a teacher prior to her marriage, and her father was a well-known educator in that section of the State where he served as county superintendent and as principal of several academies. As the older brothers and sisters secured sufficient education to meet the requirements for certification, they became teachers. All ten of the children who reached maturity taught. Eventually, three of the four brothers entered the ministry. Living in this atmosphere, Evelyn early developed a love for books and learning. Her bent for teaching was manifested by the fact that as soon as she learned a page in her primer she persisted in teaching it to the mulatto servant, Becky. Mrs. Coward recalls that Becky learned to read in this way.

Evelyn was a student at the State Normal and Industrial School at Greensboro—now Womans College of the University of North Carolina—in its formative years, graduating in the class of 1904. She attributes much of her educational philosophy and her ideals to the noble life and teaching of its president, Dr. Charles D. McIver.

After graduation she taught for two years in Washington, North Carolina, then went to Durham where she began teaching in the fourth grade. At the end of two years she was asked to take the first grade, which she accepted reluctantly. Of her work at Durham, Dr. Holland Holton of Duke University, who was her co-worker at the time, has remarked that she 'did such an outstanding job that the county superintendent of schools requested that she take the new position of primary supervisor of the county . . . I think that it may fairly be said that Mrs. Coward was as truly called to teach as any human being is called to do a worthwhile job for humanity."

In 1914, she became supervisor of the Training School at the Cullowhee Normal and Industrial School — now Western Carolina College. At that time the Training School had one critic teacher, or supervisor, and sixty-five pupils. A. C. Reynolds, then president of the institution, has said that "Mrs. Evelyn Royall Coward is a teacher in the best sense of the term . . . In her early work the practice teaching of Western Carolina Teachers College had a secure foundation."

In 1916, she was married to W. N. Coward who later became the business manager of the College. They had two daughters, Margaret Evelyn and Martha Rachel. While her children were young, Mrs. Coward discontinued teaching, but after the death of her husband in 1928, she entered the University of North Carolina for the purpose of increasing her academic standing. In 1930, she again became a member of the faculty of the Training School of Western Carolina Teachers College. She pursued her graduate work at the University of North Carolina during the summer terms and in 1940 she was granted the degree of Master of Arts. In those later years her two daughters studied at the University with her.

Throughout the seventeen years in which she served as critic teacher in the second grade, Mrs. Coward was a great asset to the Training School. Because of her intimate knowledge of the community and the school, she rendered valuable service to her co-workers in helping them to understand the children whom they were teaching. Her classroom work was superior, but her greatest contribution was in directing the work of student teachers. In conferences with them she forgot herself and was oblivious of the time element in her zeal to help them. Dean W. E. Bird of Western Carolina Teachers College, referring to his practice teaching days under her in 1914-15 and his later relationship with her on the faculty, has appraised her work as follows:

"Her name at the Training School of the College has virtually become a synonym for industry. Her school day is *all* day. This is only another way, perhaps, of saying that her feeling of obligation to her profession is unlimited in terms of time as well as of effort."

A scholar herself and a meticulous person when scholarly details were involved, she would brook no slipshod work on the part of her student teachers. She stimulated them to greater effort and advised them to keep an open mind. Her constant advice was: "If you do not love teaching and experience joy in doing it, don't teach. And when you stop growing, stop teaching."

In the spring of 1947, Mrs. Coward retired at the age of sixty-seven.

Upon request, Mrs. Coward's younger daughter, Rachel, a Medical-Social worker at Vanderbilt University, has written of her mother as a teacher:

"In a sort of analysis, I think I have felt the effect of mother's studious nature and love of teaching as far back as I can remember. I know that I was delving into the mysteries of Elson's Primer and its "This-is-father" and "This-is-mother" stories long before I was five years old. I think this furnished me with a confidence in going to school which has helped me all through my life.

"I also have memories of going on walks on Sunday afternoons when I was nine and my sister was eleven, and learning to identify Doric,

Ionic, and Corinthian columns, on the University of North Carolina buildings.

"Mother always encouraged us to read as many books as we could, and books were always part of our Santa Claus on Christmas morning. Her passion for teaching is continuing into the third generation. She began with her first grandchild, Cynthia, when the little girl was six months old. She seems to be succeeding quite well."

MARY MENDENHALL DAVIS
1850-1923

MARY E. MENDENHALL was the daughter of Elihu Mendenhall and a cousin of Mary Mendenhall Hobbs. She attended New Garden School and Westtown School in Chester, Pennsylvania. In 1877, she returned to her birth-state, North Carolina, where she began teaching in the girls' school of the New Garden School. She taught continuously in the Boarding School and Guilford College through a total of twenty years. In 1877, Mary Mendenhall (later Mary Mendenhall Hobbs) came to the Boarding School and became assistant to Mary E. Mendenhall in the girls' school.

In 1883, Mary E. Mendenhall became Secretary of the faculty. Since she did not have a degree and was ambitious to possess one, after the Boarding School became Guilford College she took college courses while teaching. She received her degree—Bachelor of Science—with the first graduating class of Guilford College in 1891.

In 1897, she married J. Franklin Davis, a member of the college faculty. He had done advanced study at Johns Hopkins University and abroad in Leipsic and Strasbourg, and was considered one of the outstanding scholars and teachers on the faculty. He and President Hobbs were close friends and counselors through many years of the building and development of Guilford College.

Being a Mendenhall, Mary E. Mendenhall Davis, had, as one might expect: strong determination, physical and moral stamina, and unfailing fidelity to responsibility. She was direct and sincere in thinking and in speech, and intolerant of anything done in a careless or slovenly manner.

Two honors came to Mary E. M. Davis at Guilford: she was the first woman and the first faculty member to be appointed on a trustee committee—and that committee was the one on endowments. Here she served with her usual determination and courage, and after 1897 she was an active assistant in the financial campaigns of the College. She took a special interest in securing contributions for the building of New Garden Hall, where girls with very small means had the opportunity of cooperative living. No service was too great or too difficult if she felt it was for the advancement of Guilford College. She was a strong power in the wise guidance of financial affairs of the young College, and of administrative policies and plans as well. However, perhaps her greatest contribution was one that cannot be measured: her inspiring influence on the religious lives of the students.

MARY FLINN DICKSON
1856-1935

THE name of Miss Mary Dickson is closely woven with early education in Morganton where she taught for about thirty years. "In her long years as a teacher there she educated a whole generation and contributed much to the intellectual life of Morganton" writes one of her early pupils. Miss Dickson was a native of Morganton and was the daughter of John A. and Elizabeth S. Greenlee Dickson.

She attended the private school of Miss Maria Cousins who came from New York soon after the War between the States and conducted a private school in Morganton for many years. Miss Dickson received her college work at Radcliffe College and took graduate work at the University of Michigan.

About the middle of the 1800's, she established a private school in a building adjacent to her home in Morganton. The school grew so rapidly that she found it necessary to move to a larger building near the center of town. Of this school, Dr. Edward Erwin, now a professor at Davidson College and a former pupil of Miss Dickson, wrote:

"The two rooms of her drab little building were comfortably and adequately equipped; the pupils were informally divided into grades. A succession of young lady assistants—Miss Dupuy, Miss Brown, Miss Richmond, Miss Thompson, and others—taught the lower grades and Latin; Miss Mary taught everything and everybody else."

She was an excellent teacher; she could impart information in an interesting way; she could secure an enormous amount of work from each pupil. She was a strict disciplinarian. When she was teaching seventh grade geography, she seemed to have eyes in the back of her head; and there was not a whisper nor a movement in all the rest of the room.

When public schools were introduced into Morganton, Miss Mary taught one of the grades. But she is remembered by her former pupils not as a limited teacher of a restricted grade but as one who could and did teach any subject in the school curriculum—except Latin. As they grew into manhood and womanhood, they never overcame a juvenile feeling of fear and trembling in her presence; but they came to know the sweetness and graciousness of her character and found in her a valued counselor and friend. In the community she was known not only as a teacher of youth but also as a devout member of her church—she was a staunch blue-stocking Presbyterian—as a leader in literary circles, and as a strong supporter of every movement for civic betterment.

In the period about 1917-1925, Miss Dickson was a member of the English staff at Winthrop College.

At the end of that period she returned to Morganton where she lived until her death, September 9, 1935.

MATTIE M. EATON
1852-1909

LAURA CLEMENT
1844-1902

MISS MATTIE EATON, known to friends and acquaintances as "Miss Mattie," beginning her teaching career at the age of fifteen, for more than forty years gave to thousands of boys and girls of Piedmont North Carolina all the education they ever had, and encouraged and adequately prepared many excellent students for entrance to institutions of higher learning. Miss Mattie's was a private school, conducted with little thought of financial reward, the tuition charges being in direct ratio to the ability to pay. For many pupils it was a "free school." For others it was a high class "boarding school," with pupils coming from a distance to enjoy the superior educational advantages offered, a number finding pleasant, home-like board and room in Miss Mattie's own home.

For Miss Mattie her school was a direct inheritance from her father, Jacob Eaton, a famous educator, proprietor and head of Clay Hill Seminary, located near Mocksville, North Carolina, in the years immediately preceding and following the Civil War. Mr. Eaton, in turn, had assumed educational leadership from his teacher, the Reverend Baxter Clegg, whose Brick Academy, in Mocksville, was built in the late eighteen forties, on the site of the present Southern Railway station. Mr. Eaton had been Mr. Clegg's first student, became his assistant, and succeeded him as head of the school.

In 1871, Miss Mattie was herself a student at her father's school, at the time ill health caused him, when she was only fifteen, to shift much of the responsibility to her shoulders. In 1874, Miss Mattie, now recognized as head of the school, was persuaded to move the old Brick

Academy site in Mocksville. Here for a number of years, tutored by her scholarly father at night, she acquired a fine classical education. which she in turn passed on to her students.

A story still extant among white haired men and women, whose fathers and mothers were among Miss Mattie's earliest pupils, concerns the respect shown her, even at fifteen, by the big boys of the school. The students were lined up at the spring, where Miss Mattie was passing out dippers of water. One big boy, in all earnestness called out, "Miss Mattie, will you condescend to stoop so low as to hand me a drink of water, if you please, Ma'am?"

On January 4, 1892, Miss Mattie, having been joined by her aunt, Miss Laura Clement, also of Mocksville, moved her school to a new building, the Mocksville Academy, later named by the students Sunnyside Seminary. Here for the next ten years, in two rooms, Miss Mattie taught the older pupils and Miss Clement taught the younger ones. In the studio, a small cottage in the school yard, a teacher was employed to give private lessons in Music and Art and to help with the costuming, the marches, dances, plays, and music of the school, especially for commencement, which was a spectacular affair requiring weeks of preparation every spring.

"Miss Laura," as she was known, was motherly, gentle, and kind. A lover of good reading, one of her greatest contributions was to instill in her pupils a love of books. In the home-like atmosphere of her classroom, in the later afternoon, after "lessons" were over, some one would call out, "Miss Laura, please read to us!" Having had experience in the rearing of not only brothers and sisters but nephews and nieces, she always kept a weather eye out for small mischief or inattention. The literature she read was so dear and familiar to her that she could continue reading without even looking at the book. A privilege much sought by the little girls was to comb Miss Laura's long, unruly dark hair, which she found great difficulty in keeping neatly arranged. While this grooming was taking place, nothing daunted, Miss Laura read on.

Quietly, earnestly, and without ostentation, religion was a daily experience in the lives of Miss Mattie and Miss Laura. Opening exercises, with Bible reading, and memorization of the Scriptures, were part of each day's routine. Older boys and girls were taught to lead in prayer and conduct the exercises.

Miss Mattie's greatest strength as a teacher lay in the fields of Composition, Literature, and Latin. She stimulated the reading of good books and much memorization of fine poetry. She was a Latin scholar and encouraged her more intellectual pupils to continue their study of the classics in college.

After the death of Miss Laura Clement on September 13, 1902, Miss Mattie, with what assistance she could find, continued her school. Upon the opening of Mocksville's first graded school in 1907, she cordially joined forces with the public schools, teaching one year before her health failed. Death came to her on November 14, 1909.

Nearly forty years after her death, a former student writing in the spring bulletin of the National Delta Kappa Gamma Society in 1947, paid the following tribute to Miss Mattie Eaton, the great friend and teacher of her youth:

"Miss Mattie was great—Miss Mattie was wonderful! The boys and girls of old Sunnyside Seminary had no doubts about the matter. She taught thoroughly and well. She opened up the treasures hidden in books. Life was a great adventure. She stimulated; she advised; she curbed; she corrected; she praised. Her keen grey eyes were crinkled from smiling, and her infectious laugh rang out loud and clear. Miss Mattie was fifty and frankly stout. But who cared? Miss Mattie had fun teaching school. Her life was rich and full with school, home, family, friends, books, the church and the great wide, wonderful world."

Miss Mattie went to heaven many years ago; but no former student of hers living today has the slightest doubt that for *her*, teaching was a good life.

HARRIET WISEMAN ELLIOTT
1884-1947

HARRIET WISEMAN ELLIOTT, a woman of parts, with a keen mind, a sturdy physique, an attractive personality, richly endowed with the qualities of leadership, gave unbounded energy and enthusiasm to the pursuit of her life goals. Early in life she became interested in the Woman Suffrage movement, drinking deeply of the inspiration of such leaders as Anna Howard Shaw and other pioneers in the struggle for women's rights. The goals of her life became the education of women and their enfranchisement. She considered education and enfranchisement twin ideas, being convinced that only an educated woman could become a good, responsible citizen. Freedom linked with an educated sense of responsibility were her watchwords, and education and politics the arenas of her gallant and enthusiastic endeavors.

Descendant of a sturdy, well-to-do pioneer family, Miss Elliott was born on July 10, 1884, in Carbondale, Illinois. She was educated at Park College, Parksville, Missouri, and at Hanover College, Hanover, Indiana, where she earned the A. B. degree in 1910 and was awarded the honorary degree of L.L.D. in 1941. Her graduate work was done at Columbia University where in 1913 she received the M.A. degree.

Armed with her new degree, Miss Elliott became in 1913, a member of the Department of History and Political Science at the State Normal and Industrial College in Greensboro. Here she was destined to remain for thirty-four years, a potent force for the education of women in the college, her adopted state, and the nation.

Miss Elliott always spoke of herself as a "teacher" at the State Normal, or at the North Carolina College for Women, or at the Woman's College of the University of North Carolina, as through the years the college changed its name. She became a leader in the development of the Normal College into a great liberal arts college for women.

As the college grew and expanded, Miss Elliott's work in political science became a full time position. Her alive, enthusiastic teaching of government attracted students to her courses so that not only those preparing to teach, who were required to take Political Science, had the benefit of her instruction, but those seeking mind-stretching electives flocked to her classes. A student said of Miss Elliott's teaching:

"As a teacher Miss Elliott awakened the students of this college to their responsibilities as participants in a democracy. She taught them to read newspapers, to cast their votes, to question again and again the why-fors of their local and national community. She forced open minds of her students, insisting that they think through for themselves the difficult problems that beset young people of our complicated world."

Miss Elliott, always a dedicated leader of great causes, worked with President Frank Porter Graham and Governor Oliver Max Gardner to organize the Greater University and to establish the Woman's College as an integral part of that university in 1934. She was a member of the first Greater University Council and used her influence to place women on the Greater University Board of Trustees.

Her broad knowledge of government, joined to a definite ability in administration, led her to plan a remarkable student-faculty set-up for the Woman's College. In consequence, in 1935, she was asked to leave the classroom and become Dean of Women in order that she might put her plan into operation.

For twelve years she worked to perfect an organization on the Woman's College campus by which students, while in college, would lead normal integrated lives in happy, beautiful, healthful, homelike surroundings, and at the same time experience the finest type of democratic community living. Her unique contribution was the establishment of an academic and personnel advisory system, with selected members of the academic faculty chosen as class chairmen and advisers of students, together with professionally trained dormitory counselors who were also part-time teachers in some academic field. Under her leadership students were given more responsibility, social activities were expanded, and student government became a fine reality. Always she kept before the students the goal of acceptance of increased responsibility along with increased freedom.

From the beginning Miss Elliott's work and influence were not confined to the college campus. It was her destiny to become a citizen

70

of North Carolina at a time when the state was entering a period of progressive change. As an ardent member of the Democratic party Miss Elliott worked in season and out of season for women's rights and fought vigorously for woman's suffrage. She was a leader in the League of Women Voters, and the American Association of University Women.

Miss Elliott's services to the state included: appointment by Governor Ehringhaus to serve with four men on the State Emergency Relief Administration, 1933-35; delegate-at-large from North Carolina to the National Democratic Convention, 1932-36; director of the educational program for the Woman's Division of the National Democratic Committee, 1934-35; alternate member of the platform committee of the Democratic Party from North Carolina, 1936; President of the North Carolina Social Service Conference, 1939-40; appointed by Governor Clyde R. Hoey a member of the North Carolina State Committee of the Conference of Southern Governors, 1940.

Not only governors but presidents sought her counsel and enlisted her services. Under President Wilson, she was in 1918-19 member of the Woman's National Defense Council during World War I. In 1940, she was a member of President Hoover's Conference on Child Health. She was appointed the only woman member on President Roosevelt's Advisory Commission of National Defense Council and later became Federal Consumer Commissioner. She had part in setting up the WAVES in World War II, and became director of the Women's Division of the War Bond Sales campaign. Secretary of the Treasury Morganthau said of her work, "She became the key person upon whom I learned to build our organization."

After the war, Miss Elliott continued to serve as adviser to the War Savings Staff, and went in 1945 to the London Conference of the United Nations Educational, Scientific, and Cultural Organization (UNESCO), as alternate adviser to the American delegation.

While on loan to the National Government, Miss Elliott returned between assignments to fulfill her policy making duties as Dean of Women. Although she was wise in her ability to organize and delegate responsibility, the students of the last few years of her life, due to her national obligations, missed her presence, her sympathetic understanding, her infectious humor, her radiant smile, her personal charm, her enthusiasm, her genuine concern for the individual student, and her inspiring idealism.

Miss Elliott was an active member of many local, state, and national educational, health, and social service organizations, before which she often spoke and led discussions. She was an orator of no mean order, possessing a big, pleasing, resonant voice which could adapt itself to a small group or fill a huge auditorium. Men as well as women admired and respected her rapier quick mind in debate, where tensions were broken by her infectious chuckle and her ability to laugh at herself.

Her last talk was given on February 7, 1947, before Alpha Chapter of Delta Kappa Gamma, of which she was an honorary member. It is significant that her discussion centered around the educational implications of the recent United Nations Educational Conference which she had attended in London.

The next day after returning from the funeral of her old friend, Oliver Max Gardner, minister to the Court of St. James, and former governor of North Carolina, Miss Elliott suffered a cerebral hemorrhage, and was later taken to her home in Carbondale, Illinois, where she died on August 6, 1947, at the age of sixty-three years.

Miss Elliott believed in democracy, practiced democracy, and taught democracy both in and outside the classroom. No more fitting memorials could have been erected to her memory than the two at the Woman's College: the yearly social science conference established in 1947 as the Harriet Elliott Social Science Forum; and the beautiful and spacious Student Union erected in 1953, and named in her honor, Elliott Hall.

Her best eulogy is expressed in the words of a former student and loyal friend: "Harriet Wiseman Elliott needs no more appropriate monument than the product of her own labor—a living memorial, the ever-widening influence of those who have caught her faith in responsible freedom and believe in it enough to live it."

SUSAN JONES EDMUNDSON
1841-1909

YEARS after the subject of this biography had passed away, a young girl greeted her new teacher in the Eureka School in Wayne County as follows: "My father said to tell you that he was once a pupil of Miss Sue and that if you are half as good a teacher as your grandmother, you'll be all right for me." Thus the way was prepared for a new teacher. The teaching career of "Miss Sue" spanned a period of forty-one years.

Susan Jones, the "Miss Sue" of the story, was born in 1841 in Warren County, the daughter of the architect of Louisburg and Chowan Colleges, Albert G. Jones. In 1857, she graduated from Chowan College and began teaching in a private school in Greene County. Here she met and married John J. Edmundson.

Her husband died soon after the War between the States, leaving Mrs. Ehmundson with four children. She tried to keep her private school open as the need for schools at this time seemed very great. As there was little money in circulation during this period, Mrs. Edmundson accepted for tuition farm products with which she fed her family.

When the public schools were established in the State, she discontinued her private school and went into public school teaching. She taught in Eureka and Pikeville Schools in Wayne County and in the schools at Wilson Mills and Faro in Johnston County. Mrs. Edmundson was a student throughout her life. And, in those days when a teacher's certificate was gained through examinations before the county Superintendent of Schools, she always made a grade of "A" which entitled her to a "First Grade Certificate," as such was termed at that time.

HETTIE WATSON FENNELL
1868-1936

IN educational philosophy and practice, Hettie Watson Fennell was ahead of her time. The basic principle of individual differences and the doctrine of interest which the psychologists were to teach at a much later date were recognized by her and were practiced in her teaching.

"Miss Hettie," as she was affectionately called, was a native of Wilmington. She was the daughter of Thomas and Mary Watson. During her childhood, she lived in the home built by Cornelius Harnett at Hilton.

She graduated from the Tileston Normal School in 1875. After her graduation, she taught in this school until it was discontinued in 1891. Following this, she taught in the Hemenway School in Wilmington for a few years, later becoming principal of that school.

About 1895, Miss Watson was married to Frederick Fennell, a merchant and farmer of Hertford County. A few years after their marriage, they sold their property and moved to Wilmington. Here Mrs. Fennell served as principal of the Lutheran Parochial School for several years. She acquired a special interest in the overgrown boys and in the under-privileged children of the parish. In the attempt to take care of the needs of the over-grown boys and to adapt school work to their interests, with the help of the boys, she initiated the first school garden in New Hanover County. She arranged for a cannery in the school where the vegetables the boys had grown were canned and sold. The proceeds of this project were used to buy materials with which the boys made office furniture. This interest in caring for individual differences continued throughout her work at the Parochial School.

Then, in about 1914, when Mrs. Fennell became principal of the newly established Cornelius Harnett School in Wilmington, she initiated the practice of having special classes for children who needed individual teaching. She advocated the principles that children differ in their ability to gain knowledge from books; that instruction should proceed from all angles as nearly as possible; that teachers should make school interesting; that material should be adapted to the capacity of the pupils; and that a pupil should not be forced to remain in school after he has reached the limit of his capacity. Thus she struggled to escape the curse of standardization so prevalent in her day. According to the prevailing philosophy and practice current at that time, all pupils were expected to conform to the same pattern of learning and they were measured by the same yardstick.

Mrs. Fennell's interest in education continued after she retired from teaching. She lectured at Parent-Teacher meetings, at teachers' institutes, and at other gatherings where she thought that the cause of education might be furthered. She was considered one of the most public spirited women of her day.

She died on March 16, 1936.

To honor the memory of this great teacher, appreciative friends have provided a silver cup which is awarded annually to the pupil in the seventh grade of the Cornelius Harnett School who has the highest scholarship record for the year.

ELIZABETH KEITH FORD

1859-1950

A teacher affects eternity; he never knows where his influence stops.   —Henry Adams

At the time of Miss Ford's death, it was said in an editorial in *The Asheville Citizen*:

"Many teachers have knowledge though not all possess the mysterious capacity for imparting knowledge in such a way that it seems to kindle new life in the spirits of the students. Miss Ford had that rare endowment."

Appropriately, then, she is included in this volume although she spent comparatively few of her ninety years actually in the classroom and made no official connections with educational organizations. The individual quality of her teaching, the illuminating power of her personality—these are continually remembered by those who knew her well. In very truth, her spirit marches on.

You who read this may envisage an imposing person. On the contrary, Miss Ford was a little over five feet tall and perhaps not at any time did she weigh more than a hundred pounds. In her tiny body, however, was Force. A firm purposefulness characterized her sprightly movements. Bright, quick brown eyes alerted one to attention. She, it is remembered clearly, gave heed to the interrogated pupil as though anticipating rich jewels of knowledge. If only vague generalities came forth, the lagging pupil was brought up sharply with Miss Ford's characteristic, crisp: "For instance, Mary?" or "For instance, Allen?"

Miss Ford's outstanding contribution to Asheville, town of her adoption, was a school for girls and boys, known simply as "Miss Ford's," established in the fall of 1902. She had lived in Asheville and its vicinity in the 80's when she came seeking health for a beloved brother whom she nursed. She was drawn to return in 1898. For three years she taught Science in the Asheville Female College and then conducted her private school for twelve years in several locations, the last being the building that today houses the Asheville Y. M. C. A.

Elizabeth Keith Ford was born on August 2, 1859, the only daughter of Frank and Rebecca Simpson Ford, at their plantation, "Sunnyside," in Bourbon County, Kentucky. One of her earliest recollections concerned an afternoon when she was sitting on a little stool by her mother who was sewing. Her father came in. The child recoiled from the expression on his face. "Becky," he said, "President Lincoln has been shot!" "O Mr. Ford!" exclaimed his wife. "What will this mean?" Thus at an early age, Elizabeth Ford came face to face with History, a subject that fascinated her all of her life.

Her early education was from private tutors and at Daughters College at Herrodsburg, Kentucky. In later years, as it became possible from time to time, she studied at the University of Chicago, the University of Cincinnati, and the University of Tennessee. Her first teaching was at Daughters College and next at Madison Institute, Richmond, Kentucky.

During the Asheville years, Miss Ford's mother lived with her as her father had died many years earlier. After her mother's death, Miss Ford retired from the teaching profession and went in 1914 to Europe for an extended tour. The outbreak of World War I sent her home. "Home" became several places where relatives and friends welcomed her. For six years she was with her best beloved niece in Tulsa, Oklahoma. For much briefer periods she lived in Colorado and Florida. Eventually, though, she came to Asheville again, her "home" in the minds of her former pupils and her many Asheville friends. Here she remained for the rest of her life, approximately fourteen years.

Miss Ford's religious affiliation for fifty-two years was with the Central Methodist Church in Asheville. She was a member of the Friendly Dozen Book Club, possibly Asheville's original woman's club. She became an honorary member of the Review Club, many of the members of which were her former pupils. She was one of the first members of Friends of the Library. These constituted the whole of her formal connections with groups. Her associations were, rather, with individuals—new friends as well as old ones, former pupils, their children, and even their grandchildren.

The young Elizabeth had had five brothers. To no sister, perhaps, had brothers been more important than to this only daughter, whose mother had frequently advised her: "You should be good to your brothers, Lizzie. Remember, you are the only sister they have." The reverse of the situation was never emphasized, apparently. All who knew the sister in later years believed she had steadfastly been "good to the brothers," even to the second and third generations.

Does such relationship explain the phenomenon that Miss Ford, tiny little lady that she was, had few if any disciplinary problems with her "big boys"? She as easily made contact with them as with her girls. They responded to her lively interests and as a rule became too much interested in the process of learning to be disciplinary cases. One of her boys, later a successful physician and the one who attended her in her final hour, once said:

"This pupil remembers a small, delicate lady whose pupils fairly trembled at the thought that each English word had to be precise and each Latin phrase perfect. But he also was to remember later his discovery that in demanding perfection she was successfully encouraging and training a regard for accuracy, truth, and faith in her pupil as though her goal were to prepare him for the eventuality of some high calling."

Miss Ford, after a lingering illness, died on February 5, 1950. Final rites were held in Paris, Kentucky, and burial was in the family plot there. Preliminary services had been conducted in the Chapel of Central Methodist Church by the pastor who had become acquainted with Miss Ford in her twilight years. He had found, however, that even in his last visits to Miss Ford he had been offered intellectual stimulus. He spoke of this and how disciplined love of good literature all her life had come to serve her well at the end of her days when increasing blindness kept her from reading. The great books she had read and the poetry she had loved and had taught so many others to appreciate were with her daily. She was not dependent on being read to, for by the hour, if she wished, she could repeat for her own delight literature that she had committed to memory.

It was revealed that in the preamble of her last will she had stated her own articles of faith: "First I would thank God for the gift of life, for family ties, and for the unmatched kindness of younger friends, my former pupils. I am thankful, too, for the joy I have found in the work of my active declining years and for the comfort and peace I have found later in the homes of friends."

On the first anniversary of her death, it was made public that a group of Miss Ford's former pupils had presented through Friends of the Library a literary collection to Sondley Reference Library of Pack Memorial Public Library, as living and lasting tribute to their greatly enjoyed and greatly beloved teacher. In announcing this gift of great importance to the library, *The Asheville Citizen-Times stated*: "Comprising books representative of the many interests of the educator, the collection is given by former students who have established themselves throughout the country and seek this opportunity to honor the person whom many regard as having pointed the way to Mecca." The collection has been voluntarily added to by other former pupils, other friends, and their children. These books are not items for museum shelves, to be seen and not touched; they are available to all who use the library. Their subject-matter reflects the varied interests that were Miss Ford's special ones: English and American Literature, Biography, History, Religion, and Natural History.

With the gift of books came a number of tributes to Miss Ford written by former pupils who to the end of her life had had close association with her.

One of these, a professor of Botany, whose interest in Nature had been stimulated by her teacher a half century before, wrote:

"She stimulated our thinking and urged us to learn to the very end of her life. Under her teaching, literature became not mere printed pages but an expression of emotions and experiences of real life. . . . A lively naturalist, she never lost her zeal for attempting to identify every plant and bird that met her keen eye."

Another, in whose home Miss Ford had frequently enjoyed the relationship that mother or grandmother might have had, wrote:

"In the life of most of us there are but few strong personalities who have influenced our lives deeply. It is not uncommon for this to have been in the person of an instructor during formative years. Miss Ford had such a deep and abiding power in the lives of her pupils. Not only did she bring to them the cold facts of knowledge and cause them to come alive in a bright flame of interest in cultural things but she furnished an example in her own life. It was a rare privilege to watch the years touch with mellow beauty the keen, richly stored mind, and the gay, sympathetic spirit—both so superbly disciplined to the end and wearing the white plume of courage."

Still another wrote:

"From the flood of grateful memories of Miss Ford as teacher and friend, outstanding are her ability to make learning an adventure and in her classroom the high code of honor which grew from her belief in us. Her genius for imparting knowledge did not cease with her active profession but was a vital part of her long life. The ideals that she strove to create in us have given us a goal which her lasting faith in us has made less impossible of attainment."

Out of the fulness of understanding, surely, it was written of Elizabeth Ford when she died: "And now that the beloved teacher has closed the door of her earthly tabernacle, her influence and her inspiration will continue even in lives unborn."

MELVILLE VINCENT FORT

1868-1939

Miss MELVILLE VINCENT FORT, head of the Department of Art, added a certain spice and piquancy to the charter membership of the faculty of the State Normal and Industrial School when she became a member in the fall of 1892. Miss Fort was young, twenty-four years old, and witty, with a pronounced twinkle in her eye. She had two hobbies, art and friends, and she cultivated both.

Miss Fort was born at Starkeville, Mississippi, May 24, 1868. She was graduated with honor from the Mississippi Industrial Institute and College and had additional training in New York. She came to the State Normal and Industrial School from a year's experience in a college in Kentucky.

According to the first college catalogue, Miss Fort offered what no doubt were "lady-like" courses in wood-carving, china painting, designing and decorative art. She also offered some very business-like courses in Industrial Art, including form study and free-hand drawing, architectural and mechanical drawing, clay modeling, and the history of art.

Talented students learned well under Miss Fort, and many became her fast friends. Under her tutelage one student made an architectual plan so well that a member of the faculty used it in building his house. Most of the students had had no opportunity to study Art before coming to the college, and to those who "couldn't draw," her sharp incisive voice sent terror to their hearts and a wavering in their lines, when she said, "You don't see it that way!" Her complimentary, "That's not bad," became a cherished memory.

Miss Fort's sprightliness and wit covered a very warm heart, which made her a favorite with the entire faculty. The names of Dr. Gove, Miss Petty, Miss Mendenhall, and Miss Fort became closely associated in the minds of the students. The last two made their home together, in the early years, at the "little green cottage" just off the campus. It was a home of friendly banter and witticism mingled with kindliness, gracious hospitality, and intelligent conversation. Miss Fort's trip in summer vacation of 1900, in which she visited the art galleries of Europe, gave added interest to both her life and her conversation.

One who became her life long friend was the wife of one of the professors, Mrs. J. Y. Joyner. A son of Mrs. Joyner says, "She was an inseparable companion of my mother. The people whom she most enjoyed were my mother and my children."

In 1919, Miss Fort resigned and moved to Raleigh where for the next few years she did part-time work in the office of the State Architect and in the Revenue Department. In Raleigh she lived in the home of the J. Y. Joyners until the death of Mrs. Joyner in 1930.

In the following years she often returned to the campus to renew old friendships. She was a cherished visitor to former faculty associates; and former students, recalling their visits to the "little green cottage," welcomed news of her.

It was while on a visit to the J. Y. Joyner family in LaGrange that Miss Fort died on July 25, 1939. She was buried in Raleigh, in the Joyner family plot.

Her best tribute is expressed in the words of one who knew and appreciated her: "She had a number of close friends, and I would say that her principal activity and hobby was the cultivation of people."

MARIANA COBB GAREISSEN
1870-1939

MRS. MARIANA COBB GAREISSEN had a long and varied career in the field of education. She was a most successful teacher; and, as a teacher of teachers and author of children's books, her influence reached beyond her classroom. Her father, Dr. W. H. H. Cobb of Goldsboro, was a surgeon in the Confederate Army. Marianna was born and reared in Goldsboro.

She attended private schools until the opening of the public schools in her home town in 1885. She completed the high school course here two years later and went to Greensboro Female College the following year. Upon completing the course offered by that institution, she began teaching at Mount Olive and at the end of two years transferred to Oxford. Then, in the fall of 1892, Miss Cobb accepted a position in the Goldsboro schools where she taught until 1895. While teaching here, she studied advanced Latin under George W. Connor who was at that time principal of the high school and later Justice of the North Carolina Supreme Court. During the same period she studied English, Literature, and History under John Spencer Bassett.

In the summer of 1895, Miss Cobb attended the Cook County Normal School and while there she visited the experimental school of John Dewey in Chicago. During that summer she came in contact with Mathilda E. Coffin, supervisor and assistant superintendent of the Detroit Schools. Miss Cobb accepted the invitation and therefore taught in Detroit until the spring of 1901. It was while teaching here that she met and married Mr. Edward Garreissen.

She returned to Goldsboro in 1906 and taught here until 1913. During the academic year 1913-1914, Mrs. Garreissen was exchange teacher in the schools of Newton, Massachusetts, then a model school system. In the fall of 1914, she returned to Goldsboro where she served as supervisor of the city schools until 1917. In the intervening summers she taught in county institutes and one summer at the University of North Carolina. She was president of the Primary Department of the North Carolina State Teachers Association in 1917. Dr. J. Y. Joyner, then State Superintendent of Public Instruction, asked Mrs. Garreissen to assist in presenting the new bill for State Certification of Teachers to the Legislature of 1917-1918. Because of her services here, Dr. Joyner later wrote her a letter of thanks for her "splendid presentation and valuable aid."

It was during these years that the teachers of North Carolina began to feel the force of Mrs. Gareissen's influence which was strengthened and deepened throughout subsequent years.

In 1918, Mrs. Gareissen became a member of the staff of the Newson Publishing Company of New York City to demonstrate their books and methods. Until her retirement from this position in 1938, she went into practically every eastern state from Maine to Texas and as far west as Ohio and Arkansas. Meanwhile she lectured from convention platforms, taught in summer schools, demonstrated in institutes and in many school systems, presented arguments for book adoptions before state governors and legislative committees, thus helping to form the thought and practices of hundreds of teachers in various states. Requests for her services were so numerous that she was forced to budget her time and to travel widely and constantly.

Yet while engaged in these manifold activities, and often while "on the road," Mrs. Gareissen found time to put into concrete expression some of her basic psychological teachings. She wrote for the Newsom Company the pre-primer, *Easy Steps to Playtime,* and in collaboration with Mrs. Geneva Johnston Hecox, Superintendent of Primary Grades in Washington, D. C., wrote the primer called *Our Pets.*

During the last five or six years of her long teaching career Mrs. Gareissen's contacts with the teachers of North Carolina were renewed as she worked in the schools with members of the State Department of Education. As she went from one end of the State to the other, her heart was frequently gladdened by expressions of warm appreciation from teachers and school authorities whom she had helped.

On April 10, 1939, Mrs. Gareissen passed away in Houston, Texas, at the home of her only daughter.

MARY OWEN GRAHAM
1872-

MARY OWEN GRAHAM, teacher, school administrator, college president and civic leader was born in Wilmington, North Carolina, on October 13, 1872, the daughter of Archibald and Eliza Owen Barry Graham. She is a member of a distinguished North Carolina family whose ancestry is a blending of Scotch, French, Welsh, and English. To her own illustrious record is added that of her brother, Dr. Edward Kidder Graham, president of the University of North Carolina from 1913 to 1918, and of his son, Dr. Edward Kidder Graham, Jr., who is carrying on an educational career of the same high tradition. Her uncle, Dr. Alexander Graham, ranked foremost among educators in North Carolina. He originated the graded school system in Fayetteville, and was for many years superintendent of the Charlotte city schools. His son, Dr. Frank Porter Graham, has added honor to the name as president of the University of North Carolina, as United States Senator, and as mediator to foreign countries.

When Miss Graham was very young, her family moved to Charlotte, North Carolina, and Charlotte has remained her home, though she has been away for periods of time. Her education was received in private schools, in the Charlotte city schools and in Charlotte Female Institute, now Queens College, where she received her A. B. degree in 1890. She studied at the summer schools of the Universities of North Carolina and Tennessee and in 1907 attended Teachers College of Columbia University.

Miss Graham's contributions to education and to the civic life of the state have been varied. She was first of all an enthusiastic and devoted teacher. She taught in the graded schools of Charlotte from 1892 to 1907. There was a shortage of teachers in those days, too, and Miss Graham says that at times she had as many as ninety children in her primary class, and never less than sixty-five. Broader fields of service called and from 1908 to 1912 she was a member of the Department of Education of the North Carolina College for Women in charge of training primary teachers. It was during this time of her emphasis on work in the primary field that she organized and became the first president of the North Carolina Primary Teachers Association. This group wielded unusual professional strength for a number of years until, under her guidance, it became a part of the North Carolina Teachers Assembly. She edited for the Primary Teachers Association a booklet entitled "Literature and Stories for Primary Grades." She also edited in collaboration with Ann Michaux Williams, a manual for teachers and students for teaching phonics. For some years there was a rewarding sale for this book.

Always interested in teacher training, Miss Graham often spent her summers in furthering this cause. She was an instructor in North Carolina State College Summer School in 1906. She conducted courses in Methods in Teaching in many County Institutes in North Carolina from 1907-1914. She was instructor in the School of Methods in Fredericksburg, Virginia, in 1908. She taught courses in Primary Methods in the Summer School of the University of North Carolina from 1908 to 1913.

She was Assistant Superintendent of Education in Mecklenburg County, North Carolina, from 1912 to 1916. She instituted Community Week in the county. This was participated in by each school district and it culminated in commencements at the end of ten days. There were many dramatic incidents as a result of this and Mecklenburg had a fine educational awakening. Because of its success the Governor by proclamation made Community Week a state wide enterprise.

Miss Graham served as president of Peace Institute, Raleigh, North Carolina, from 1916 until 1924. This proved to be the crowning experience of her life's work. To it she brought her usual devotion to duty, wisdom gleaned from her years of experience, her innate abilities and strength of character, and her great personal magnetism. Devoted to home, church, and state, she imbued the girls who went to Peace with these ideals. Her aim was for the full and rounded development of the girls mentally, physically, spiritually, and socially. As one means to this end, student government was instituted at Peace.

She foresaw the need of accrediting of junior colleges and had the work of Peace scheduled for two years of preparatory and two years of college work, with the name being changed to Peace Junior College. There were excellent departments in piano, violin, art, dramatics, and business in addition to the regular liberal arts courses. The students were especially prepared to discover special aptitudes. The majority of the students went on to higher educational institutions and so excellent was their training at Peace that they stood among the best.

Under Miss Graham's leadership, her professional staff and the alumnae of Peace became vital groups, each contributing richly to the success of the school. In addition, Miss Graham enlisted the interest of various individuals, one of whom was Mrs. William N. Reynolds of Winston-Salem, who expended much time studying the needs of the college and left it in her will a bequest of $100,000. It was during Miss Graham's administration that plans were initiated for renovation and enlargement of the school facilities which resulted in a plant of durability and unusual charm.

A woman of the attainments of "Miss Mary Owen", as she was affectionately called, was sought for many state offices and services. To these she brought a heart of interest, and she performed them with a distinction which reflected honor on the womanhood of the state. She spoke impressively and effectively on the floor of assemblies in which she held membership and she often spoke before Senate and

House committees of the legislature. She was the first woman to serve as president of the North Carolina Teachers Association, in 1914-15, and as Committee Woman from North Carolina on the National Democratic Committee from 1918 to 1927. Other capacities in which she served were: member of the State Board of examiners; trustee of the North Carolina State School for the Blind, 1916 to 1922; member of the Committee of 100 for Public Welfare; vice-president of the State Literary and Historical Association; member of the South Atlantic Committee, Y. W. C. A.; speaker for the War Committee of World War I, and president of the Albemarle Presbyterial, organization of Presbyterian Women of the Church.

Before retiring she was a member of many professional and cultural organizations of national, state and local nature. These included the National Education Association; the Federation of Women's Clubs; League of Women Voters; Y. W. C. A.; D. A. R.; U. D. C.; Business and Professional Women and the Bessie Dewey Book Club. She is an honorary member of the Altrusa Club.

Miss Mary Owen Graham is claimed with pride by North Carolina as a woman of noble traits and as an educator of influence.

MARIA DANIEL GRAHAM
1876-1945

MARIA DANIEL GRAHAM was born in a family that has made rich contribution to the history of education in North Carolina. She was reared in the school atmosphere, and spent her life in the schoolroom, giving nearly half a century to the service of teaching and in her native state.

The daughter of John and Frances Daniel Graham, she was born in the Shady Grove section of Warren County, October 11, 1876, in the shadow of her father's school, the Fork Academy.

John Graham when a young man went from the upper Cape Fear region to teach in Warren County and spent the remainder of his long life teaching in that county. While the schools he taught were under three names at different periods and in different localities, they were always known as "The Graham Schools". They were all preparatory boarding schools noted for the excellent preparation of their students for college or life. The course of study was always on a solid, classical foundation, with heavy courses in Latin, Greek and mathematics. The boarding department was always managed by Mrs. Graham and had the home atmosphere.

The first of the schools was the Fork Academy, a few miles from

Warrenton, in the country. After a few years the school building was burned and he moved to another part of the county and opened Ridgeway High School, which for several years flourished, but that also, was destroyed by fire. Then he made his final move to Warrenton where he put new life into the old Warrenton Academy, changing its name to Warrenton High School. This continued to be a "Graham School" until the public school was extended to include the high school, then he retired.

Other members of his family besides John Graham have gained distinction in the field of education. His brother Alexander Graham, built up the public schools of Charlotte. Two of his nephews, Edward Kidder Graham and Frank Graham have been president of the University of North Carolina. One niece, Mary Owen Graham, was president of Peace Institute. The six children of John Graham were all prepared for college in their father's schools. The eldest son died as he was ready to enter college. Two others besides Maria followed the teaching profession. The eldest daughter, Amma, began teaching the elementary department and French in her father's school immediately after finishing college and taught with him until the last Graham school closed. His son William spent most of his life teaching, part of the time in his father's school. The other two daughters, Flora and Virginia, both taught in their father's school for a while but married early.

Maria's early school days were spent in the Fork Academy and her high school days in the Ridgeway High School. She knew from childhood that she wanted to be a teacher and chose a school that specialized in teacher training, George Peabody Normal College, later George Peabody Teachers College, graduating from there with the degree of L. I. (Licentiate of Instruction) in 1895.

She spent two years, 1903-1905, studying at Teachers College, Columbia University, receiving the B. S. degree. She later returned to Teachers College for another year, getting the M. A. degree from Columbia University in 1925. She attended the University of Michigan the summer of 1940 and did some work at the University of North Carolina in the summer.

Her first teaching was a one-teacher rural school in Shelby County, Tennessee, from 1895-1897. She taught for the next six years in her father's schools, first in Ridgeway and then in Warrenton, and then for a period of three years, from 1905 to 1908, making in all nine years, that she spent teaching in her father's school. The year 1908-1909 she taught mathematics in the Goldsboro High School.

When East Carolina Teachers College was opened in 1909 she was elected teacher of mathematics and remained with this school for thirty-six years, throughout its changes from a two-year normal school to a well-established standard four-year teachers college, East Carolina Teachers College. She retired in 1945.

She returned to Warrenton, her old home, to be with her family the remainder of her life. She lived less than two years. She died on March 31, 1947, after a lingering illness.

Miss Graham was peculiarly fitted for teacher-training work not only because of her extensive work in teachers colleges but because she also had solid, basic work in an all-round education that made her a valuable member of the faculty in working out a well-balanced course of study. Throughout her years of teaching she taught both elementary and high school work and covered a wide range of subjects, including Latin, Greek, English and History, as well as mathematics. According to her statement, she considered Greek and Mathematics her specialties, but was also prepared to teach philosophy, phychology, and physics. Mathematics was, however, the subject to which she devoted most of her life.

Many of the so-called new methods now used in mathematics workshops are like those Miss Graham used in her teaching. While she never neglected sound basic principles, she was always on the alert for new methods and new ideas, and watched for opportunities to guide her students to make practical application of these principles. Whenever there was construction on the campus, there her students would be found making their own measurements for practical problems. The Greenville tobacco market also provided problem material for them.

Miss Graham was a woman of strong convictions and had the courage to stand by her convictions. She had great influence over her students. She was especially a favorite with the boys, perhaps because of her work in her father's school, where most of the boarding pupils were boys and perhaps because boys as a rule find mathematics their favorite subject. She followed with great interest the boys in service, keeping up with them. In World War II she had news bulletins mailed to the boys and had a bulletin board on which she kept reports on her boys.

She was faculty adviser for a number of classes, beginning with the class of 1914, and served as adviser for various student organizations. Her work with the Young Women's Christian Association was distinctive. She was adviser for that from the time it was organized until her retirement. She was a member of the Methodist Church and actively interested in its societies.

Maria Graham was a master teacher. She taught her students not only mathematics but trained them to teach mathematics and they are now carrying on her work in their classrooms in all parts of the state.

MINNIE G. GRAY

1861-1947

MINNIE G. GRAY, christened Amelia Garrett in old St. Thomas Church, Windsor, Bertie County, North Carolina, was born in Windsor in 1861. The site of this little town on the Cashie River was a donation of her great-grandfather, William Gray, being a part of an original land grant from the Crown. Minnie Gray's ancestors were people of wealth and culture, active in the affairs of both town and county. They met with courage the reverses following the War between the States which swept away their fortune.

When she was very young, her family moved to the Brimmage Plantation on the Cashie River, some distance from the county seat. As no schools were accessible, her education began under parental tutelage. Later she spent several winters in the home of a relative where, with the young cousins, she studied under a governess, an able and inspiring teacher. After school hours, the many plantation activities and the long rides and rambles through fields and woods contributed to her all-round development. Winter evenings were spent around an open fire where the father of the family made his listeners familiar with the well-beloved characters of English and American literature.

At the age of sixteen, this ambitious girl, needing funds for further schooling, assumed the position of nursery governess for two little girls who also enjoyed plantation life at Elmwood, on Salmon Creek. There she was a much-loved member of a delightful household.

After two years of teaching, she was enrolled, in 1879, as a pupil in St. Katherine's Hall, a select school for young ladies in Jackson, North Carolina, under the supervision of the Misses Copeland assisted by their bachelor brother. There, seizing every opportunity to acquire knowledge in the subjects she loved—literature, music, and art—she made an excellent record.

At the end of her second year in this institution, duty called her back to the little farm home one mile from Windsor to which the family had moved after the death of her father. Here Minnie Gray shared with her brother the care of their invalid mother and a delicate sister. In this modest cottage, she assumed the management of the household with great proficiency.

No obstacle ever daunted Minnie Gray. When a cousin offered to give her music lessons, she was confronted with the handicap of having no piano on which to practice. With great ingenuity, she fashioned a keyboard of white cardboard and pasted on it pine bark carved to represent black keys. Each day she practiced on this mute instrument. So skilled did she become in finger movement and sight reading that several years later when she began teaching, she added a course in music to her academic subjects and taught this with marked success. At a later period, in order to coach some students in French, she took a correspondence course and bought French records for her victrola.

As Minnie watched the efforts of her brother to care for the family financially, she resolved to help. But when she announced her intention of renting a school building in Windsor and opening a school on her own initiative, she was met with determined opposition by her family. This project would entail her walking two miles each day to and from school in order to look after the needs of her mother and sister. Also, it would mean the borrowing of money for necessary equipment.

However, despite dire predictions, she persisted. Thus did "Miss Minnie's" private school come into being. The long walk twice each day over country roads, the tasks of building fires, providing water, supplying all facilities for schoolroom cleanliness, were not the only demands she met in addition to the main duty of teaching seven grades. Many a little child whose parents were unable to pay the small tuition fee or to provide decent clothing was kept in school by the generosity of this teacher with the understanding heart. Her faith and courage helped her to solve many problems, and the little school grew into an institution that served the best interests of the community.

Moreover, in those days of infrequent entertainments, the Christmas commencement programs put on by "Miss Minnie's" pupils were greatly enjoyed. On these occasions the costumes of the participants and the stage setting bore testimony to the artistic taste of the teacher.

Many of the leading citizens of Windsor received their early training under her thorough instruction at this time. Gentle speech and manners, refined personal habits, honesty, obedience, and reverence for God were stressed in her curriculum. Fortunate was the child with such a teacher!

Then the day came when Miss Gray's school and the Windsor Academy, hitherto operated as a private school for older boys and girls, joined forces with Miss Gray as assistant to a young student from the University of North Carolina. In this capacity she served with two other Carolina graduates who were in turn in charge of the Academy. With the establishment of the Windsor Graded Schools, however, the doors of the Academy were closed.

During the years that followed, Miss Gray taught in the public schools of Selma, Oxford, Winston-Salem, and Rocky Mount. She laid aside her much loved work in Winston-Salem to return to her brother's home to nurse her sister in her last illness. She later taught in Rocky Mount for more than twenty-five years. Her work was most satisfactory and she made friends among pupils and patrons. For some time after her retirement, she gave a few hours each week to instructing a number of pupils interested in art.

The lack of a college diploma, perhaps, intensified Miss Gray's desire for greater scholarship and through the years she was not only a teacher but an earnest student as well. "Thou that teachest another, teachest thou not thyself?" brought from her a nod of affirmation. She attended summer sessions at State College, the University of North Carolina, and Columbia University. In retirement, her chief concern was with the present and she kept informed on current events. Still possessing the enthusiasm of youth and finding joy in the companionship of young friends, she rejoiced in the many new fields of service open to the young women of today and for those who ventured therein she had words of encouragement and cheer. Many have been the lives touched and inspired to nobler striving because of Minnie Gray's loyalty and faith in all things good. Surely from the beginning to the end she enjoyed the abundant life, and in her old age could say with Tennyson's Ulysses: "How dull it is—To rust unburnish'd, not to shine in use!"

LULA JANE GREY
1864-1939

LULA JANE GREY, daughter of Hugh A. and Jane Parks Grey, was born on September 9, 1864, in Union County in the Old Providence Church neighborhood. Her father was connected with schools in some capacity practically all his life except the years he was in the Confederate Army. Therefore it was natural that his daughter should choose teaching as her life work. Three of her five brothers were also prominent in educational work whereas a fourth brother went into the ministry. And another brother who was a very successful business man gave the Jane Grey Parks Library to Davidson College in memory of his mother.

Miss Lula was educated at the Charlotte Female Institute, now Queens College. She began her teaching in Montgomery County in the home of the Reverend McIntire. From there she went to Lawrenceville, Georgia, to assist in a school conducted by her brother, W. R. Grey, who soon thereafter became a member of the faculty of Davidson College where he taught for about fifty years. A short time after her brother left Lawrenceville, Miss Lula came back to Mooresville, North Carolina, to teach with another brother, Hugh A. Grey, Jr., in the Mooresville Academy. Here she taught the primary grades from about 1888 until 1902. At this time she returned to the Charlotte Female Institute to teach. Then finally she taught in Mitchell College in Statesville.

In her later years Miss Lula retired from teaching and went to live in Hendersonville where her brothers Captain James Grey and Charles L. Grey were living. She remained here until her death on April 26, 1939. She is buried in Mooresville beside her brother Hugh A. Grey, Jr.

It was at Mooresville that Miss Lula's influence made the most lasting impression. The following appraisal comes from one of her former Mooresville pupils:

"This is dedicated to one in whose life and personality were so integrated the high qualities of teacher, gentlewoman, and Christian that it would be impossible to separate these in evaluating the measure of her influence upon the lives of us who were so fortunate as to have been her pupils, to teacher extraordinary, Miss Lula Jane Grey.

"No modern, progressive methods of teaching have ever obtained any more excellent results than those employed by "Miss Lula," probably because her methods embodied what is best in the modern science of teaching. Thoroughness, honesty, energy, seem to me to have been the key-notes of her method. No student ever passed from her elementary class room without having mastered the basic principles of English grammar and of sentence structure, so that both the written and the spoken language had become his or her ready tool for use in the general educational process. With the same thoroughness, the arithmetical process of addition, subtraction, multiplication, division, and fractions—common and decimal—were mastered. Long before anyone ever heard of intelligence quotients, Miss Lula's patient persistence helped many students with limited intelligence to acquire an excellent knowledge of the processes mentioned above and of other essential fundamentals.

"To neither teacher nor to pupil was there any 'royal road to learning.' Both accepted as natural the tedious hours of work that lay in the accomplishment of the learning task. This did not mean, however, that the teacher placed upon pupils discouragingly impossible tasks, nor that she failed to make the process of learning as interesting as it was possible to make it. One early recalls, for example, that reading could become a pleasure, after having been introduced during weekly Friday afternoon reading periods, to such interesting characters as Little Lord Fauntleroy, Sara Crewe, Little Women, and David Copperfield. Probably one of Miss Lula's greatest accomplishments as a teacher was the fact that she inspired, in one way or another, so many of her pupils with an energy and zeal that surmounted many of the difficult phases of learning.

"Miss Lula's influence was not limited, however, to the purely academic phases of class-room instruction. Her practical Christianity, which manifested itself in an abiding faith, an intellectual and moral sturdiness, an unqualified honesty, a hatred of all shams, a courage, a cheerfulness, a good will toward everyone; and her standards of refined culture have been reflected, at least to some degree, in the lives of all her students; and there are many among these who feel that she gave to them a priceless heritage of high concepts of worthy living."

DR. ANNA M. GOVE
1867-1948

"THE memory of Dr. Anna M. Gove that I expect to carry through life is not that of a learned physician, or a tireless worker for the common good, or a gracious lady whose poise and manner could grace any social circles, though Dr. Gove was all of these. Rather, I like to think of her as a personal friend that I knew and loved. . . . What kept Dr. Gove from resembling, even faintly a saint on a pedestal, was an ever present, quiet but patent sense of humor, a soft spoken quip, a manifest feeling of intimate friendliness that charmed the hearts of high and low and made them feel at ease in her presence. And so I like to think of Dr. Gove, just as I knew her—at once a joy, a solace, and an inspiration."

Thus a former student summarized the life and work of Dr. Anna M. Gove, who as physician, teacher, mentor, and friend served the students, alumnae, and faculty of the Woman's College of the University of North Carolina for more than half a century.

When Dr. Anna M. Gove came to the then State Normal and Industrial School at the beginning of its second year, 1893, she was truly pioneering in the field of health education and in the acceptance of medicine as a proper career for women. In North Carolina there were only two other women physicians, Dr. Annie Alexander of Charlotte and a Dr. Jones of Goldsboro. In many communities a woman physician was looked upon as a curiosity.

In Greensboro the ground had been broken by the first resident physician, Dr. Miriam Bitting, who had remained one year. When Dr. Gove arrived the students with youthful openmindedness readily accepted "the lady doctress," as she was sometimes called. The parents were more hesitant. One mother wrote in 1893, "Please don't teach Mary so much about her insides. It ain't decent."

The doctors, frankly curious about this intruder into their profession, were somewhat awkward and embarrassed in her presence. One country doctor, who read Latin with the ease that he did English, in the spring of 1894, when the state medical society met in Greensboro, drove into town, not so much to attend the sessions as "to see what the female lady doctress looked like." A physician who had come to see his niece, kept his hat on when Dr. Gove came into the room, explaining that he "didn't know how to treat a lady doctor." When Dr. Gove replied that she would be satisfied to be treated as he would treat any other lady, he removed his hat. However, the doctors, we have Dr. Gove's own word for it, were always courteous and kind. Indeed they could hardly have been otherwise in the face of her dignity, professional courtesy, and sound training.

Dr. Gove's quiet modesty probably prevented the full realization of how exceptional were her background and training. Anna M. Gove, born July 6, 1867, descendant of an eminent New England family, a native of Whitefield, New Hampshire, where her father was a physician and early graduate of Dartmouth, grew up in a home of the finest culture, and was given the best education that New England could afford. While she received the loving care of an only child, in her bringing up there was no softness. Her training in manners was so thorough that her taste in conduct was to become almost infallible; and the doing of the considerate, gracious thing became second nature. She was expected to stand on her own feet and to do her duty with courage and without complaint.

Much of her early education came from her father as he made his professional rounds in a buckboard made to carry only one. If the little Anna were very good and promised to hold on tightly, she was allowed to accompany him, and then to minister to the family pets when she returned home.

Following her own and her father's plan that she should become a well-educated woman and physician, Dr. Gove, after private schooling in Whitefield, was graduated from the St. Johnsbury Academy, Vermont. This was followed by a pre-medical course at the Massachusetts Institute of Technology. There she joined a small band of girls unusual in both their ability and in their ambition "to master the course at the hardest school in New England." Dr. Gove always remembered her years in Boston as golden years, both because of the goodly fellowship of pioneers and the stimulating instruction.

From Boston she went to New York, graduating in 1892 from the Woman's College of the New York Infirmary (later consolidated with Cornell University Medical School). The year 1892-93 she spent as an intern at the New York Infant Asylum. Forty years later her "chief" was to recall how she did "A-1 medical work," how she "seemed a born physician" and soon won the hearts of all by her marvelous tact and her kindness, to say nothing of the fact that "not even an atom of dust dared attach itself to her."

With this background and training, young Dr. Gove, then twenty-six years of age, small and dignified, gentle and charming, arrived in the fall of 1893 to take up her duties as resident physician, head of the Department of Physiology and Physical Culture, and teacher of Physiology and Hygiene at the newly established State Normal and Industrial School in Greensboro.

A less courageous soul might have been daunted by the task before her. The new school was almost totally lacking in facilities for the care of the sick, with no dispensary, no infirmary, nor rooms set aside for such use, no office except the classroom, no nurse, no office assistant, and, indeed no hospital in the town of Greensboro.

Four to six girls were housed in each dormitory room, and room-mates were supposed to care for the ailing one. On pads hung outside the dining room, illnesses were reported. The doctor visited the sick each day and in addition made daily inspections of all rooms, once for orderliness and in the afternoon to see if the windows were open during the required hour of outdoor exercise. Dr. Gove also taught Physiology and Hygiene, the general objective being "to give students such knowledge as will make them reverence and care for their bodies and such training as will give them strength and conduce to their happiness."

Dr. Gove's strength lay in preventive medicine. The president's report of September, 1910, states, "The prevention of sickness has been the main object of our resident physician." an early alumna said, "Dr. Gove has worked tirelessly to prevent handicaps among us. She has been willing to do the unexciting, laborious day by day duties of the mother of a large family."

While willing to perform any medical duty from the president's house to the home of the janitor, Dr. Gove's brilliant mind was forging ahead. Dr. Will Beall, her consulting physician for many years, said, "From the beginning her work with the college has been progressively upward."

Under her guidance the health facilities of the college improved year by year. The new infirmary built in 1896 at first had only a colored care-taker, later a practical nurse, and still later a trained nurse. A new large well-equipped infirmary, completed in 1912 under the direct supervision of Dr. Gove, was the first well-equipped infirmary for women students in this part of the United States. Medical and physical examinations were begun when only two colleges, Amherst and Vassar, required them. The college was one of the first in the country and the very first in North Carolina to add chest X-rays to these examinations.

As the years passed, under her direction a sturdy Department of Health, with a Personal Hygiene Course required of all freshmen, was set up. With her stimulation and encouragement the Department of Physical Culture gradually developed into a nationally recognized Department of Physical Education with two years of Physical Education required of all students.

Improvements in health facilities in the college paralleled Dr. Gove's own growth and development. The itinerary of her study and travels reads like a saga: leave of absence 1896-97 for graduate study in Vienna and attendance at the International Medical Association meeting in Moscow as a delegate from New Hampshire and North Carolina; summer vacation 1899 at the University of Chicago; summer of 1901 at Cornell University; on leave 1901-03 she taught physiology at Vassar and did private practice in Yonkers, New York; on leave 1913-14 for study in Vienna, together with a Mediterranean cruise, including six weeks in Constantinople and a return trip through western Europe. While on leave in 1917 for study at the Post Graduate Hospital in New York, she signed up for Red Cross work in World War I and went to Europe. Returning to the college in 1920, she studied at the University of Michigan the summers of 1924 and 1928. Her last leave of absence was in 1926-27 for a trip around the world, including China, Japan, Korea, French Indo-China, and India.

As a physician, Dr. Gove practiced the highest professional ethics, being affiliated with and a participant in the deliberations of more than a dozen medical, health, and civic organizations on the local, national, and international levels. A professional honor which she prized was a life membership in the American Medical Association of Vienna.

Many honors were bestowed upon Dr. Gove. In 1936, the college infirmary became the Anna M. Gove Infirmary; and the new infirmary completed in 1953 bears her name.

Although Dr. Gove actually taught and lectured in the classroom only in the early years, she was in reality the teacher supreme both by precept and example. So recognized, she was in 1938 elected to the first honorary membership of North Carolina's Alpha Chapter of Delta Kappa Gamma.

In 1951 a $21,000 bequest given in her memory by her cousin Miss Maria C. Brace of Baltimore, to the Woman's College Library, will be used to purchase a special collection of fine and rare books, each volume bearing her name plate.

In her will Dr. Gove honored herself by bequeathing to the college a $5000 scholarship in the name of Mrs. Charles Duncan McIver.

In 1936 Dr. Gove retired but continued to keep her office and serve in an advisory capacity. With her retirement her home became even more a mecca for alumnae, faculty, and friends. Furnished with heirloom antiques and interesting objects from her world travels, her living room became the center for those who sought genteel companionship and sympathetic understanding. On chilly Sunday afternoons groups would gather around a crackling wood fire and a box of chocolates to listen to the symphony and chat with Dr. Gove. Mattie would appear in the door to announce dinner, Mattie Booker, colored, whose beautiful affection and devotion had served Dr. Gove for many years. People, even the Mattie Bookers, were Dr. Gove's hobby. She was above all thoughtful, thoughtful of the little things that make people feel warm inside.

On January 28, 1948, at the age of eighty, Dr. Gove died. As the fire in her house of friendship went out the college, the alumnae, and the community mourned the passing of a life that had meant so much to so many.

Epitomizing her fine and rare personality, the day of her funeral, on her desk there sat, all day long, a small white vase containing three green and golden orchids—lady's slippers.

MARGARET WINIFRED HALIBURTON
1855-1928

MARGARET HALIBURTON rendered invaluable service as a master teacher and as an author of textbooks at a time when such were most needed, as it was not until about the turn of the century that the Old North State began to wake from its "Rip Van Winkle" sleep. At that time, a real educational revival took place in North Carolina. One of the results of this awakening was the establishment, in 1892, of the North Carolina State Normal and Industrial School at Greensboro. Leaders were now beginning to look for people who were capable of training teachers, and Miss Haliburton was among those chosen.

Margaret Haliburton was a native of Burke County. She was graduated from Greensboro Female College—now Greensboro College for Women—in 1877. She began teaching in Salisbury the following year. During her early teaching years, she proved herself a master teacher, a rank she continued to hold.

About the middle of the 1880's, she accepted a position in the public schools of Asheville. Here, under the inspiration and leadership of Dr. P. P. Claxton, who was superintendent of the city schools at the time, she was in the midst of a type of superior teaching when suddenly she and Dr. Claxton were called to the newly-established teacher training institution at Greensboro. Miss Haliburton served in its practice school from 1893 to 1901. Her student teachers often remarked that her keen analytical mind enabled her to size up a situation quickly and that she pointed out to them their potentialities and responsibilities for service, thus inspiring them to do their very best.

It was while Miss Haliburton was connected with teacher training at what is now Womans College of the University of North Carolina that in collaboration with her co-worker, Dr. Claxton, she published her first book, *Paraphrase of Grimm's Fairy Tales* as a supplement to the First Reader.

In 1903, she accepted the position of Primary Supervisor in the State Normal School at Farmville, Virginia, which place she held until 1909. During this period she issued *Phonics in Reading; a Manual and Drill Book*, and *Playmates Primer*. From 1909 to 1912, she was engaged in study and in writing textbooks at Columbia University. In 1912 came the series of Readers which bore her name and also *Teaching Poetry in the Grades* by Haliburton and Agnes G. Smith. Her Readers were adopted in North Carolina and in a number of other states. In philosophy and concept, her Primers, especially, were in advance of their time. They were founded on the principle of activity, a basic characteristic of childhood. In addition to textbooks, Miss Haliburton wrote a number of articles for periodicals.

When she left Columbia University in 1913, she went to Waco,

94

Texas, as Assistant Superintendent of Schools. She continued in this position until about the time of her death which occurred in 1928 when she was seventy-three years of age. She was buried at Connelly Springs, North Carolina. On her tombstone is this inscription:

A PIONEER EDUCATOR AND AUTHOR OF NORTH CAROLINA
"I will lift up mine eyes unto the hills."

At the National Convention of the Delta Kappa Gamma Society in 1942, the North Carolina delegation presented a figurine of Miss Haliburton. It was returned to the State in 1953 and was placed in the Hall of History in Raleigh with several other figurines from North Carolina.

The following is a complete list of Miss Haliburton's publications:

P. P. Claxton and M. W. Haliburton: *Paraphrase of Grimm's Fairy Tales; Supplement to First Reader*. Richmond, B. F. Johnson Publishing Company, 1900.

P. P. Claxton and M. W. Haliburton: *Phonics in Reading; a Manual*. Richmond, B. F. Johnson Publishing Company, 1908.

M. W. Haliburton and F. T. Norvell: *Graded Classics*, First to Fifth Readers. Richmond, B. F. Johnson Publishing Company, 1901.

M. W. Haliburton: *Playmates; a Primer*. Richmond, B. F. Johnson Publishing Company, 1906.

M. W. Haliburton: *The Haliburton Readers,* 6 books. New York, D. C. Heath and Company, 1917.

M. W. Haliburton: *Haliburton Teacher's Manual to Accompany the Haliburton Readers*. New York, D. C. Heath and Company, 1917.

M. W. Haliburton and A. G. Smith: *Teaching Poetry in the Grades*. Boston, Houghton Mifflin Company, 1911. (Riverside Educational Monographs).

ANNIE JONES HART

1844-1931

A N indomitable will of the spirit in victory over physical handicaps in the life of Miss Annie Jones Hart inculcated into three generations of her pupils an appreciation of the finer things of life. Her neat black dress covered a misshapened back, that to her was always a veritable thorn in the flesh, but over which she triumphed and lived above it in a life of service.

Born in upper South Carolina in 1844, the only child of Derrill A. Hart and Margaret Kennedy Hart, she was educated in Columbia and fitted for her life of teaching. Immediately after 1865 Miss Hart began her career as a teacher in Wilmington, being associated with a relative,

Miss Kate Kennedy, who was conducting a school for girls in a one story building situated on the west side of Third Street between Market and Princess Streets.

Misses Kennedy and Hart's Female School, after Miss Kennedy's marriage to Dr. A. J. De Rossett in 1877, was conducted by Miss Hart and Miss Mary Brown, ably assisted by Miss Hobday of Virginia and, for a time, by Mrs. A. M. Waddell and Mrs. Deveruz Lippitt, instructors in music and painting. Later the school was moved across Third Street next to the Court House and finally to the house on Orange Street, erected by St. John's Lodge in 1801 for Masonic purposes, and preserved today as St. John's Tavern.

Miss Hart was endowed with varied natural talents through which she developed in her pupils an appreciation of real culture. She possessed a full rich alto voice and for many years assisted in the choir of St. James Episcopal Church. She was a composer of music and in her possession was a thick manuscript containing her musical compositions, among them plays and operettas. Her composition for the children's Easter service is still used at St. James Church, where from the church tower each Easter Sunday afternoon is heard from the lips of children of a later generation her carol, "Waken, children, children of the King."

In the early days of her teaching, her ideas were so advanced as to include physical education through calisthenics, games, and play. Copies of the commencement programs, dating as early as June, 1869, reveal cultural training in literature, music, dramatic art, and physical education. Excerpts from the Wilmington *Journal* of 1869 and 1870 give accounts of the presence of the editor and other patrons of the school at the School Examination in primary geography, arithmetic, logic, algebra, astronomy, and French. Particularly impressed was the editor by "a young lady going through the most intricate problems in algebra with the facility of a venerable professor, and another reading and speaking French almost with the fluency of a native." Original compositions revealed "real poetry of thought . . . and good sense and humor in verse."

Miss Hart was so highly regarded by the educators of Wilmington that in 1898, when a change was being made in the administration of the public schools, the Chairman of the Board of Education, Mr. James H. Chadbourn, tried to persuade her to become superintendent of the public schools. After much consideration, on account of personal reasons and loyalty to her own school, she thought best not to accept. The private school was continued by Miss Hart and Miss Brown until June, 1920, when they expressed through the Wilmington *Morning Star* their ". . . regret at this severance of many ties, as well as their sincere thanks for long-continued unsolicited patronage."

Eleven years later, on September 9, 1931, the indomitable spirit of Annie Jones Hart was released after eighty-seven years of gallant living. The community in which she lived and served has been enriched spiritually and culturally by a great teacher.

MARGARET HEARNE
1852-1949

On April 14, 1945, just prior to the organization of the Omicron Chapter of Delta Kappa Gamma in Wilson, Miss Margaret Hearne, at the age of ninety-three, was received as an honorary member. The service conducted at her bedside was very impressive. Those who knew this veteran teacher were happy that this honor could be bestowed upon her in recognition of her contribution in molding the characters of the men and women of her loved town of Wilson.

Margaret Hearne's family moved to Wilson from Edgecombe County in 1857 when she was five years old. Here Margaret attended the following private schools: D. S. Richardson's Private School for Girls, Miss Mattie Harper's Select School for Girls, and Professor De Berniere Hooper's School for Girls.

After completing her education at the age of seventeen, she founded a private school of her own for boys and girls. Her school was located in the same frame building used as her parents' home and her brother's newspaper office.

However, with the establishment of the first public school in Wilson in 1881, Miss Hearne gave up her private school and became one of the first public school teachers of the city. She remained a member of the faculty until two years later when the public school closed. Following this, she taught in Silas E. Warren's Collegiate Institute in Wilson; but when the Wilson public school reopened, she again became one of the faculty and was reelected each year until she retired in 1927 at the age of seventy-five. During the War between the States, Miss Hearne was one of the few teachers who remained in Wilson teaching the town's children.

In appreciation for her fifty-three years' service and for the influence which she had exerted over the hundreds of children, the local school board granted this noble teacher the first and only pension ever given by the city to a member of the teaching profession. The school in which she taught so many years was named *The Margaret Hearne School* in her honor, and in the auditorium hangs an oil portrait of Miss Hearne which was presented by her former pupils.

"Miss Mag," as she was affectionately called, had the happy faculty of remembering her former pupils whether their estate were high or low. She pointed with pride to a number of outstanding people under whom she had taught. Among these were P. P. Claxton, Dr. Collier Cobb, Dr. Eugene Branson, Judge George W. Connor, and Dr. Charles L. Coon.

Miss Hearne died in Wilson at the age of ninety-seven.

MOLLIE HEATH

1935

ALL things seem to have worked together to make Miss Mollie Heath a great teacher. The influence that her teacher-mother had exerted throughout her early environment and training, her strong and sincere love for children, her Peter Pan spirit that kept her close to children during her seventy-two years, her recognition of the progress being made in primary education, and her determination to keep pace—these taken together made her a loving and inspiring teacher.

For several generations, "Miss Mollie" was a "personification" of the New Bern schools as described by her home newspaper when reporting her death on September 2, 1935. For fifty years she had been receiving pupils in the primary grades, teaching them elements of the art of living in addition to primer lessons, and "following them with her kindly interest through the advanced grades into college and out into the world."

However, New Bern did not wait until Miss Mollie Heath was dead to express its appreciation. At the end of her forty-fourth year of teaching in New Bern, in Sunday School as well as in day school, the high school juniors had her as an honor guest at their banquet; the seniors dedicated the Annual to her; and the town named its new primary school building for her.

About this time in a feature article about "Miss Mollie," Gertrude Carraway wrote that the kiddies did not consider any party a real success if this teacher were absent. Some of the pupils showed Miss Carraway little sisters named for her; and one baby even bore the name "Miss Mollie." Miss Carraway told, also, about the pupil who wanted two fathers and two mothers: his own father and George Washington and his own mother and "Miss Mollie."

Apparently at every stage, Miss Heath satisfied her pupils, her patrons, and her fellow-citizens. Yet in the meantime, however, she was not satisfied with herself. Although she was constantly being enriched by her increasing fund of experience and she had in her possession a life certificate, she studied throughout many summers. Columbia University, the University of California, the University of Tennessee, the University of North Carolina, and the University of Virginia are among the institutions whose summer sessions she attended.

Most of her teaching in the regular school year was done in the New Bern public schools. For a few years, when the public schools were closed by an injunction because a citizen had objected to "paying taxes to educate other people's children," Miss Health taught a private school. During a few summers she taught in Greenville, North Carolina, and other places.

Miss Heath always loved her profession. Possibilities in other fields never appealed to her. A saving sense of humor and a sound philosophy of life kept her zestful and efficient. A superintendent under whom she taught paid her this tribute: "I know that it is not in the power of human beings to bless lives more richly than she did." A close friend and fellow teacher wrote of her: "Rarly are so many virtues crowded into the life of one woman."

THE HILLIARD SISTERS

1859-1941

THE Francis Hilliard School was for seventeen years one of the educational landmarks of Oxford, North Carolina. It was the successor of Granville Institute, a boarding and day school established in 1888 by Miss Betty Clarke, under the auspices of the Episcopal Church. In 1892, the school property, located on the north corner of New College and Lee Streets was purchased by the Reverend Francis W. Hilliard. The same summer, his daughters, who had recently finished their courses at Goucher College, took charge. The school appears not to have taken the name of the Francis W. Hilliard School for Women until 1897, the year (it is believed) in which the parental Hilliards moved from Edenton to Oxford.

The Reverend Francis W. Hilliard (1832-1910), a native of Massachusetts, a graduate of Harvard and class poet, had married in 1857 Maria Nash Johnston, daughter of the rector of the historic St. Paul's Episcopal Church in Edenton, North Carolina; and had later become himself the rector there. Two of his three teaching daughters were born in the rectory in Edenton—the eldest, Margaret Burgwyn, about 1859, and Elizabeth Haven about 1868. The second daughter, Katherine Haven, was born in Plymouth, North Carolina, January 15, 1861. These maiden ladies of the "old school," descendants of the New England Craigie family and of the North Carolina families of Nash and Iredell, had long and useful careers worthy of their distinguished lineage.

Margaret Hilliard was an outstanding student in German and English at Goucher College, and became an "inspirational teacher of the best in literature, in German, and in the cultural arts." The college credits gained in English under her instruction bear witness to her exceptional ability. A woman of unusually strong and impressive character, active not only in the cultural, but also in the religious and civic life of the community, she was presumably the mainstay of the school in its later period. Miss Margaret died, after years of invalidism, on December 31, 1936, in the family home which had housed also the Hilliard School.

99

Katherine Hilliard also earned the reputation of "inspirational teacher," and this "not only in her own field—Latin, French and Math—but also in English and History." She was a member of the first class (of five members) to be graduated, in 1892, from Goucher College. It was soon after her graduation that she began her work in the Hilliard School, as vice-principal. After about ten years there, she went to Omaha, where she won a high reputation as a teacher of English in the Omaha High School. In 1925 she retired to return home, but taught again for several years in the Oxford High School. Most of the final winter of her life was spent in Winter Park, Florida. She passed away in her Oxford home on August 3, 1941.

Miss Katherine's character was especially marked by devoutness and modesty. She was a devoted student and teacher of the Bible, a faithful supporter of Christian missions and the ideals of Christian unity, and a staunch friend. After her death, the *Goucher Alumnae Quarterly* (Nov., 1941) carried a two-page sketch of this early graduate and also a paragraph about her in its 1892 class notes, ending thus: "She and her sister Margaret left on everybody a decided impression: They were original in their outlook, sympathetic in their relations to others and contributed a colorful and highly-prized page to the early days of our college."

Elizabeth Hilliard, who died at her home after a brief illness, two years before Katherine, on June 12, 1939, was perhaps the most vivacious and versatile of the three teaching sisters. She earned the A. B. degree from the University of Chicago and the M. A. from Columbia University, and studied voice and piano at Peabody Conservatory and dramatics at Goucher College. Naturally enough, she became a leader in the dramatic and musical activities of Oxford. She taught for many years in the Hilliard School, with notable success in music and dramatics. Nor did she become idle in her later years. Long after the closing of the school, Miss Elizabeth was serving as secretary of an Art Study class organized by the Art Department of the Oxford Woman's Club. Like her sisters, she was a faithful and zealous member of St. Stephens Episcopal Church in her home otwn. And, like her sisters and parents, she lies buried in beautiful Elmwood Cemetery in Oxford.

There is no doubt that the Hilliard School, "which became widely known throughout the state," was one of the best of its kind for girls in North Carolina. Its founder and teachers had studied at Harvard and Chicago and Columbia and Goucher. "Their aim," in the words of Miss Katherine Hilliard, "was to give to their pupils a thorough college preparatory course that would be accepted at any college, and to arouse in them a desire to continue their studies in some college or university of national standing." A number of their graduates were admitted to Goucher on certificate from the school, some even receiving advanced credit for postgraduate work.

The Hilliard sisters will long be remembered in Oxford, not only for their high academic and ethical standards and superior teaching abilities, but for their remarkably strong personalities. Nor should the inspiring presence of their parents in the school be forgotten. The Reverend Francis W. Hilliard died in the summer of 1910 in Memphis, Tennessee, and was buried in Elmwood Cemetery, Oxford, by the side of his wife who had died only one year earlier.

Among the valued assistants in the school were Miss Nina Horner, later Mrs. W. S. Manning of Spartanburg, South Carolina, who taught history when fresh from her course at Harvard—and, in the primary department, the late Mrs. Archibald A. Hicks and Miss Willie Skinner.

In 1909, owing to illness and death in the family, the Francis Hilliard School was closed; but, like Oxford College and the Horner Military School, it had done its share in winning for earlier Oxford the litle, "the Athens of North Carolina."

MARY MENDENHALL HOBBS

1852-1930

MARY MENDENHALL HOBBS, pioneer teacher, writer lecturer, and—most important of all—pioneer leader in promoting higher education for women, was given, in 1921, by the University of North Carolina, an honorary degree of Doctor of Literature. At their ceremonial, the following citation was given:

"Deeply imbued with faith in the widening destiny of women, for more than three decades, she has stood forth in the light, immeasurably courageous in advocacy of complete and full-orbed education, whether under church or state, for youth and maid alike. Whether advancing the noble cause of higher education; widening the channels of religious influence of the Society of Friends, both locally and nationally; or vitalizing the consciousness—it has been with the spirit and the pen of the literary artist that she has kindled the emotions of her generation. In recognition of this contribution to our mental and spiritual life, the University of North Carolina will now confer upon her the degree of Doctor of Literature."

Mary Mendenhall was the eldest daughter of Nereus and Oriana Mendenhall, and was born August 30, 1852. Nereus Mendenhall served as teacher and superintendent of New Garden Boarding School intermittently from 1849 to 1867. Thus, Mary Mendenhall was reared in the Quaker tradition and in an atmosphere of religious education and service, and to this ideal she devoted her whole life.

She was educated at the New Garden School and at Howland School at Cayuga Lake, New York. Early in life she was given by her father the ideal that girls should be trained as carefully as boys. Later, while completing her education at the Howland School, she was imbued with the idea that girls should be educated as human beings, and not merely as females.

In 1878, Mary Mendenhall returned to New Garden Boarding School to teach Latin and History in the girls' school. Then, two years later she married Dr. L. Lyndon Hobbs who was at that time the Superintendent of the School. They had known each other from childhood. From their simple Quaker home, through nearly a half-century, there radiated confidence, enthusiasm, and inspiration for the school that was so close to their hearts and for the College that grew from the Boarding School. In 1888, Dr. Hobbs became the first President of the newly organized Guilford College, but Mary Mendenhall Hobbs did not limit her interest or her pioneering efforts for this institution. While continuing to teach till almost 1900, her concern for an educated womanhood in North Carolina increased until it became of paramount importance to her.

At Guilford College she labored diligently to equalize opportunities for girls. Probably her most distinctive contribution to the College was the idea of the co-operative residence hall for girls. Here the girls lived as a family, cooked and served meals together, and shared the labor of caring for the Hall. This made considerable reduction in the living expenses of each girl, while at the same time the group shared comradeship and service along the path of education and toward a finer and richer foundation for life. The first efforts in this direction took the form of several cottages. But when this did not prove as satisfactory as expected, the plan was transferred to a residence hall, named by Mrs. Hobbs "New Garden Hall." After her death, July 20, 1930, the name was changed in her honor to "Mary Hobbs Hall."

The writing and lectures of Mrs. Hobbs contributed substantially to the strong forward movement toward higher education for women that took place in the late years of the 19th century and the early years of the 20th century. In 1889, Dr. Charles Duncan McIver was working valiantly for the establishment of the State Normal and Industrial School for Girls. Because this project was so completely in line with her thinking, Mrs. Hobbs entered wholeheartedly into the campaign and spared no effort to aid Dr. McIver in achieving his purpose. She spoke at local meetings and conventions of many women's organizations and wrote newspaper articles liberally. With the combination of Mrs. Hobbs' great intellectual vigor, her deep earnestness and devotion to the cause of women's education, and her ability to write convincingly, she gave strong assistance to the establishment of the school that is now the Woman's College of the University of North Carolina.

In addition to all the activities in which she was engaged, Mary M. Hobbs raised a family of five children and created a home that all Guilford loved as an integral part of college life. She sincerely believed that "there wasn't any limit to what a person could do if he didn't care who got the credit." Hers was a radiant and joyful personality with an inspiring influence, especially on the lives of young people. While enjoying a wide range of interests, her chief interest was always in people. Here she revealed her rich gift for friendship.

After Mary Hobbs' passing, an editorial in *The Greensboro News* stated:

"Her real distinction was in the character of her thinking. It was straight, true, and wholesome; magnificent in its simplicity, its directness, and its earnestness."

Josephus Daniels (whose wife was of Quaker ancestry) wrote of Mrs. Hobbs: "She was easily the foremost woman in North Carolina in knowledge of world conditions and in the advocacy of practical Christian plans." And the President of the Board of Trustees of Guilford College said: "We feel that a great spirit has departed from us and left us filled with solemn awe."

ANNIE L. HUGHES
1851-1932

ANNIE L. HUGHES, born September 3, 1851, in the Eno Presbyterian Church community, near Cedar Grove, North Carolina, was an outstanding teacher in Reidsville, North Carolina, and in Orange County for sixty years.

Her grandfather, Joseph D. Hughes, came to the Eno community in the early 1800's, at the request of the Reverend Samuel Paisley, to teach a school near the church. Then, later, one of Joseph D.'s ten sons, Samuel W. Hughes, father of Annie L., founded the Cedar Grove Academy in 1845. This school was moved during the War between the States to his home place, two miles away, and afterwards called Hughes Academy. This Academy was a boys' preparatory school and enrolled students from several Southern states, including Texas. Here were also included in the enrollment the younger of the Hughes family as well as those of kinsmen and neighbors; and other teachers were employed. In this Academy, Annie was prepared for college; and she entered Concord Female College, a Presbyterian school in Statesville, where she was graduated June 27, 1867. Also, as the years passed, she attended many summer schools at the State University and at other colleges.

After graduation at the age of sixteen, she taught in the Hughes Academy for about ten years; then for a time taught a private school for the children and neighbors of Mr. Cunningham in Caswell County. About 1880, she went to Reidsville to assist Miss Emma Scales, owner and principal of the Reidsville Female Seminary. In about five years she bought the school and remained as its principal until September, 1901. This Seminary was a preparatory school for girls, but included in the lower grades some boys through the age of twelve.

In 1901, she sold the Seminary, to the regret of the people of Reidsville. And at the request of her uncle and other relatives and friends at Cedar Grove, she bought the Cedar Grove Academy which had been closed for several years after a flourishing existence from 1889 to the middle 1900's. In this school she prepared both boys and girls for college. Entrance examinations were not required of her graduates for admission to the University, Davidson, and other colleges where her reputation as a thorough teacher was well known.

In 1915, in the midst of the era of consolidation, the Cedar Grove Academy was sold to Orange County. Until that time the only public, or "free" school, at Cedar Grove had been a log cabin, one-teacher, four months' school. Miss Hughes taught in this new county school for several years; was principal of the high school in Milton, North Carolina, for about three years; then taught Latin in the Hillsboro High School for several years.

Still active in body and alert in mind, she retired after sixty years of experience in private and public school teaching, but she continued to serve others until the day of her death, which came suddenly in Hillsboro, July 5, 1932. The last few years were spent as a useful and cheerful member of her family and of the community where she happened to be. Although she had built a home in which to spend her last years, her family gave her little time to spend there. She divided most of the last months between her sister, Mrs. C. W. Johnston of Chapel Hill, and her nephew, Samuel W. Hughes of Hillsboro. At whatever place she was, she was a comfort and an inspiration. Her influence, both as a teacher and a Christian leader, is still felt, especially among her former students, many of whom have expressed the feeling that she has a "building of God, an house not made with hands, eternal in the heavens."

MINNIE LOU JAMISON
1866-1948

MINNIE LOU JAMISON, connected in various capacities with the Woman's College of the University of North Carolina for more than half a century, was the embodiment of selfless loyalty and joyous service. A member of the first student body of the State Normal and Industrial School in 1892, student assistant in the Department of Home Economics in 1894-95, a member of the first regular graduating class in

1895-96, she was invited by President Charles Duncan McIver to join the Home Economics faculty in 1896. From that day forward for fifty-two years it was her fortune and her delight to serve the college, the state, and generation after generation of college girls.

Miss Jamison was born October 9, 1866 near Mooresville, North Carolina, of sturdy Scotch-Irish parentage, the daughter of Louise Kilpatrick Jamison and Miles Stanhope Jamison. Her early life was spent in the shadow of Prospect Presbyyterian Church, Rowan County; and her education received in church, home, and at the academy nearby stressed the Christian ideals followed throughout her long life of love and service.

After several years of teaching under what were primitive conditions in the public schools of Rowan, Iredell, and Cabarrus Counties, her love of her pupils led her to seek a better education in order to be of greater service in the classroom. She began to dream and to save her money to that end. Her story is characteristic of the pioneer college women of that day. She said, "I came to the State Normal and Industrial School with just enough money to eke out my existence for the year (1892). . . . I took little odd jobs that year, many of which the janitors do now and receive much better pay—I am glad." And she added:

"During my student days I had one good dress. Before my junior year I made it over into an Eton jacket suit for my best Sunday dress. Those were strenuous days, but I do not regret them. I cherish them."

No one of those first students embraced more wholeheartedly than did Miss Jamison the ideal of President McIver, that when you educate a woman you educate a family. The greatest moment of her life was when Dr. McIver invited her to join the Home Economics faculty at a salary of thirty-three and one-third dollars a month. Now she could have a part in preparing women to meet what she considered their first obligation, the establishment and preservation of the home.

Her early students marvel that so much was done with so little, as with meager equipment she laid the foundations of a great school of Home Economics. She not only taught them the practical skills of cooking and sewing, but she held before them the ideal of an educated woman in every home. While she taught "how to make a cake that will keep your husband in a good humor" or "how to budget your time, money, and work," she likewise taught by her own life and example the true meaning of the thirteenth chapter of First Corinthians.

In 1897 Miss Jamison added to her duties by becoming assistant lady principal to Miss Sue May Kirkland. As she said, "From that date, my life with students in the dormitory became my happiest work." While holding high standards of conduct, Miss Jamison, always young in heart, sympathized with and understood the problems of youth. What a book she could have written on the "Love Affairs of College Girls."

Miss Jamison was a pioneer in Home Economics teaching, not only on campus but throughout the State, helping her graduates initiate and set up programs in the high schools, and in 1900 she helped her sister, Lillie Hope Jamison, organize the first work in Home Economics in the Durham City Schools.

From 1915 to 1922, in connection with the extension division of the College, she worked with rural adults; first, in 1915-16 under the Smith-Lever Act and in cooperation with the State and Federal Departments of Agriculture she went over the State organizing the older women into community clubs; and second, in 1917-18 as secretary of the College Volunteer Workers in North Carolina, she put on so effective a program as to merit high praise from Herbert Hoover, the National Food Administrator.

A bulletin, "A Study in Foods and Household Equipment," prepared by Miss Jamison in 1916, received three printings and was circulated throughout the United States and several foreign countries.

Returning to the campus in 1924 after two years of illness, the result of an accident, Miss Jamison was given charge of freshmen, a position she held for the next twelve years, and one she considered her greatest challenge. She said, "My long years of experience have taught me that in every freshman there is a finer self to be developed."

Under her leadership freshman classes beautified the campus with shrubs and flowers and "Keep off the grass" became their slogan. The annual formal banquet became a dance with young men invited from the city and the near-by colleges. Under Miss Jamison's direction the campus, once called "no man's land" by Miss Elliott became a place of normal, happy social life.

In 1936 Miss Jamison on semi-retirement, became adviser in social affairs and was given charge of the Students' Building. She often said, "I wish the college would give me more to do."

At mail time she was to be seen daily on the steps of Students' Building greeting passing students with her cheery "Hello" and often a question about some alumna, probably the student's mother. They called her "the lady with the white powder puff hair."

She was greatly interested in the children of the alumnae. One alumna whose own marriage had been given Miss Jamison's blessing, received a letter concerning her son who had been "courting" on campus. "I'm glad he's given that girl up," wrote Miss Jamison. "She deceives her father and she is not good enough for my grandson."

With her distinctive personality and cordial social graces Miss Jamison was an ideal campus hostess. No gathering of visitors, especially alumnae, was complete without her cordial greeting, and "to pour" was her prerogative.

Miss Jamison was appreciated while she lived. In 1939-40, her last freshman class, as seniors, dedicated *Pine Needles,* the college yearbook, to her; and that same year the name of West Dormitory was changed to Jamison Hall.

In 1941, on the fiftieth anniversary of the opening of the college, a glowing tribute was paid the life and work of Miss Jamison in the anniversary publication, "Educate a Woman." A student was heard to remark, "How wonderful that she was here to read that for herself!"

Just five days before her death on January 23, 1948 at the age of eighty-one years, Miss Jamison was on the campus for the last time.

Students, alumnae, and friends mourned her passing and reverently attended her funeral at the Presbyterian Church of the Covenant. On a cold winter day Minnie Lou Jamison came home to old Prospect Presbyterian Church to rest with her fathers.

Her best tribute is summarized in the college annual dedication of 1939: "Educator, Counselor, Believer in Youth, Miss Minnie Lou Jamison has served the college and the state since her graduation. Her work has been as distinctive for excellence as for length of service."

MABELLE KIZER JOHNSTON
Retired 1945

M RS. T. EDGAR JOHNSTON'S professional career in teaching, supervising, and teacher training extended over a period of more than forty years. She was noted for her excellent teaching on whatever level her work happened to be. She served on various State Committees through which she made her influence felt. Perhaps she is best known for her organization and supervision of teacher training on the high school level as an emergency measure for the great teacher shortage during and immediately following World War I.

A native of Virginia, Mabelle Kizer, at the age of eight, moved with her parents to Salisbury, North Carolina. She completed the work offered in the Salisbury city schools and studied two years in Miss Jennie Caldwell's private school. She continued her studies at Mont Amoena Seminary, a Lutheran Junior College located at Mount Pleasant, North Carolina. Later she received a degree from Catawba College.

In 1897, Miss Kizer was married to T. Edgar Johnston of Salisbury. However, her home duties did not interfere with her professional career. She had begun teaching as an assistant to her father, R. G. Kizer, who was Superintendent of the Salisbury City Schools and of Rowan County. Soon after her marriage, she began teaching in the Salisbury schools. Here she was fortunate to have had the supervision and inspiration of three of the State's leading educators of that day who succeeded one another as head of the Salisbury schools: Charles L. Coon, I. C. Griffin, and A. T. Allen. Mrs. Johnston took advantage of the help of these leaders, also continued her studies through summer schools at the University of North Carolina, Columbia University, Peabody College, and Duke University.

She became very prominent in educational circles in the State. In 1917, E. C. Brooks, State Superintendent of Schools, appointed her as one of the six members of the State Board of Examiners and Institute Conductors. As a member of this board she had a voice in abolishing written examinations for teachers' certificates, also in setting up six weeks summer schools for teacher training to replace the two weeks' institutes previously held. For several years Mrs. Johnston served as one of the State Supervisors of County Summer Schools.

In the 1920's she did outstanding work in teacher training in the State.

Because of the lack of trained teachers to fill the public schools the Department of Education in 1910 established a plan of training teachers on the high school level. It continued this work with some modifications until 1929. After 1917 when the State took over the certification of all teachers a graduate of an accredited high school which offered teacher training was issued an Elementary Certificate. In the early 1920's Mrs. Johnston was supervisor of all schools where this work was being done. This was an arduous task. From sea coast on the east to Franklin on the west, she traveled visiting twenty-one schools where this work was being carried on. She offered encouragement and practical help to the instructors and inspired the students with ambition to do their best. In 1925 a regulation was passed by which admission to the teacher training departments was based upon high school graduation. Mrs. Johnston was instrumental in getting those in authority to allow college credit for a year's work in these training centers. Not only did the project aid in furnishing teachers to tide the State over an emergency, but numbers of students entered college, graduated, and went into the teaching profession. The personal testimony of these students was invariably: "What I am and what I have been able to do, I owe in large measure to Mrs. Johnston."

In 1928 when Mrs. Johnston was about to leave this work, the instructors who had worked under her supervision showed their appreciation for her untiring efforts by giving her a life membership in the National Education Association.

Following her work as Supervisor of Teacher Training, Mrs. Johnston joined the staff of Catawba College as instructor in Education. Here she remained until her retirement in 1945. She still retains her interest in educational activities through contacts with former associates and students who seek her advice. She lives in Salisbury.

MRS. MOLLIE ROBERTS JONES
1875-1945

BECAUSE of her long and varied experience, Mollie Roberts Jones may be classified as teacher, school principal, college president, and community worker. With her husband, she was co-founder of Pineland College at Salemburg, North Carolina, and served as its president for twenty years.

Mollie, the daughter of Bright Roberts and his wife, Mary A. Jones Roberts, was born at Carbonton, North Carolina, March 16, 1875.

The period in which Mollie grew up was economically a very difficult one for the farmer in the Southern States, and she experienced financial difficulties in attaining her education. However, she was ambitious and, by teaching at intervals during her college career, she managed to complete the requirements for a Bachelor's degree from Guilford College in 1896. Later she studied at Saddler's Business College in Baltimore and attended summer sessions at Columbia University.

For the first six years after Mollie's graduation from Guilford College, 1896-1901, she served as: teacher, Siloam Academy, 1897; teacher, Guilford College Graded School, 1899-1900; principal, Corinth Academy, Conley, Virginia, 1900-1901. Then, in the fall of 1901, she became a member of the faculty at Salemburg Academy and here in December of the next year she married her principal, G. F. Edwards.

Together, Mr. and Mrs. Edwards planned ambitiously toward the growth and expansion of the Academy; and the people of the community shared this ambition, granting them four acres of land including the school building which they were then using. However, in 1907, Mr. Edwards died and Mrs. Edwards was left in sole charge of the school with no funds for carrying it on. But friends came to her aid with donations and she managed to keep the school alive.

In 1908, Mrs. Edwards married W. J. Jones who had recently come to the village as pastor of the Salemburg Baptist Church. Mr. Jones possessed unusual business and executive ability; and the couple worked together for the advancement of the school in the realization that there was a great need in this region at this period for a boarding school for girls. Within ten years the school grew rapidly in equipment, enrollment, and reputation. In 1919, the name was changed from Salemburg Academy to Pineland School for Girls of which Mrs. Jones was principal. By 1927, the school had become Pineland Junior College for Young Women and thus Mrs. Jones was now a college president.

Since there was a growing demand for a school for boys in conjunction with the one for girls, Edwards Military Institute was established for boys in 1935. This school was coordinate with the school for girls, and the two schools were chartered as Pineland College. Mr. and Mrs. Jones were co-founders and co-presidents of the two schools and served as co-presidents until the death of Mrs. Jones in 1945.

The student body of Pineland College through the years of its existence has been drawn from a wide area and from different classes of society. Mrs. Jones helped girls from broken homes, from poverty stricken families—in fact, from all social groups—with a rare sympathy and understanding. Great was her influence!

In addition to her work as teacher and educator, Mrs. Jones was active in local and State, civic and political organizations. She served as Commissioner of the town of Salemburg, secretary of the local organization for rural development, and vice-chairman of the Democratic party in Sampson County. In 1912, she was elected president of the Farm Women's Organization. Her activities in State organizations included membership on the Equalization Fund Commission, the Interracial Commission, and the State Forestry Association. She frequently spoke before clubs. She taught a Sunday School class in the Salemburg Baptist Church for forty-three years.

ELIZABETH KELLY
1879-1933

ELIZABETH KELLY, the North Carolina mountain woman who raised her voice against illiteracy in her own State and one of the earliest supervisors in North Carolina, was born in Macon County, November 1, 1879. She was the daughter of Mark L. and Elizabeth Hyatt Kelly, both of whom were pioneer teachers in their mountain region.

At the age of four, Elizabeth, a precocious child, started to school to Miss Angie McPherson, and at sixteen she was teaching in a rural school in her home county. She later attended Womans College of the University of North Carolina, then returned to Franklin to teach.

Her work as a teacher attracted wide attention, and in 1912, when rural school supervision was introduced into the State, Miss Kelly was asked to accept the position of supervisor in Johnston County which position she held for four years. These were pioneer days in rural school work. To Miss Kelly, ideals taught in the schoolroom were of no value unless they could be put to work toward improving society. Therefore, in addition to organizing the schools of the county into groups and holding inspiring and constructive meetings in each group, she gave individual help to individual teachers and took much interest in the corn clubs, the canning clubs, and the rural health clubs. Because of her work along these lines, she was asked to teach a course in "Rural Organization" in the summer school at State College in Raleigh. In an article relating

110

to the plans for this summer school, the *Raleigh News and Observer* stated: "Under the Bickett administration Rural is the word and Johnston's widely known supervisor is credited with knowing more about building up the Bickett kingdom than any woman now engaged in the public school work."

The 1917 session of the General Assembly of North Carolina appropriated $25,000 a year for two years for the purpose of conducting schools for adult illiterates. One section of this law provided that the organization and direction of this work be placed in the hands of the State Superintendent of Public Instruction. J. Y. Joyner, Superintendent at that time, appointed Miss Kelly Commissioner of School for Illiterates.

Shortly after entering upon her new duties, Miss Kelly issued to all county superintendents a letter which contained the following:

"First I would suggest that you make a careful survey of your county and locate all illiterates more than fourteen years old. Your best chance of doing this will be by means of teachers and pupils in your schools . . . You may have other and better plans for your own particular county. If so, we are anxious to know what they are, that we may all plan and work together to the end that the census of 1920 may find us well on toward the goal of North Carolina freed from illiteracy."

In order to strengthen the teaching force for the work in adult illiteracy, Miss Kelly organized in connection with the regular summer school of Asheville Teachers College of 1918 the first school for teachers of native adult beginners ever attempted in the United States. In an issue that spring the *Asheville Citizen* stated:

"America's first school for training teachers for work with adult illiterates will be opened in Asheville next June under the direction of Miss Elizabeth Kelly, director of the adult illiterate work of the State Department of Education. She will be assisted by Mrs. Elizabeth Morris and Professor Alton C. Roberts."

An examination of the newspapers of the period shows that this work with illiterates received publicity from mountains to coast. Mrs. W. T. Bost wrote in the *Greensboro Daily News*, June 29, 1919:

"She (Miss Kelly) is so ardently interested in her chosen work that she goes on the assumption that everybody else is a welfare worker, and it occurs to her that now when such vast possibilities for service are opening up, there might be a few drones and parasites inhabiting the earth."

Since Miss Kelly was a pioneer in this work of adult illiteracy, one of her problems was to obtain material to put into the hands of those being taught. In her attempt to meet this need she arranged a primer based on material taken from the Bible. She reasoned that all

111

adults were familiar with Bible stories from having heard them so often.

Her work received considerable recognition outside the State, and Miss Kelly was invited to speak before various organizations. At the request of Miss Mabel Carney she spoke before the Rural Life Conference at Columbia University in the summer of 1919, and later she gave a series of radio talks on the Farm Life Program in Chicago. She also appeared in the 1921 volume of *Who's Who in America.*

In 1923, Miss Kelly was elected president of the North Carolina Education Association. It was during her presidency that the Association adopted the plan of dividing the State into six districts and holding an annual meeting in each district in addition to the State-wide delegated meeting each spring. In her message before the Association in March, 1924, Miss Kelly said:

"The Education Association under the new plan of organization proposes to use its annual meeting for deciding which old plans and policies are to be retained and what new ones are to be adopted. The district meetings are to be used as a sort of laboratory for testing policies."

The burden of her theme during her presidency was the equalization of educational opportunity for all children of elementary school age. Since she had served on the board for the Equalizing Fund which the State had set up in 1918, she realized the inadequacy of this arrangement to accomplish what was desired for the elementary school.

Miss Kelly's broad interests in the welfare of people and her reputation for doing things well led to her appointment on several other boards and committees. Governor Bickett appointed her a trustee of the Caswell Training School in 1917. Later, Governor McLean made her a member of the Board of Trustees of the Cullowhee Normal School, now Western Carolina Teachers College.

She was active in the cause of woman suffrage and made a number of speeches on the subject during the summer of 1920 when the ratification of the Nineteenth Amendment to the Federal Constitution was to come before a special legislative assembly in North Carolina. The following from the Rocky Mount paper serves as an amusing illustration:

"Miss Elizabeth Kelly will be the speaker before the regular weekly session of the Current Topics Club at the Y. M. C. A. Monday evening . . . While Miss Kelly has not announced her subject she has requested the committee to speak on "Woman Suffrage" from the woman's viewpoint . . . Miss Kelly's coming will mark an unprecedented event in the history of the local organization as no woman speaker has ever appeared before it during its several years of existence."

When North Carolina discontinued her appropriation for the work in adult illiteracy in 1924, Miss Kelly was invited by the Tobacco Growers' Cooperative Association to take charge of its new Department of Women's work.

After spending about six years here, Miss Kelly returned in 1931 to her home in Franklin to care for her aged mother. However, her public activities did not cease. She accepted the chairmanship of the Red Cross in Macon County and so well did she serve here that the editor of the *Red Cross Journal* gave her special recognition.

Numerous amusing stories concerning Miss Kelly are told by her friends. Among them is the following: While attending a summer conference of Welfare Workers, she was on a program with a Boston speaker. This speaker referred sympathetically to the "poor mountain whites" and the possibilities of helping them. At the close of the lecture, Miss Kelly was introduced. She—the personification of her rock-ribbed mountains; a woman of about six feet, three inches, weighing over two hundred pounds—rose and said: "I am one of those 'poor mountain whites' about whom the gentleman has just been talking."

In the fall of 1932, her services to her mountain people and to her State were interrupted by a serious illness. When, in October, she underwent an operation, she was told that her case was beyond the skill of any surgeon. On January 22, 1933, she passed away at the age of fifty-four. A quotation from an editorial in her home town paper, the *Franklin Press*, seems a fitting close to this sketch regarding her public services: "She gave of herself so generously and she had so much to give."

FLORA MAHN KENDALL
1863-1936

FOR nearly forty years, Flora Mahn Kendall taught music in Goldsboro. She was an outstanding piano teacher and a specialist in teaching music to small children.

Mrs. Kendall was a native of Wilmington, North Carolina. She was educated at Greensboro Female College, now Greensboro College, graduating in 1882 as valedictorian of her class. Later she studied music with Katherine Burroughs of Detroit, Michigan, and became an accredited teacher of the Burroughs Kindergarten Method.

She vitalized her work through group meetings held in her studio where the lives and works of great musicians were studied.

Mrs. Kendall was active in church work. For several years she was choir director at Saint Paul's Methodist Church. And she served as superintendent of the Beginners' Department of the Sunday School of this church for twenty-five years.

She died in Goldsboro, August 13, 1936.

SUE MAY KIRKLAND
——1914

THE position of lady principal, "custodian of manners and morals," of the eighteen nineties laid the ground work for the deanship of today. Miss Sue May Kirkland who was the lady principal of the State Normal and Industrial School for the first twenty-two years of its existence, was in the first catalogue of 1892 noted as responsible for "habits and manners," while in subsequent catalogues she was designated as "lady principal, referee in matters social and domestic," until in the catalogue of 1898-99, when her title became simply, "lady principal."

Miss Kirkland was an extremely important person on the Normal School campus. She was responsible for all social functions as well as the students' correct manners, habits, and conduct in the dormitories and in their social life on and off campus.

This new adventure in state-supported higher education for young women was indeed fortunate in the sturdy personality and fine cultural background of its lady principal. A native of Hillsboro, descendant of a long line of distinguished ancestry, Miss Kirkland was born and bred a true Southern lady. She was educated at the famous finishing school, Nash and Kollock's Select School for Young Ladies, in Hillsboro. Here she experienced the best in culture and correct deportment for young ladies of the period. To this educational background she added experience as a member of the faculty of Peace Institute, Raleigh, a select Presbyterian school for girls.

President Julius I. Foust in his biennial report for 1912-14 paid the following tribute to Miss Kirkland's influence on the life of the students:

"From the opening of the College twenty-two years ago Miss Kirkland has been one of the most important factors in its life. On account of her position she was brought into closer contact with the students than any other member of the Faculty, and for that reason it is impossible to estimate the influence that she exerted, not only upon the life of the institution, but also upon the life of the State through the young women who came under her care and supervision. Miss Kirkland possessed one of those strong, positive characters that made a deep impression upon all with whom she came in contact. . . . Her sympathy for young people was strong and deep, and she met their problems with a fine spirit of cooperation which was always returned by the students."

Miss Kirkland impressed her standards and ideals upon the students as probably no other member of the first faculty did. An early alumna wrote:

"In my picture gallery of memories whether I see Miss Kirkland in her sitting room, moving majestically down the halls, presiding in the dining room or at some social function, she was always a queenly, stately,

114

dignified, commanding personality for whom I had great respect, accompanied at first with a feeling of awe, later with admiration and love. We spoke of her as Queen Victoria. She was always a handsome, well-dressed woman; the rustle of her silk skirts impressed us; also her fine heirloom jewelry, and her lovely hands."

She was a lady "to the manor born" and taught the amenities of life both by precept and example. Amanda, her personal maid, arranged her hair, cared for her wardrobe, and kept her suite in apple-pie order. Her rose garden, carefully tended, abounded in fragrant loveliness.

At her place in the dining hall her own silver service was in daily use. It was a coveted honor to be invited to sit at her table. Remembered and long used in many alumnae homes was Miss Kirkland's blessing: "Bless us, O Lord, and make us ever thankful for these and all thy mercies. For Christ's sake, Amen."

She set a high standard of morals and manners for her girls. She encouraged the development of the social graces and the religious life. Regular church attendance was arranged for and expected.

A suggestion from Miss Kirkland was equivalent to a command. Two frequent reminders were: "Ladies never hurry." and "Where are your gloves? No lady goes shopping or to church without them."

Many stories are extant depicting Miss Kirkland's dignity. It is said that on one occasion when walking sedately down the aisle of the First Presbyterian Church, she suffered a severe fall. An usher, a handsome young dentist, a favorite of Miss Kirkland, rushed to her aid and asked solicitiously, "Are you hurt, Miss Kirkland?" To which she replied, "No, but my dignity is crushed forever."

Miss Kirkland's extreme dignity was off-set by a gracious manner, a lovely smile, a keen sense of humor, and eyes that could twinkle gaily. A tradition handed down by students is to this effect: Miss Boddie on seeing two students sitting unchaperoned in the parlor talking to two young men, took the matter to Miss Kirkland. "When you and I were young, we were never permitted to receive gentlemen without a chaperon," complained Miss Boddie. To which Miss Kirkland replied with a twinkle, "Yes, and see what it did for us."

With the same twinkle in her eyes she is said to have corrected a visitor's salutation of "Mrs. Kirkland," with, "*Miss* Kirkland, by choice."

Miss Kirkland's strict standards of decorum were typical of the period. Early catalogues carried the statement: "Visits of young men must be restricted to holiday occasions and those stated times when the young ladies will announce that they are 'At Home' to their friends generally." Notwithstanding rules and regulations many a successful romance blossomed on campus and received proper chaperonage in Miss Kirkland's parlours.

On June 8, 1914, while she was on a visit to her sister, Mrs. C. C. Crow, in Raleigh, death came to Miss Kirkland. On the following day she was laid to rest in Oak Wood cemetery. Her age remains a lady's secret.

Memorial services, held at the Founder's Day exercises of the college on October 4, 1914, were devoted to eulogies of Miss Kirkland. On that occasion President Foust said, "Her influence and the inspiration of her life have become one of the best possessions of this college. Such a life lived with sincerity cannot entirely pass from us."

From the private papers of the late Dr. W. C. Smith comes this tribute: "Ever cheerful, ever dignified; gifted in intellect, gracious in manner, helpful in counsel, loyal to truth . . . We had her presence . . . we have her life."

Her life-like portrait hangs in Kirkland Hall, a reminder to present day students of the importance of gracious living even in the atomic age.

LAURA LAZENBY
1864-1941

UNDER the inspiration of Charles B. Aycock, Charles D. McIver, and J. Y. Joyner, at which time the public schools were waking up and the private schools were filling the gap between the old and the new, Laura Lazenby began her teaching career in Rowan County.

Laura was born in the Cool Spring community of Iredell County, June 16, 1864, ten days before her father, Daniel O. Lazenby entered the Confederate Army.

She had learned her letters at home, using the newspapers as a primer, before she started to school to Mrs. Jane Hill at the Allison school house near Turnersburg. She received her elementary education in the "free' or public schools of that day, these being supplemented by subscription schools. Her preparatory work was done at the Mount Bethel private school and at Cool Spring Academy where she studied two years. She continued her education at Simonton Academy, now Mitchell College, and at the Thomasville Female Academy.

To become a teacher had been Miss Lazenby's ambition from girlhood. When she left school at Thomasville, the opportunity of realizing that wish came to pass: the neighbors asked her to start a "subscription school" for their "children." To this she agreed; but when she reached the little log schoolhouse in the grove the first morning, she was surprised to meet pupils taller and older than she. However, summoning courage for the task, she made a start and here she continued to teach for several months.

About 1892, Miss Lazenby went to Statesville to take the customary examination given to teachers and was issued a certificate. In 1893, she was elected to a teaching position in the graded schools of Statesville. She continued to teach in this system for forty years.

Miss Lazenby was very fond of teaching which she termed "one triumph after another over the impossible." She gave her best efforts to her work.

Because of ill health, she was forced to retire in 1934. She passed away on September 3, 1941.

LILY WEBB LONG
1847-1929

A MONG the names of women educators in North Carolina that of Miss Lily Webb Long stands pre-eminent. Most of her life was spent in the field of education, but she is remembered chiefly for her work at Queens College, which she loved and served under its various names for several decades.

Born in Hillsboro, North Carolina, June 12, 1847, "Miss Lily" was the daughter of Dr. Osmond and Helen Webb Long, from whom she inherited those splendid traits of mind and heart which so well fitted her for the great role she was to play in the education of the women of the State.

Miss Long began her teaching career at the age of seventeen and from that time her life was dedicated to the education of young women.

She taught at Peace Institute and in the Charlotte Graded School, then in the Charlotte Female Institute, which was successively presided over by Dr. and Mrs. Robert Burwell, Dr. Robert Chapman, and Dr. W. R. Atkinson.

At this school she so endeared herself to the girls who came under her tutelage, as well as to their parents, that when Dr. W. R. Atkinson closed the Institute in 1890 and moved to Columbia, South Carolina, she was asked to open a school for girls.

In organizing this school she had the active assistance of several prominent women of Charlotte whose daughters had been her pupils. In 1891 the Charlotte Seminary was opened on North Tryon Street, near the corner of East Ninth.

Miss Long was Principal of this Seminary for five years and was ably assisted in the various departments by several of Charlotte's most gifted teachers. During this time many girls were prepared to take their places in the religious, cultural, and social life of the city—many of them following in Miss Long's footsteps to become teachers.

When, in 1896, the Presbyterians of Mecklenburg and Concord decided to establish a college in Charlotte, Miss Long was asked to bring her Seminary into the organization and to become the first President of

117

the Presbyterian College for Women. This office she filled with great distinction for several years.

To know "Miss Lily" during these years was indeed to love her. With her personal charm and culture and her appearance, she was a shining example of all that a gentlewoman should be. Always standing firmly for what she believed to be right, she was a wise teacher, a patient and helpful counselor to "her girls." The achievement in scholarship, growth in character, and success in their chosen fields of these girls continued to be a source of pride and joy to Miss Long throughout the remaining years of her life.

In 1899, when Dr. James R. Bridges assumed the presidency of the Presbyterian College for Women, Miss Long became Dean. For this work she was exceptionally well fitted, and she continued in this position until her retirement in 1910.

The Lily Long Dormitory, one of the lovely buildings on Queens campus, stands as a memorial to her loyalty to the institution which she served so long and so well.

In many ways the Alumnae Association has paid tribute to Miss Long's splendid service to Queens College. In 1925 she was made the first Life Member of that organization. Following her death, on September 4, 1929, the Association established the Lily Long Memorial Scholarship Fund to be used by worthy young women attending college. On June 3, 1950, the Association presented to the college a handsome portrait of Miss Long. This portrait, painted by Dayrell Kortheuer, hangs in the parlor of Burwell Hall.

"Miss Lily" also gave freely of her time and talents to the Second Presbyterian Church, of which she was for many years a loyal and devoted member; to the Woman's Club, which she served in many capacities and of which she was the only Honorary Vice-President; and to the Cranford Book Club (the first to be organized in the city), of which she was a charter member.

She was an active member of Mecklenburg Chapter Daughters of the American Revolution, and a charter member of Stonewall Jackson Chapter United Daughters of the Confederacy. In 1926, the latter organization established at Queens College the Lily Long Scholarship Loan Fund for the use of girls of Confederate ancestry. This fund has been used continuously since its establishment.

Perhaps no more fitting tribute could be paid Miss Long than that by Mrs. A. A. McGeachy on May 26, 1914, at the last meeting of the Alumnae Association in the old building of Presbyterian College for Women on North College Street. Mrs. McGreachy, herself one of "Miss Lily's girls", said in part:

"One who has perhaps participated in the education of more girls than any woman in North Carolina; whose influence extends far an wide, into homes made by women who have learned to know and admire

118

the traits that made up her splendid womanhood: modesty, unselfishness, self-control, broad thinking, right living; who forgets injury and remembers kindness; who has spent her life in an effort to ennoble the lives around her—Miss Lily Long."

EMMA AUGUSTA LEHMAN
1841-1918

To the thousands of "Salem girls" scattered from Maryland to Texas, the memories of their happy years in Salem Academy and College center about a frail, keen-eyed little figure in cap and gown, their beloved senior teacher, Miss Emma Lehman. Year by year for fifty-four years the quiet but pervasive personality of Emma Lehman, her brilliant mind and undaunted spirit, made for the steady upbuilding of Salem Academy and College. Her fruitful years bear record to the impress upon the plastic hearts and minds of young womanhood throughout this period of active service which she gave with selfless devotion to her Alma Mater. Into the warp and woof of the history of education in North Carolina are woven the quiet but vitalizing years of this beloved teacher in the classrooms of Old Salem.

Born August 28, 1841, of music-loving, staunch Moravian stock, in the village of Bethania, North Carolina, Emma Augusta Lehman, daughter of Eugene Christian Lehman and Amanda Sophia Butner Lehman, gave promise of unusual mental powers at an early age when at thirteen she entered Salem Academy and in three years completed the course.

At sixteen, she began her teaching career in a free school near her home; and, though many of her pupils were as old or older than herself, she succeeded in winning their respect. Meantime she was earning, in addition to her $64.00 for four months' work, a Number One Teachers' Certificate. She taught in other free schools until 1864, when at the age of twenty-three she was called to her Alma Mater. Here, in the stimulating, congenial atmosphere of her beloved Moravian school, she passed the remaining years of her long and useful life.

Many stories have been handed down, telling of Miss Lehman's creative ability as a teacher, of her individualism, her original and inspiring methods in the classroom, her insight into the heart of a piece of literature, and her gift of making her "girls" feel and see its hidden beauties.

Although it is as a teacher of English that Miss Lehman is best known, her professional experience included other college subjects of a widely differing nature. Indeed, her versatility was truly remarkable.

119

In addition to English she taught Art, gave piano lessons, and with great enthusiasm carried on courses in Botany and Astronomy. It is even a tradition of the college that in the days when ideals were high and funds were low, whenever it was necessary to add a subject to the curriculum (shorthand or flute-playing, for instance) Miss Lehman was called upon first to teach herself the subject and then she was expected to teach it to others.

So great was her interest in Botany that she won wide recognition along this line. She was so original and so thorough in this study that she actually discovered a hitherto unidentified plant which the State botanist of New York named *Monotropsis Lehmani* in her honor. Then, on one occasion, she had reason to differ with the distinguished botanist, Dr. Asa Gray who contended that there was no such thing as a yellow trillium. She convinced Dr. Gray to the contrary by sending him specimens of yellow trillium from her own locality.

Furthermore, her versatility found expression in many other forms of activity. Apart from her teaching and her duties as organizer of the senior class and Senior Teacher, she prepared talks for clubs and contributed numerous articles on a variety of subjects to current newspapers and magazines; she was antiquarian and historian of her native village and her college, and as such was constantly called upon to assist in celebrations and anniversary programs; she published in book form an account of her summer in Europe, 1889; she gave talks on mushrooms and stars; she did clay modeling and hammered brass; she worked handsome pictures in wool; and, in between times, she wrote poetry.

Many of her poems breathe a spiritual outlook on life, expressive of her deeply spiritual nature. Her one slim volume of verse, brought out as a commencement gift to her seniors in 1904 reflects this same inner beauty. She read her Bible constantly and fed her heart on the hymns of her church. On the evening before her homegoing she recited with her sister all four stanzas of a beloved hymn.

An hour spent in the gracious home of Miss Lehman's niece, Mrs. E. T. Kapp, makes vivid the background of this pioneer teacher. Here are her books and mementoes; her scrap books filled with her whimsical stories of owls and bees, butterflies and birds, with dainty etchings of old Moravian homes, with poems and sketches never published. Also, here are specimens of her handiwork—hammered brass, bits of molded clay, and wood carving, among the last a charming set of decoys (an ancient hen and her biddies); the lovely old melodeon and music books, giving a hint of the days when Miss Lehman's father was director of the village orchestra and Miss Lehman, a bright-eyed three-year-old sat under the drop-leaf table in the parlor while the clarionette and the violin, the flutes and the trombones, tuned up for the weekly practice.

That hour's visit made the past glow with life as bits of stories were dropped—stories that gave a personal touch of the time when great-grandfather Lehman came back from Philadelphia in 1845, bringing with

120

him a wonderful new remedy for malaria—quinine—$60.00 an ounce, and with the help of his little Emma he rolled the quinine into tiny balls for use in the family in spite of the dire threats of local doctors that such dosage, even if it cured malaria, would cause the bones to rot. Another story told of an evening on the roof of the village buggy shop when young Emma and her aunt watched until midnight for old Jupiter to rise. And, finally, there was the big rag doll Miss Lehman and another Salem teacher made for President Cleveland's little Ruth, and with it was the letter of appreciation for the gift in the Presidnt's own hand-writing.

It is pleasing to know that Miss Lehman had the joy for realizing the esteem and respect with which she was held. Her girls presented her at one commencement a loving cup filled with gold coins and at another time with a golden book filled with loving messages. The handsome stone steps in front of Annex Hall were given in her honor. And the College, in recognition of her fifty years of service bestowed upon her in 1914 the honorary degree of Master of Arts.

N. MELDONA LIVINGSTONE

1873-1948

THE name of N. Meldona Livingstone deserves a place in any group of pioneer women teachers in North Carolina because she inspired and developed an effective educational program in a section where the State was doing very little for education. Beginning in a one-teacher school in Rutherford County, her qualities of leadership and superior teaching ability soon spread to adjoining counties and culminated in the establishment of a high school in an area where there was none.

"Miss Meldona," as she was known to the people in that group of counties where she served for fifty years, was born in Tennessee of native North Carolina parents. Her father, Lindsay W. Livingstone of Rutherford County, was married to Martha Morgan of McDowell County soon after the close of the War between the States and later migrated to Tennessee. On July 9, 1873, the subject of this sketch was born on a little farm near Newport.

Little Meldona started to school at the age of four, and at the age of six she was reading well. By the time she was ten, she was spelling the big words in Webster's Blue Back Spelling Book. In spite of the difficulties of the times, she managed to attend high school. Then, at the age of fifteen, she began to teach in the rural schools in order to finance her further education. Through persistent effort she finally graduated from Carson and Newman College.

For awhile after graduation she continued to teach in east Tennessee, but a desire to return to the region from which her parents had come led her to seek a position in North Carolina. Therefore in the fall of 1894 she began teaching in the Holly Springs community in Rutherford County. The writer (Cordelia Camp) at that time a little girl of ten, was among the eighty pupils present on the first day of school to greet "Miss Meldona," and her recollections of the occasion are very vivid. Some of the pupils—the group ranged in age from six to twenty-one—were seated in the large one-room building while others remained outside. Soon a buggy drove up to the front, and the teacher got out. The little girl seated near the fireplace now surveyed a slim woman nearly six feet tall wearing a blue flannel dress with flowing skirt and tight basque according to the fashion of the day. Her black hair was combed back from her forehead and arranged in a knot near the crown of her head and adorned with an ornamental hairpin.

An indescribable feeling ran through that group of pupils—a recognition that here was a teacher who differed from any it had had before.

Soon the new teacher stepped to the door and rang a handbell which brought all pupils into the room. Then, reading a chapter from the Bible, she said: "Let us stand and engage in prayer." This was an activity to which we had not been accustomed. The impression of those years when "Miss Meldona" taught in that school still remain. She possessed that indescribable something which Emerson called "the oversoul." Because of her influence many young men and women from that community went out later and made a contribution to the world.

In spite of the large number of pupils and nine grades of work carried on in that school, there were few disciplinary problems. An attempted analysis of Miss Livingstone's success as a teacher would seem to indicate that it was due to her magnetic personality and her untiring efforts plus the esteem in which she was held by both pupils and parents. Doubtless her pedagogical devices and teaching techniques aided.

Another phase of this teacher's work which still looms large in the writer's mind was the fact that the school was made the intellectual and social center of the community. The three months provided by the county were extended to eight by the patrons; and throughout the term there were speaking contests, programs, a debating society carried on by the adults of the community, and the like. Characterizing this period in retrospect, J. S. Lynch, a student and later the president of the Huntley-Hill Stockton Company of Winston-Salem, wrote:

"Miss Livingstone ranks among the pioneer teachers of Nirth Carolina. She established an eight months' school term where three months had been the custom. Under her leadership the community and the children caught a vision which led to a school spirit unsurpassed in the area where she worked."

After serving three years in the Holly Springs community, Miss

Livingstone went to the village of Ellenboro where for several years she carried on in a similar way to that already described.

She was succeeded at Holly Springs by her brother-in-law, the Reverend D. J. Hunt. The educational movement these two teachers started attracted wide attention. As a result, in 1900, Round Hill Academy was established by the Green River Baptist Association in the area where they were working. Mr. Hunt was made principal of the new institution and Miss Livingstone became "Lady Principal." The school drew students from all the surrounding counties. In addition to preparing students for college it offered a teacher training course on the secondary level. The part played by the "Lady Principal" is best expressed in the words of Mrs. Clara Morris Hargiss, a student in the Academy: "During my school days at Round Hill I was impressed with Miss Livingstone's versatility; she could teach anything in the curriculum." The monetary reward was often very meager. Speaking of the work in later years, Miss Livingstone said: "Although Mr. Hunt and I made many sacrifices at Round Hill, I still remember my work there with pleasure and rejoice that so many young men and women went out from that school and rendered valuable service."

After eight years at Round Hill, Miss Livingstone accepted the principalship of the public school at Grover. In a few years the school grew to a standard school. In later years, Dr. Lyle G. Ellis, a former student and then a practicing physician in Connecticut, wrote:

"Miss Livingstone was a natural leader, of firm character, and endowed with unusual energy. Many young people were influenced by her high standards of conduct, living, and sound teaching."

In the spring of 1944, "Miss Meldona" retired at the age of seventy. She continued to live in Grover. On February 22, 1948, she passed away. Among the remarks made by former students attending the funeral, perhaps the words of Mrs. Effie Lynch McCall are typical of the esteem in which this pioneer was held: "As a child I thought that Miss Livingstone was the most remarkable person I ever knew, except my mother; I still think so."

JANE GRACEY LOGAN

1747-1830

ALL women who cast their lots with pioneers were selfreliant and courageous, and Jane Gracey Logan is a supreme example of relentless determination and indomitable courage, also. The account of her reactions to frontier conditions, the story of her making a home and a living for her children and at the same time teaching them, should bring to this generation a vivid consciousness of a great heritage from that pioneer era. Here were no small towns with private schools nor large plantations with private tutors. The children of the pioneers learned to read, to write, and to figure, around their parents' knees, in front of log fires, after the long days of work were over.

Some time prior to 1780, Captain James Logan and his wife, Jane Gracey Logan, migrated from the vicinity of old Centre Meeting House in Iredell County (where Jane was born and reared) to the foot of the Blue Ridge Mountains near the present town of Old Fort.

Although General Griffith Rutherford, in 1776, at the head of the colonial militia from the Carolinas and Virginia had marched against the Overhill Cherokees and had burned their villages, laid waste their fields, and broken their power, the Indians, during the hunting season, continued to roam east of the Ridge. The settlers, fearing Indian tomahawks and scalping knives, were always, at a moment's notice, ready to flee to forts which had been built as places of refuge.

Sometime during the winter of 1779-1780 the Logans and their neighbors were warned by courier that Indians were in the vicinity. This meant for the settlers to hasten to the nearest fort, which was the one at Pleasant Gardens. Mr. Logan sent his wife and four children ahead of him. He soon followed, having hidden the cow and having buried the gold he had panned from a nearby stream.

The families which had sought refuge in the fort remained there during the winter. In January of that year, 1780, two babies were born in the fort. One of them was Rebecca, daughter of James and Jane Logan.

In order that the baby might have sufficient food, Mr. Logan, accompanied by his ten-year-old son, John, went out for the cow. They were returning, when Indians fired from ambush at Mr. Logan. The report of the gun frightened the pony on which John had been tied, one foot to the other, by cords that passed under the belly of the animal. The pony carried John to the fort safely. In fright and terror, he told his mother of the attack on his father and added that he heard arrows whizzing behind him all the way.

When friends ventured out to look for Mr. Logan, they found him where he had fallen. He had been killed and scalped.

When "spring broke," the refugees returned to their cabins, and among them were Jane Gracey Logan and her five children, ranging in ages from infant Rebecca to ten-year-old John. Although she was not accustomed to work in the fields, she and John made a crop. Neither of them knew plow language so John rode one of the horses to pull the reins as his mother directed, "to the old mare's side" or "to the pony's side." She followed the plow.

During the next autumn, Mrs. Logan was afraid to remain in the cabin at night for fear that Indians might descend upon the white settlement again. So, when it began to grow dark, she would gather up her children and take them into the nearby woods to a hole which she had hollowed out underneath the roots of a huge tree that had been uprooted during a storm. She would wrap each child in his blanket and tuck him snugly into the hole, then place herself in front and pull leaves up over all.

One night she had to return to the cabin for milk for hungry Rebecca. Before reaching their hiding place again, she was startled by Robert's screaming, "Mammy! Mammy! Indians!" In the moonlight, she could see Robert bounding toward her, his blanket flying in the air. She hastened to him and was frantically smothering his sobs when John reached them and assured his mother that what had frightened Robert was a rabbit running through the woods.

Amid such hazards and days of hard labor in the home and in the field, Jane Gracey Logan, an educated woman for her day, taught her children reading, writing and arithmetic.

One example of her excellent teaching was Robert who, at maturity, served ably as a surveyor and a teacher.

As a surveyor: Many of the early State grants, and the plats that accompany them, describing land entries in McDowell and surrounding counties in western North Carolina, were executed by Robert Logan. The accuracy of his spelling and the neatness and the meticulousness of his drawings are evidence of the efficiency of his mother as a teacher, the one who prepared him for his life work. Also, during the period of intense land speculations in western North Carolina, near the close of the eighteenth century, Robert Logan was the official surveyor of the State for the county of Burke which then extended to the Mississippi. He was a member of the party that in 1799 surveyed and marked out the boundary line between North Carolina and Tennessee.

As a teacher: It is believed that Robert Logan taught the first school in what is now McDowell County. He is credited in his immediate community of having taught the first school of neighborhood children in a one room cabin which he built for that urpose. And it is evident that he was well prepared for the work of teaching.

The location of the Jane Gracey Logan cabin is known, and it was here that this splendid woman taught her children and it was here that Robert Logan taught the children of the neighborhood. It was a noble institution in every sense of the term.

NORA KINCAID MARBUT

1862-1938

U P to about 1900 the early education of North Carolina children was largely in the hands of men and women who possessed a love of learning coupled with an emotional drive to pass their knowledge on to others. Teaching did not provide an avenue for social or economic advancement. In that period the town of Morganton was blest with three women who fall into the category of persons with a burning desire to teach: Misses Maria Cousins and Mary Dickson and Mrs. W. R. Marbut.

The last of this trio, Nora Kincaid Marbut, was born January 4, 1862, to John Bristol Kincaid and Adeline Mull Kincaid of Morganton. She attended private schools in Morganton and was graduated from Griffin Female College, Griffin, Georgia, in 1880.

In 1882, she married William Robert Marbut; and, in 1887, she returned to Morganton where she began her teaching career. She taught in the public schools a few years, then organized a private school, operating it until about 1912 when the public schools of the town became better organized. She then returned to the Morganton Graded School and there she remained until her retirement.

In her private school, Mrs. Marbut taught first grade onward through college preparation courses, using an assistant for the younger children. She was so completely consecrated to her work and so thorough with it that her pupils later stood well in their college classes. The late Dr. Forney of Greensboro Womans College once said that pupils from Mrs. Marbut's private school of Morganton were unusually well equipped in English for their secretarial courses.

Mrs. Marbut's life was completely absorbed in her work and she was very conscientious. She was one of the early teachers to realize the importance of Art, Literature, and Nature in the curriculum, and she aroused her pupils' interest in each of these subjects. She even spent time with her pupils on field trips.

Always an eager student with an active interest in national and international affairs, Mrs. Marbut did not hesitate to form and express her own opinions. She had a sense of responsibility for the underprivileged, and was charitable and kind to the unfortunate. With a rigid concept of duty and a deep and abiding interest in each pupil, she strove for the building of character without which she believed no one could achieve lasting happiness and usefulness in life.

Mrs. Marbut died October 19, 1938.

GERTRUDE WHITTIER MENDENHALL
1861-1926

FROM the first day of its opening in 1892, for thirty-four years, the spirit and personality of Gertrude Whittier Mendenhall wove themselves into the warp and woof of the fabric of the North Carolina State Normal and Industrial School, as year by year it developed from Normal School to College for Women. Her ideals, her standards, her integrity played upon the thinking and action of students and faculty alike. She was so highly respected and honored for her character and scholarship that President Charles Duncan McIver is reported to have declared that he would keep Miss Mendenhall on his faculty even if she could not teach at all.

The "gentle Quaker," Gertrude Whittier Mendenhall, born April 9, 1861 at Guilford College, North Carolina, was descended from a long line of intelligent, educated Friends. Having completed the course at New Garden Boarding School (now Guilford College), she entered Wellesley in 1881, where she received the B. S. degree in 1885.

She first became a member of the faculty of Peace Institute, Raleigh; but when in 1888 New Garden Boarding School became Guilford College, true to her Quaker traditions, she returned to become a charter member of the faculty of this newly reorganized institution. While at Peace Institute Miss Mendenhall had been so impressed by the spirit of Charles Duncan McIver that, when in 1892 he invited her to become a charter member of his faculty and head of the Department of Mathematics at the State Normal and Industrial School then opening in Greensboro, with a sense of real adventure, she accepted.

Miss Mendenhall, a teacher of high native intelligence, the most thorough scholarship, and the greatest respect for her subject, manifested infinite patience and understanding when dealing with students. It must have tried her patience to attempt to teach Mathematics to the students from the North Carolina schools of the day, whose background, in the majority of cases, was meager, indeed.

A student of the early years says: "In the fall of 1895 I entered her class; and then began for me four years of happy misery; for I loved her and I did not love mathematics, neither could I understand it; but there was never a time when she did not understand me, and make it possible for my poor mathematical brain to achieve the impossible."

It was true that Miss Mendenhall inspired students to attempt "the impossible." One student relates: "And I did work for her! Everybody did, for you knew you'd die if that summons came, 'Lina, take the next theorem', and you couldn't do it. You would never be able to look her in the eyes again."

Miss Mendenhall was above all things just and rigidly fair but also firm, with the ability to condemn, even severely, when necessary. She was quite canny in her estimates of her students. They reported: "She always knew when you had tried and couldn't from the time you couldn't because you hadn't tried; and how completely by word or even look could she rebuke the careless and reward the diligent, and with what kind and often unappreciated firmness would guide the blind who were trying to see."

Her subject was to Miss Mendenhall a personal thing. To her mind, it taught truth and necessitated straight thinking. Certainly in her own life she demonstrated the high qualities which she claimed for the study of Mathematics.

It was common for those who knew Miss Mendenhall to speak of her "conscience," and respect it, too. When grading time came Miss Mendenhall really wrestled with her conscionce. But "truth was truth" and some had to receive low grades and even fail!

As a person Miss Mendenhall was gentle, shy, lovable, with a hunger for being loved. She possessed a quaint, quiet, delightfully dry humor. Her sudden smile, illuminating her usually calm countenance, was the essence of sweetness. Said a friend: "Such capacity for friendship she had! How companionable she was! With her advent there always came a warm, friendly atmosphere. Her multitudinous acts of kindness were not prompted by a cold sense of duty, but were the spontaneous and natural expression of her loving heart. Love was what her soul sought from you."

Miss Mendenhall daily lived on a plane that few of us comprehend as possible, but she was always approachable. A sense of superiority was unknown to her, because she possessed the wholesome virtues of sound common sense and a keen sense of humor.

Her students were her friends. She remembered all holidays for those who sat at her table in the dining hall. At Christmas she presented each with dainty neckware. At Easter, after she moved to the "Little Green Cottage," on Spring Garden Street, she gave her girls an egg hunt on the lawn. It was a treat to be invited to supper. At parting in the spring she gave forget-me-nots from her garden, many of which were taken home, planted, and cherished for years.

A former student describes her personal appearance thus: "We looked upon her with respect, mingled with awe, as she sat erect on the platform through chapel exercises, and gazed out at us over the rims of her glasses, which always slid a little way down on her nose, thus giving her a more severe aspect than she was entitled to. Of course, she wore, nine times out of ten, the white shirtwaist, stiff collar, white or brown tie, and brown skirt that somehow seemed a vertiable part of our everyday Miss Mendenhall." However, while her appearance was demure and neat, her clothes were made of excellent material.

From the beginning to the end of her career, Miss Mendenhall was an influential and highly respected member of the faculty. No important committee was ever complete without her. She was not only a charter member of the faculty but she was also a charter member of the faculty council and of the smaller, more select body, the faculty cabinet. Among the faculty she was known as a thorough scholar, with sane judgment, sound common sense, honesty, and breadth of view in facing issues. She was the epitome of faithfulness and fairness in carrying out any piece of faculty business.

Miss Mendenhall was truly a follower of the Christ. Her religion was a part of her everyday living. In a message to the Alumnae on Founder's Day, October, 1925, a year before her death, she wrote: "Is there not danger in this age of much materialism that we shall think too little of things of the spirit and our growth in grace and in knowledge of the truth?"

Miss Mendenhall was a life-long member of the Society of Friends and gave much time and devotion to work of the Yearly Meeting and to the development of Guilford College. She was an active member of the Advisory Committee of the college from 1906 to her death, and she was for many years secretary of the Yearly Meeting.

Walter W. Haviland of the Friends Select School of Philadelphia paid a beautiful tribute to Miss Mendenhall in behalf of that wider circle of friends, those beyond the immediate vicinity in which she had lived and moved: "What was said of Edwin Dowde that 'he never failed in all his life to help any other man, within his conscience,' was true in the highest sense of her."

On April 15, 1926, Miss Mendenhall died and was interred in the family plot in the quiet country burying ground of old Deep River Church, near Greensboro.

Appropriately in her will she had made provision for a scholarship at the Woman's College to be awarded to the Sophomore member of the student body showing the most promise in the field of Mathematics and who desires to pursue higher work in Mathematics or allied sciences.

In 1950, the College honored the memory of Miss Mendenhall by naming a newly completed dormitory Mendenhall Hall.

Two tributes, one from a former colleague and one from a friend and former student express the love and esteem in which Miss Mendenhall was held.

Said Dr. J. Y. Joyner, former dean of the faculty:

"One of the choicest spirits, most lovable characters, sweetest influences in that first little faculty of men and women was Gertrude Whittier Mendenhall. She was a wise counselor in perplexing crises; she was a peace-maker in hot and honest disagreement and discussions; she was a comforter in times of sorrow and discouragement; she was an inspiration in the quiet courage of her convictions, devotion to duty, to high ideals. She had no sympathy with show and sham and shirking. . . . It was not what she said but what she was, and she moved so quietly among students and faculty, that left all the stronger and nobler that touched the hem of her spiritual robe.

An alumna who knew her longest and best paid her this tribute:

"For what am I most grateful to Miss Mendenhall? For not disappointing me. As a child I thought she was a rare, noble woman—as a woman, knowing more of human nature and life's pressures upon it, I *know* that is lives like hers that give dignity to human existence."

DORA MILLER
1857-1943

MISS ANNA MEDORA MILLER died August 17, 1943, in Kinston, North Carolina, at the age of eighty-six. But "Miss Dora's" influence lives on in many lives. Numerous Kinstonians testify admiringly and affectionately to this teacher's firmness, thoroughness, and patience.

Miss Miller's first teaching experience was in a public school in Jones County, but she soon set up her own school in the home of her brother, George Edgar Miller, in Kinston. Later she held her classes in a small building just back of St. Mary's Episcopal Church of which she was a devoted member.

For thirty years she taught children from the first grade through the seventh. Her enrollment was limited to twenty pupils as thoroughness was her motto. If one week were required to master one page, a week was devoted to that page. One of her pupils recalls the daily pronunciation class and the spelling matches based on Webster's Blue Back Speller.

When Miss Miller's teaching days ended in 1903, she became custodian of the little nucleus of books that formed Kinston's "public library." Serving for small pay, she kept alive through the years a spark of interest among the citizens in a city-owned library. Discouragements must have been overwhelming at times. Not only was her salary meager, but appropriations were negligible and public interest was slight. Twice during her period of service in the library the quarters were moved. Her labor and faith, however, were justified for she lived to see a modern library established with a trained librarian in charge.

Miss Miller's own training was through private tutors and Kinston College—long defunct—of which Dr. Richard Lewis was head. She read extensively; and she retained interest in civic and world affairs to the end of her life. Perhaps the secret of her influence may be best summarized in her own words which she expressed so frequently: "I love to live."

130

THE MINORS
JULIA BRENT ALLEN MINOR
1850-1919

"PIONEER worker for public education in Granville County--" what better words could tell the story of a mother of nine children who taught forty-one years in the public schools of her native county and gave to the State six daughters each of whom achieved outstanding success in their chosen fields of teaching in both public schools and colleges in several states. These daughters are: Hettie Minor Hicks, Music and Kindergarten Education; Eva Minor, Music (deceased); Daisy Elizabeth Minor Skinner, Art; Julia Brent Minor Moore, Foreign Languages; Lillian Patrick Minor, Elementary Education; and Alleine Richard Minor, Music. Also, for exceptionally meritorious and distinguished service in the Ypres Sommes combat area in World War I, Colonel Sidney Minor won the Distinguished Service Medal of his country.

Julia Brent Allen Minor, daughter of William A. Allen and Emeline Henry Allen, was born near old Corinth Church in Granville County on April 24, 1850, and died at her home in Oxford January 19, 1919. When Julia was a small child her father died after which her mother moved to Oxford in order that her children might receive the best educational advantages of that time. At the age of sixteen, in February, 1866, Julia Brent Allen was graduated with honors from old St. John's College (later Oxford College) receiving a diploma in "academic learning and music." This was during the presidency of Dr. J. H. Mills. One year later she began her work as a teacher in a small rural school near Oxford in Granville County.

On September 20, 1870, Julia Brent Allen was married to the young Confederate Captain, Richard Van Buren Minor, whose death on March 8, 1892, left Mrs. Minor with the sole responsibility of rearing and educating her nine children, an undertaking magnificently accomplished as is attested to by the record of her children's successes. In fact, each child secured a college education.

After Mrs. Minor's marriage, she continued teaching in the private school at Minor's Mill, then later entered the Oxford public school system where she remained for the rest of her teaching career until illness made it necessary for her to retire.

When she began teaching in Oxford, there was no satisfactory building in which to house the children enrolled in the public school, so at her own expense she equipped a room in her own home and taught there for many years. Her pupils spent long hours practicing their Friday afternoon exercises or commencement speeches under the oak trees in her yard where they could have room to "exercise their lungs." They were required to speak plainly enough for her to hear them from where she sat on the porch to "direct" their "gestures."

Not only did she teach the three "R's," but she knew the intimate home life of each of her pupils wherever she taught. Night after night the midnight oil burned as she sewed a garment for a destitute new baby or child in her school community. Never a Christmas passed without a blazing Christmas tree at the school. The tree was decorated with gifts for all the community and was made possible by the generosity of the town of Oxford. The gifts were wrappd and distributed by personal friends and neighbors.

Though a shy and retiring personality, Mrs. Minor never failed to respond to a call for service to education. When the bond issue to establish the graded school in Oxford was to be voted on, she, aided by her oldest son and daughter, materially influenced the passage of the issue by her eloquent campaign prior to the election.

Her services were sought by educational leaders in many distant places in the State but Mrs. Minor preferred to remain in her native county and town to serve her own community and keep "Minorwood" as a home for her family. Her services have been beautifully described by a former pupil who wrote after Mrs. Minor's death:

"In her going I am made to realize the passing of one whose good influences upon my life have extended almost from infancy. She served her day and generation well, and in her passing her community, her county, and her State are much poorer. I doubt not that if the long roll of those who came under her influence as a teacher could be called and each should answer as to the early influences that were most helpful and formative in his life, he would include after the name of his own parents the name of Mrs. Minor."

The following lines seem a fitting close to this sketch:
The teacher lives forever.
On and on he shall go, singing.
Singing still the songs he taught to the world's youth
'Till lapping waters shall bear them o'er and o'er
And argosy and crew ride safe to port."

EVA MINOR
1875-1945

EVA MINOR, daughter of Julia Brent Allen Minor and Richard Van Buren Minor, was born at Minorwood (the old Minor home) at Oxford, North Carolina, November 28, 1875, and died December 17, 1945, following a severe paralytic stroke. Her ability as a teacher and composer of music, as a rare singer, as one who inspired youth from early childhood to maturity to know and appreciate music, made her a success in life remembered and "loved most by those who knew her best." She had an intellectual and social heritage which made her an inspiration to her students by "precept as well as by example." No person gave more freely of his time and effort to help those who came to her than did Eva Minor.

Miss Minor's early education was received in the public and private schools of Oxford during which time her teachers made possible the development of her musical talent. This talent had manifested itself at the early age of three years when she could play many simple melodies on the piano with "both hands." Among her teachers whom she always referred to as "My inspirations" were Miss Annie Hamme of Oxford, at that time recognized as an outstanding musician in North Carolina and a Miss Marvin of the faculty of the old Oxford College. Miss Minor was graduated in Music by Greensboro Female College, now Greensboro College, and pursued her studies further in Philadelphia and in New York. She also attended Columbia University, Cornell's School of Music, Chautauqua, New York, and Long Island.

In her early years she taught in both public and private schools in Oxford, making a significant contribution to the Oxford Orphanage when she developed the well-known "Singing Class." Many times she said that her work at the State School for the Deaf and Blind children in Raleigh was the most challenging and satisfying work that she had ever accomplished. In 1905, Miss Minor was elected Head of the Music Department of the State Teachers College, Farmville, Virginia, which position she held for eight years.

Working with future teachers was for her a happy experience, but she preferred to work with growing boys and girls so she returned to her native State as Supervisor of Music in the Durham City schools for a long period of time. "Undoubtedly," said one who worked with her during her supervisory service, "she laid the foundation for the sound program of public school music from the first grade throughout high school now effective in our city. She had an unusually difficult task in trying to direct the music program without assistance in both white and colored schools. She was instrumental in organizing high school orchestras and in having special training given members of the orchestra."

Her last years were spent in Lexington, North Carolina, as Director of Church Music and Recreation, as well as Director of her own private studio for Music Education. In this city she composed the "Dedication Theme to the Mothers of America," which made its first appearance in all the Lexington churches on Mothers Day, May, 1941. Here, too, the original music for the Education Pageant written by her sister was composed. The success of young children taught by her unique method of musical instruction and the simple, practical materials used in the work, won recognition to such an extent that these materials were being prepared for publication at the time of her death.

Like her mother, she was always ready to help teachers add new life to classroom situations. Consequently summer vacations were spent instructing teachers at Eastern State Teachers College and at State College in Raleigh and in working in county-wide teachers' meetings in Halifax, Davidson, and Bertie Counties in North Carolina.

When illness compelled Miss Minor to retire from work in Lexington, she returned to her native Oxford to spend what proved to be only a few months with members of her family. Her ruling passion was strong even in her last weeks, for just four days before the final summons came, she was helping a young nephew with some of the rudiments of music. Thus her active life ended as she would have had it end: imparting to a child something that had made her own presence such a benefit to the music world of childhood.

MARGARET ELIOT MITCHELL
1835-1905

ELIZA NORTH MITCHELL GRANT
1833-1883

THE two Mitchell sisters for whom Mitchell College received its present name were the daughters of the Connecticut-born Dr. Elisha Mitchell who in 1857 lost his life while exploring the peak that now bears his name. Their mother, Maria North Mitchell, was also of New England birth.

Since Chapel Hill, the home town of the Mitchell family, afforded so little opportunity for the education of women at that period, both girls were sent to New England for their education.

When quite young, Margaret volunteered for foreign mission service, but because of her health she was not accepted. Then, some time in the 1850's she began teaching in a private school in Chapel Hill. A few years later she was joined by her sister Eliza who in 1853 had married Richard S. Grant of Norfolk, Virginia. Soon after their marriage the young couple went to Texas to live. Some five or six years after this, Mr. Grant was fatally shot by a bandit. Eliza with her two children started back to Chapel Hill, and the younger of the two died on the way. Since it was financially necessary for her to work, she began teaching with her sister.

During the Reconstruction Period this private school in Chapel Hill was forced to close, and the Mitchell sisters went to Oxford, North Carolina, and took charge of the Oxford Female Academy.

Mrs. Lucy Fort of Oxford who was a student of the Academy when the Mitchell sisters were in charge recalled Eliza (Mrs. Grant)) as "a fine looking lady with black hair and Margaret as a lovable and somewhat comical looking pedagogue with long corkscrew curls bobbing on either side of her dainty cap whenever she laughed."

In 1874, Eliza Mitchell Grant accepted the presidency of what was then called Simonton Female College in Statesville. The next year Margaret and her mother moved to Statesville and Margaret became associated with Eliza in the work of the college. Here the two sisters worked cooperatively and successfully from 1875 until Mrs. Grant's death in 1883.

That the work of the Mitchell sisters was distinctive throughout the period in which they served is attested by the following excerpt from the history page of the Mitchell College catalog of 1950:

"After the Civil War, the college, failing as a financial enterprise, was bought by R. F. Simonton of Statesville and for the next 23 years was called Simonton Female College.

The college won its first substantial success from 1875 to 1883 under the guidance of Mrs. Eliza Mitchell Grant and her sister, Margaret Elliott Mitchell."

Margaret Mitchell, always near sighted, was in her last days afflicted with cataracts in both eyes. She retired from teaching in 1884 and devoted her time to her home in Statesville and to work in the Presbyterian church. She died in 1905 and was buried in Oakwood Cemetery beside her sister Eliza. The Presbyterian Board of Foreign Missions received a substantial bequest from her estate.

After the sisters had passed on, their name was honored by having the college named for them. Again to quote from the above mentioned catalog:

"In 1915, that is, in the sixty-first year of the life of the college, Concord Presbytery, urged by the alumnae and approved by the trustees, changed the name of the institution to Mitchell College. The name was given to honor Mrs. Eliza Mitchell Grant and Miss Margaret Elliott Mitchell, daughters of Dr. Elisha Mitchell, scientist, educator, and Christian gentleman."

HATTIE MOORE
1825-1910

Miss HATTIE MOORE was born on a rice plantation near Wilmington. Her father was Alexander Duncan Moore, a direct descendant of General James Moore, Revolutionary hero of Wilmington. Her mother was Harriet Osborne Moore, a sister of Judge James W. Osborne of Charlotte. Hattie was the oldest of fourteen children.

When the slaves were freed at the close of the War between the

States, the rice plantation had to be abandoned; and the Moore family moved to Mecklenburg County, living for a short time at "Rosedale," near Croft.

From "Rosedale," Miss Hattie went to Charlotte where she opened a private school in West Seventh Street on the site of the present St. Peters Parish House. Many citizens of Charlotte received their early schooling here. Among these were Miss Fannie B. Moore, Miss Mary Armand, and Miss Betty Nash, all of whom, later, had a part in teaching the youth of Charlotte. Miss Charlee Hutchinson, then in her teens, assisted Miss Moore as teacher.

A tribute once paid Miss Moore's teaching is as follows: When Mrs. J. H. McAden said to Dr. Alexander Graham, head of the Charlotte City Schools, that her daughter Ella would soon go from Miss Moore's private school to his school system, Dr. Graham replied: "Good! All the pupils we have gotten from her are good ones. They are especially fine readers."

Miss Hattie discontinued her school about 1888. According to rumor, she walked into the schoolroom one morning and said: "Children, go home. I can't stand you a minute longer."

After the closing of the school, she moved into the little gray cottage at 311 West Church Street, which was her home for the remainder of her life. Into that home she received five orphaned children of her brother, two girls and three boys, the eldest fifteen or sixteen years old and the youngest five or six years of age. This was their home until they were ready to go out into the world.

Here Miss Hattie built a little greenhouse in which she grew rare flowers and plants. She had a fine garden, also. At the age of seventy-five, she planted a maple tree in her front yard which is standing there at the present time. Some friends exclaimed, "Imagine planting a tree when you are seventy-five years old; you will never live to enjoy it!" To this, Miss Hattie replied: "But other people will."

Miss Hattie's church activities were very dear to her. At an early age, she organized the little girls of St. Peters Episcopal Church into a society called the "Busy Bees," and these children, by sewing and by making and selling candy, raised the money with which was purchased the lot on which St. Peters Hospital was built. It was in this hospital that Miss Hattie spent the last months of her long and useful life.

MRS. R. L. MOORE
1876-1950

FOR nearly fifty years Mrs. R. L. Moore was an outstanding person on the campus at Mars Hill College. Her extraordinary business management plus her willingness to sacrifice home life for the institution put the college on the road to financial security with a vital program for growth and expansion.

Born Edna Sophronia Corpening, she was the oldest of the nine children of Albert Gallatin Corpening of Burke County, North Carolina. The site of her early home is now covered by the waters of Lake James. This home was burned when Edna was quite young and the family moved to another of her father's farms in Caldwell County. Her father, a pioneer teacher as well as a landowner and farmer, met his wife Sarah Cannon while he was teaching at Riverbend near the present town of Gastonia.

Edna received her formal education at Amherst Academy, located between Lenoir and Morganton, under the Reverend R. L. Patton, a noted educator of that day. Her father employed a special music teacher for the home, also a teacher to instruct the girls in "fancy sewing." Reverend Patton was succeeded at Amherst by R. L. Moore under whom Edna continued her studies and at the same time assisted in teaching the lower grades.

On June 11, 1895, on her nineteenth birthday, she was married to her principal, R. L. Moore. Two years later Mr. Moore was called to lead the struggling school at Mars Hill. This institution was founded by the Baptist Church in 1856; but because of the War between the States and Reconstruction days followed by the poor economic condition of the 1880's the school was at a very low ebb when Mr. Moore assumed the leadership in 1897.

Mrs. Moore soon realized that the business cares of the indebted institution were too great for Mr. Moore to carry in addition to his other administrative duties and his academic work. Therefore, she volunteered her service and took over all financial responsibilities. In fact, the financial condition of the school was such as to necessitate Mr. and Mrs. Moore's sacrificing their own home life in order to maintain the girls' dormitory. Here Mrs. Moore served as dietitian, cook, housekeeper, nurse, and mother to the girls as well as hostess to the guests. Because of the meager equipment and supplies in the dormitory she graciously contributed the use of her wedding silver, china, glassware, and linens. It is said that during a blizzard, when snow was blowing into the poorly constructed dormitory, Mrs. Moore felt such concern for the students that she took the blankets from her own bed and gave them to the girls. She and Mr. Moore made themselves as comfortable as possible under the cover of coats and woolen clothing. During the summer months with the help of the girls she did considerable canning of fruits and vegetables for the winter supply of the dormitory.

In 1913, when the financial conditions of the college had improved, Mrs. Moore was relieved of the many duties she had assumed earlier, and she and Mr. Moore built a house and established their own home in Mars Hill. Yet she continued as bursar of the college until her health failed in 1946.

Mrs. Moore was not only a successful business executive but she was a consecrated leader in the church and community. She served as superintendent of the Junior Department in the Sunday School of the Mars Hill Baptist Church for twenty-five years; and for thirty-five years she was superintendent of the Womans Missionary Union of the French Broad Association.

In addition to her activities in school, church, and community, Mrs. Moore reared two children, E. C. Moore of Asheville and Mrs. Oren E. Roberts of Mars Hill.

Mrs. Moore suffered a severe heart attack on October 19, 1949, from which she never recovered. Her husband passed away on December 16, 1949, and Mrs. Moore's death occurred on February 14, 1950.

EUNICE STACY MACKAY
1884-1947

FOR forty-three years Eunice Stacy MacKay taught in the schools of North Carolina and other states of the South; and the last seventeen of these years she taught in Smithfield, North Carolina. A. G. Glenn, Principal of the Smithfield School, upon receiving the announcement of her death on February 12, 1947, said of her: "By precept and example she sought to inculcate high ideals in the young people under her charge; her influence will endure in the lives of those whom she taught and our community and state are richer because of her life and work." Entering the teaching profession during the first decade of the twentieth century, Miss MacKay early became imbued with the spirit of the educational revival in the state of North Carolina led by Governor Aycock, Dr. Alderman, Dr. McIver, and others.

Born in Harnett County on June 7, 1884, Eunice MacKay attended the public schools of that county. For three years she was a student at Flora Macdonald College. Realizing the importance of in-service training, she enrolled as a senior at the University of North Carolina in the fall of 1928. She received the A. B. degree in 1929; and during subsequent summers she continued her studies, receiving the degree of Master of Arts in June, 1931.

Miss MacKay began her first teaching at Averysboro in her home county. Later she taught in South Carolina; in Buford, Georgia; and in Beechwood, Kentucky. Returning to North Carolina, she taught four years in the Manteo High School. From there she moved to Lincolnton where she served ten years as teacher of History and director of Dramatics in the high school. Out of her experiences with play-production in the Lincolnton school came the article, "Dramatics in the High School," published in *North Carolina Education* in May, 1925.

After her graduation from the University of North Carolina, Miss MacKay began her work as teacher of History in the Smithfield High School. Here she continued this work for seventeen years until a month before her death.

Having the conviction that knowledge was her needed instrument, she proceeded to lay the foundation for her professional work through sound scholarship and diligent study early in life. Her respect for the basic dignity of man, her high regard for the accumulated wisdom of the ages, and her emphasis upon spiritual values were foundation stones in the structure of her professional life.

In her classroom there was ever an atmosphere of creative development, of warm comradeship. To lead her students to acquire new facts and ideas, to develop increased skills, to show evidence of critical thinking—these were goals toward which Miss MacKay worked with high courage and unflagging zeal.

One of the finest tributes to her life has come from one of her former students, Mr. L. R. Jordan, student at Amherst College, Massachusetts, to the Editor of *The Smithfield* (North Carolina) *Herald* on February 21, 1947. It is as follows:

"The news of the death of Miss Eunice MacKay was received today with much sorrow; for in the passing of this beloved educator I have suffered a personal loss, as have my family and community.

Remembrances of instruction in the Smithfield Public Schools and of Miss MacKay are inseparable; for she played one of the major roles in this drama of memories.

What success I have achieved thus far in College belongs in large part to the thoroughness and devotion with which this great lady pursued her profession. Mourning can never pay even partial tribute to such a citizen! Only hard work toward the improvement of our public school system can ever show our appreciation and love for the untiring efforts, sacrificial devotion, and inspiring love of one who recognized her duty, set to work, never compromised her ideals and achieved success."

But hers was not a personal success, but a success reflecting in the lives of the hundreds of Johnston County boys and girls who were fortunate enough to enjoy the generous light of her wisdom.

EUNICE McDOWELL
1859-1946

THE name of Eunice McDowell is closely linked with Chowan College. Her father, the Reverend Archibald McDowell, was head of the college when Eunice was born. Here she took her undergraduate work, then later studied at Columbia University.

Miss McDowell began teaching at Vine Hill Academy in Scotland Neck, North Carolina, in 1882. Here she served as principal until at which time she accepted the position of principal of the Female Seminary at Franklin, Virginia. She continued this work for eight years.

Her following record shows that she was on on the faculties of Greensboro College of Women; Meredith College; Bessie Tift College, Forsythe, Georgia; and Averette College, Danville, Virginia.

After these forty years of teaching, Miss McDowell returned in 1920 to Chowan College where she taught Bible and Latin. Then, in 1925, she was made dean of women of that institution.

Her activity as a teacher ended in 1937 as the result of a serious illness. However, her interest remained with her Alma Mater until June 29, 1946, when death claimed her.

JANE S. McKIMMON
1867-

PIONEER work of all kinds requires strength of character, and quite often little praise results from it. This was the case in the early stages of Home Demonstration work among the farm women in North Carolina, and yet recognition and honor lie at the feet of Jane S. Mc-Kimmon, who is generally recognized throughout the State as the guiding genius of the work. Through her work and through the efforts of many staunch souls who were not easily discouraged, the women and girls all over rural North Carolina are coming into their own and have been taught to make their lives fuller, more comfortable, and more efficient through an improved standard of the country home; and, since North Carolina is a rural state with no large cities, this means that all homes have been improved. Mrs. McKimmon, pioneer leader in Home Demonstration work, can aptly be described by two lines from Milton: "Grace is in all her steps, heaven in her eyes . . . in every gesture, dignity and love."

Mrs. McKimmon, of direct Scotch descent, was the daughter of William Simpson who was born in New York soon after his parents arrived from Scotland. The Simpson family later settled in Virginia and it was here that William Simpson was married to Anne Cannon, also a native of Glascow. Immediately after their marriage, Mr. and Mrs. Simpson moved to Raleigh where Mrs. McKimmon was born—Jane Simpson.

It was at Peace Institute, Raleigh, she was educated. She later married Charles McKimmon. She has found time to rear to maturity four children amid all her busy outside life.

In 1927 and 1929, Mrs. McKimmon earned B. S. and M. S. degrees from North Carolina State College in Raleigh. In 1933, because of her outstanding leadership in a great educational organization for farm women, the University of North Carolina conferred upon her an honorary degree of Doctor of Laws (LL. D.).

Home Demonstration work began in 1911, when Mrs. McKimmon was appointed State Home Demonstration Agent. She was active in the work of the organization until February, 1937, when she retired from administrative duties to write a book on the history of Home Demonstration work. The book, entitled *When We're Green We Grow*, symbolizes the driving force back of a successful career. Here it is evident that Mrs. McKimmon, leader and teacher, loved to work with people.

She has lived to see the dreams for her organization of Home Demonstration work grow from fourteen counties when organized in 1911-12 to an organization of one hundred counties today. In *When We're Green We Grow*, she says: "It has been a ready and receptive people with whom I have worked, a people who were green and ready to grow; and I have seen the sap rise, the leaves put forth, and a multitude of blossoms bring forth fruit in its season."

Hers has been a long life of service for an organization and work that she so deeply believed in and loved with heart and soul. Experience showed her:

"There was something in the people with whom we worked, out there in the country, that let us know that spirit was stronger than any obstacle which could be placed in our paths.

Someone has called home demonstration work The Country Woman's College. I think it is a good name for our organization. It is through the wide variety of home economics subjects taught by trained home economists that the best in farm family living is brought into our farm homes."

Homemakers must get their education from where they are with what they have. "To teach adults," says Dr. McKimmon, "you must present ideas that matter to them."

Home demonstration agents are guided by the same general principles as college and high school teachers. Dr. McKimmon was very pleased when her staff of state and field workers were classified as members of the State College faculty.

141

All through her years as State Home Demonstration Agent, she was given the privilege by the Dean of Agriculture and Director of Extension at North Carolina State College of working on an equal footing with the men in the extension organization. This, she says, was the only basis for any real success.

Jane Simpson McKimmon has been a living symbol of courage and faith, always radiating light and learning among all the people with whom she worked. She did not work because of her love for Home Economics, but because of her love of people. North Carolina farm families return that love.

HELEN GRAHAM McMASTER
1859-1930

THE teaching career of Helen McMaster began at Columbia College, South Carolina, but most of her work was connected with the early days of Mars Hill College in North Carolina. Miss McMaster was one of fourteen children of Colonel Fitz William McMaster and Mary Jane MacFie McMaster of Columbia, South Carolina.

No record of her life would be complete without an account of her father's interest in the cause of education.

At the age of fourteen, Fitz William McMaster entered South Carolina College at Columbia and upon graduation he served as secretary to the president and librarian of the college for eight years. In the meantime he married Mary Jane MacFie of Columbia. Later he joined the Confederate Army and rose to the rank of colonel. At the close of the war, he became a lawyer of note. He was very civic minded and, being aware of the South's need of public schools, he felt that here was the hope of these surviving states. Therefore, through Colonel McMaster's tireless labor in overcoming prejudices and opposition, the city schools of Columbia, South Carolina, were planned and the foundation laid for a Winthrop Training School for Teachers. This training school later became Winthrop College at Rock Hill, South Carolina.

With such a background, it is not surprising that Helen McMaster became a great teacher and advocated education for all and the training of teachers. Her sister has said: "Helen literally set at father's feet in her thirst for education." Also, in her classes—her education was largely in private schools—she was very studious and a lover of literature.

After teaching at Columbia College for several years, Miss McMaster's health failed and she went to Asheville, North Carolina, on the advice of her physician. Here she lived in the home of Captain Melvin Carter, a relative, and was governess to his children.

Then, one day in 1889, Mr. John Robert Sams of Mars Hill came to the Carter home. He was in search of someone to teach in his community during that summer. He offered Miss McMaster the position which she accepted. Thus she began teaching in an old school house which stood at what is now Mars Hill College. The college had been founded in the year 1857 but after the war the struggle was too great for the sessions to continue and the work was suspended for a period. It was during this time that Miss McMaster conducted her private school. In her own words she had "a room filled with bright-faced boys and girls." Meantime she was realizing that there were splendid opportunities for a school at Mars Hill.

With the beginning of the fall term, Mr. Zeb Hunter and Helen McMaster were in charge; and soon after, at her suggestion, a school board was established. The school continued to grow in size and in interest. From 1890 to 1893, it was conducted by Mr. Thomas Hufham and Miss McMaster. Then Dr. John E. White joined them in the last year of her stay at Mars Hill. At this time 100 pupils were enrolled.

Miss McMaster is responsible for putting the school on a college basis. Through her, an interest in higher education was received.

After her years of service at Mars Hill, this educational leader returned to Columbia, South Carolina, and taught for several years in a private school. Yet she went back to Mars Hill many times. Here she rejoiced over the progress of the college and found pleasure in meeting her former students in whom she continued her great interest. At such reunions there would be nostalgic accounts of plays dramatized, the reading of Shakespeare, and exercises in calisthenics. One former pupil recalled "how she had enjoyed Miss Helen's reading poetry and how every child was given drawing lessons and how every day there was a Bible lesson for all." She was told by certain ones that had it not been for her they would never have continued their studies. Some of these had eventually graduated from the University of North Carolina, Carolina State College, and Harvard University.

From the many tributes paid Miss McMaster are the two following ones: Miss Mary Carter once spoke beautifully of "Cousin Helen's charm, her sweetness, and her brilliant mind"; and Mrs. Virginia McMaster Foard says: "Helen McMaster was a brilliant teacher and a great woman in her love and unselfishness . . . She was a courageous person. She was tall and handsome with a pleasing personality."

Helen McMaster had devoted friends in every class of society. She made everyone feel at ease in her presence. Her passion for teaching extended throughout her household as she did not have a servant whom she did not teach to read the Bible. When she lay on her bier in 1930, her negro cook of seven years summed up the characteristic relationship that had existed between mistress and servant by saying: "Sweet lady, I hope I shall see you again."

Miss McMaster's ideas were ahead of her time. Therefore, she was a pioneer and a pioneer is a pathfinder, one who goes before to remove obstacles and prepares the way for others. With this interpretation of a pioneer we can easily classify Helen Graham McMaster as a pioneer in the field of education.

MARY HINTON CARRAWAY PARKER

1842-1930

HIGH on the list of notable pioneer teachers in North Carolina stands the name of Mary Hinton Carraway or, as she was generally called, "Miss Mollie."

Her life covered nineteen years before the War Between the States and stretched almost a third of a century into the 1900's.

Her early years were normal and uneventful, conditioned by the surroundings in which she lived. She was born to William Pope Carraway and his wife Temperance Ranselear Middleton Carraway on June 24, 1842, and was named for her maternal grandmother. She grew up at her father's home, Veinnicci, which was about four miles from Goldsboro, North Carolina. It was a typical Southern plantation, with many slaves. On a beautiful saddle horse given her by her father she would frequently accompany him on his daily rounds.

Two and a half miles away was the small village of Everettesville, where she attended her first school, completing her studies at the early age of fourteen.

She was next sent to Wayne Female College, in Goldsboro, partly because her father was one of the prominent stockholders. Here, as elsewhere, she proved to be an outstanding student, completing her college course at the age of fifteen. Her diploma, signed by President T. M. Frost, was dated May 27, 1858. Subjects in which this document credited her with proficiency were classic and English literature and "those branches of science usually taught in the female colleges of the United States." Her classical training included both Greek and Latin, and to these were added French and music.

Not satisfied with her preparation, she went back for a year of post-graduate work, at the same time doing some teaching in the college. Her studies during this period included music and law. It has been said that she was one of the first women in North Carolina to study law. At commencement in 1859 Dr. Charles Deems, in behalf of the College, presented her with a gold medal for the fine quality of her work. This souvenir, still treasured by her granddaughter, bears the inscription "Mary Hinton Carraway, M.A.," a Greek motto, and the date 1857. Her graduation address, written in a meticulous hand, and composed in Latin, has also been preserved. News items published that year attest to her ability and to the respect and affection she won by her teaching.

At the age of eighteen she went back to Everettesville, to teach in the school she had attended as a child. Here, however, she noted many changes. The planters of the neighborhood had banded together to improve the academy; and her father had given it a tract of twenty-five acres, adding permission to the school authorities to cut firewood from his adjacent property. A church and many lovely homes had been built in the village. Names of some of the prominent families of Everettesville included Collier, Cobb, Moore, Everett, Lane, Whitfield, Hines, Daniel, Hooks, and McKinney. She taught there for a few years and was dearly loved by her pupils. Many of them were a great deal older than she.

That her musical ability was unusual was proved by an incident which occurred during the war. A negro musician, called Blind Tom, gave a concert in Goldsboro which she attended. He had a stunt which he had figured out. He played one tune with his right hand, another with his left, and sang the third tune. It was a tricky combination. After completing his concert he would invite any one in the audience who would like to do so, to try it. When he gave the invitation, Miss Mollie got up and he showed her how it was done. It took only a few minutes to master the technique—one which stayed with her for the next half-century and which she demonstrated at an Old Folks' Party given by her church in Greensboro fifty-six years later.

At one time Miss Mollie kept a diary. The dates covered by this record are the fall of 1860 and the spring of 1861. It mentions the declaration of war and the departure of the local troops. During the war she did much work in Goldsboro, making bandages, sewing for the Conferedate soldiers, and anything else she could.

Still another interest, one which led the mind to the utmost bounds of the earth, was the collecting and pressing of botanical speciments (foliage and flowers), from numerous parts of the world. Under each specimen was the name of the place from which it had come, who secured it for her, and any other pertinent information. Items ranged from Siberia to Australia, Gettysburg to Lucknow. There was even one leaf secured in Africa by the Stanley expedition that went to find Livingston.

Proof that she was skilled with the needle is seen in some of her handiwork now owned by her grand-daughter. There is lace as fine as a spider-web, a filmy handkerchief, minutely intricate embroidery, and the daintiest of baby clothes. In making a baby dress which she completed on her fifty-eighth birthday (for her grand-daughter), she used a Number 12 needle and Number 200 thread.

145

Another aspect of her personality was her capacity for friendship. One of the best friends she ever had was Dr. C. F. Deems, her pastor. He had come South to represent the American Bible Society for the state of North Carolina, was later made third president of Greensboro College (1850-54). He also served as the pastor of the Methodist church attended by the Carraway family. His letters to her are gems. Miss Mollie became engaged to his son, Lt. Theodore Deems; but the young man met his death on the battlefield of Gettysburg. His daughter Minnie visited her often; and in July 1868 she made a visit to the Deems family in New York, seeing many places of interest, including West Point. She stayed until time to return for the opening of her school in the fall.

There is an interesting anecdote about this pastor and the Carraway family Bible. When Dr. Deems baptized the baby, Charles Deems Carraway, he had written the name in the family Bible. During the war one of the Northern armies camped on the Carraway plantation right near the house, and a soldier had gone off with that Bible with the family records in it. Dr. Deems had earlier moved to New York and established the Church of the Strangers. One day his assistant came back from paying some pastoral calls and asked him if he knew of a family in North Carolina who were named Carraway. He replied, "Yes indeed, they are my best friends down there. Why do you ask?"

The assistant said that while paying some calls he had noticed in an old family Bible the name of Charles Deems Carraway and wondered about it. Dr. Deems said, "Yes, he was named for me." He went to see the woman who had it and she sold him that the Bible was a war relic and she would not give it up unless someone from the Carraway family came for it. So Dr. Deems got in touch with the Carraways, who sent a member to New York and regained their Bible.

Besides the theft of the Bible, the war brought many hardships. As the Yankees camped near by, the family lost food, supplies, and personal property. The fields were not worked. Then in July after the surrender in 1865 Miss Mollie's father died, and from that time on she and her mother had the responsibility of the family and the plantation. She had many brothers and sisters. Her sisters died early; and at the time of her father's death the ages of her broters living were nine, thirteen, and seventeen. Only two lived to manhood.

Miss Mollie was married on June 18,1873, at the age of thirty-one, to Captain Joseph A. Parker, a widower with four daughters. He was from Nansemond County, Virginia. To them were born three boys and one girl. The boys were William Carraway Parker, James Alfred Parker, and Thomas Wesley Parker. The one girl was Temperance Rebecca Parker, later Mrs. Alvis Lea Harris.

Soon after their marriage they went to Laurinburg, N. C., to

146

live. Here the school facilities were very poor, so she started her own private school. It grew until it required two or three assistants. In 1885 she attended the first normal school for teachers, which was held in Wilson. She never ceased to be a learner. She was a born teacher and gave her pupils inspiration to live a higher life. She enjoyed coaching the school plays and church programs, such as bazaars, Easter concerts, and Christmas plays. This was her most important period as a teacher, a mother, and a community leader. Here she taught for twenty-eight years.

Her later life was spent in Reidsville and Greensboro. In 1901, when she was sixty, she went to Reidsville to live with her daughter. They later moved to Greensboro, where she frequently encountered former students who greeted her with exprssions of apprciation and affection.

To the very last of her long span of life her mind was active and inquiring. She studied the dictionary each day for new words and meanings, never content with what she knew. She could truly say, with Tennyson,

"...all experience is an arch wherethro'
Gleams that untravell'd world, whose margin fades
Forever and forever when I move."

Her children, grandchildren, and one great-grandchild were very close to her.

She died on March 8, 1930, at the home of her daughter in Greensboro and was buried in Laurinburg, N. C. She was survived by nine grandsons and -daughters and one great-grandchild.

Her pupils do not forget her, nor the inspiration she gave. Her descendants honor her memory. And North Carolina owes her the esteem due to those who give their day and time more than the age asks of them—a plus quality of personal enrichment.

BROOKS STRAYHORN PARKER
1897-1930

MRS. Brooks Strayhorn Parker was one of the educational leaders in Durham County during the years when the consolidation of rural schools was taking place. She spent most of her life in this county. Here she was educated; here she taught in several of the county schools; and here she engaged in church and community activities.

She was born in 1897, the daughter of Jeppie Cole Strayhorn and Eugene Strayhorn. Her father died when she was six years old. Her mother married again, but she died when Brooks was twelve years

147

old. Her stepfather saw that she had a high school education. As she lived with relatives during these early years, adjustment to the different households was necessary. She developed into a woman of strong character with a perseverance that enabled her to carry out any project that she undertook. Also, she had a keen sense of humor that helped her straighten out difficult situations.

Brooks graduated from the Durham High School in 1914, studied that summer at Trinity College Summer School, then began teaching in the fall. Her first school was in Orange County, but she soon moved into Durham County where she lived with her uncle and aunt, Mr. and Mrs. W. L. Cole. While living here, she continued teaching during the school terms and attended summer schools at Duke University. She received her degree from Duke in 1930. She taught in the following schools in Durham County: Bethesda, East Durham, Bragtown, West Durham, Southview, and Glenn. She was principal of the Glenn School for three years. In 1930, she was elected principal of Hillandale School.

In 1921, Miss Strayhorn was married to M. E. Parker, a dairyman of Durham County. During the nine years of her married life, she not only continued to teach and to go to college, but she also assisted her husband in paying off a large indebtedness on the dairy by helping him in the actual work of the dairy.

Mrs. Parker was vitally interested in the consolidation of schools which was taking place at that period. She used her influence in the consolidation of the Bragtown and Hillandale schools and was responsible for the location of the latter school. She was leader of the first May Day program to be held in Durham County.

Until she moved to Durham, she was a member of the Christian Church. Here she joined the Bethany Methodist Church in which she took an active interest.

Mrs. Parker met her death in an automobile accident in September, 1950, just a few weeks after she had completed her work at Duke for an A.B. degree, and at the time she was making plans for the principalship of Hillandale School, to which position she had been elected in the summer of that same year.

The Glenn School, Durham County, erected and dedicated a memoral to her, at which time fitting memorial exercises were held.

SOPHIA ARMS PARTRIDGE
1817-1881

ONE of the early boarding schools for girls, for which Raleigh was later noted, opened in 1846 and closed in 1851; and again it was in session from 1858 until 1865. Said to be the first boarding school in Raleigh, the Select School for Young Ladies was also the only school which, open before the War between the States, continued throughout this troubled period.

Miss Sophia Arms Partridge, a "thorough gentlewoman of great culture and refinement and a most efficient teacher," was responsible for this notable school. Born on May 15, 1817, at Vienna, New York, she came South because of the ill health of her sister and located at Louisburg, North Carolina, where she taught a school for girls. Then, in 1846, she established her Select School for Young Ladies in Raleigh and was assisted by her two sisters, Martha and Caroline (later Mrs. James Jordon) and her aunt, Mrs. John Bobbitt. In 1816, Mrs. Bobbitt, then Miss Harriet Partridge, "a lady from Massachusetts who is eminently qualified for the important trust," had taken charge of Louisburg Female Academy.

The new school grew rapidly in popularity. Some of Miss Partridge's students folowed her to Raleigh; and though most of the young women came from Raleigh and vicinity, there were students from states as far away as Mississippi. Many prominent families were represented.

In an old roll book, the records are written in finest penmanship; some of the names marked with M indicate those who took Music. Art was also an important subject; and along with it Miss Partridge taught fine needlework, embroideries, and all the dainty handwork that young ladies of that day were supposed to master. But whatever the subject, she strove to inculcate high ideals of living: love of God; love of nature; love of the good, the true, and the beautiful.

Nor did she ever lose sight of the social graces. Her young ladies were taught how to enter and leave a room, and under her training no young lady would have thought of crossing her knees or of exposing more than a glimpse of slender ankles. Calling days provided practice of social amenities. Dressed in best attire, young ladies were wont to call on their teachers or to act as hostesses to the teachers who, in turn, called on them.

Miss Sophia was strict in her requirements, tolerating no shoddy work. Yet, as one of her admirers put it, she never lost control of her temper but had "a most admirable disposition" and a happy faculty of correcting without leaving a sting. Her students loved her and respected her judgements.

Her personal accomplishments were considerable. She received many prizes from the State Fair for her paintings and was widely recognized for her artistic talent. *The Arator* (meaning the plowman), a monthly newspaper published by Thomas J. Lemany about the middle of the century, carried on its front page a composite design suggestive of the State of North Carolina: the Capitol, a railway train, a man plowing, and a small cottage. The sketch for the cut was made by Miss Partridge.

There is a lovely old book, out of print today, called *A Wreath from the Woods of Carolina*, published in New York in 1859 by the General Protestant Episcopal Sunday School Union and Church Book Society. The book was illustrated with colored flower plates by Miss Partridge, though neither her name nor that of the author of the stories appears in the book. The foreword reads:

"The writer of these stories has always considered flowers a most happy and charming medium through which to direct the opening minds of children to love and adoration of their great Creator. Prompted by this consideration and hoping they will afford pleasure as well as profit to the youthful reader, she now presents a volume illustrated with engravings of the beautiful wild flowers connected with each story."

The frontispiece is a wreath of honeysuckle, lupine, wild pinks, and other wild flowers native to North Carolina.

Miss Partridge always identified herself with her adopted City and State. During the War between the States, she worked for the soldiers, nursing the wounded and organizing the women and girls to help at the hospital.

And thus she served until after 1864, when, failing in health, she was forced to give up teaching. Her last years were spent with her flowers, her paintings, and her books. She died in 1881, a woman greatly beloved.

Warm, vital, and courageous, possessed of a prodigious faith in life, such pioneer women as Miss Partridge contributed to their generation a quality of living which will not die—a quality that goes on living through others, even after memories of its sources have faded. Of Sophia Partridge someone has said: "Though she has been dead for over a half a century, so vital was her personality and so great was her contribution to the educational life of Raleigh, she still lives."

ANNIE PERKINS
1873-

ANNIE Perkins Day was celebrated on May 22, 1946, in Farmville to honor the teacher who was retiring after having taught in Pitt County for fifty years. On that day, the citizens of Farmville at a picnic at the Recreation Centre crowned "Miss Annie" and presented her with the keys of the city and a love gift of $1300. Photographers from *Life Magazine* were there to make a graphic record of the celebration that had started with the serving of breakfast in bed to "Queen Ann" and was to last the livelong day.

Miss Perkins was born in Greenville where she studied at the Forbes School on Evans Street and later at the Seminary, owned and operated by the Methodist Church. She was for a time a student at Salem College; after she began teaching, she studied for a number of summers at State College and at the University of North Carolina. At the beginning of her first summer school at the University, in her course in teaching the primary subjects, the first topic was teaching phonics through the use of passages from the Bible.

For three years before she began her long period of service in the public schools of Farmville, Miss Perkins taught in rural schools near Farmville and in a private primary school in Greenville where she had from twenty-five to thirty pupils at a time and where she discovered that pupils can be amazingly successful in teaching one another. Today she wonders why that possibility is not more generally recognized.

In her teaching in Greenville and in Farmville, she stressed mental arithmetic. In a store recently she heard one of her pupils of long ago say to a clerk, "Don't let Miss Annie see you using a pencil for such simple figuring!" Her former pupils have much to thank her for, besides phonics and mental arithmetic, and they know it. In the success of many who started their schooling with her, Miss Perkins finds happiness.

The school is not the only institution she has served long and well. She is a member of the Farmvile Baptist Church, the Farmville Literary Club, the Woman's Club, the Merry Matrons' Club, the Rebecca Winborne Chapter of the U.D.C., and of the Col. Alexander McAlister Chapter of the D.A.R. In the North Carolina Federation of Women's Clubs, she has been an officer; in most of the other organizations of which she is a member, she has been president; in several she was a charter member.

In many a group, when she appears, some will say, "Here's Miss Annie. Good!" and others show that they are having the same thought.

151

MARY M. PETTY
1863-

ANNIE M. PETTY
1871-

THE Petty sisters, Miss Annie and Miss Mary, have devoted a sum total of almost ninety years of active service in the schools of North Carolina, and now in retirement continue their intense interest in and keen alertness to the educational problems of the day. Their contributions have been and are different, but each in her particular sphere has many firsts to her credit.

Daughters of Mr. and Mrs. William Clinton Petty of Bush Hill, which in 1887 became Archdale, Randolph County, North Carolina, they were reared in a sturdy Quaker home, where books and learning were cherished and religion was of everyday concern.

Their early education was obtained from excellent teachers in a neighborhood school, for the erection of which their father and his neighbors contributed from five to one hundred dollars apiece. Education and religion being close allies in the thinking of Friends, the children attended school down stairs on week days, and church services up stairs on Sundays.

Miss Mary, the elder of the two sisters, after attending the neighborhood school, completed her preparatory education at New Garden Boarding School, now Guilford College. In 1881, together with her intimate friend, Gertrude Mendenhall, she entered Wellesly, where she majored in Science and took special work in Machematics, receiving the B. S. degree in 1885.

Her first position was at Statesville College, now Mitchell College, where she occupied the chair, or as she delights to call it, the "settee" of Mathematics. In the meantime, New Garden Boarding School, having been raised to college rank, as Guilford College, in 1888, the year of its opening, Miss Petty became a charter member of its faculty, as teacher of Mathematics and Latin.

After five years on the Guilford College faculty, she in 1893, followed by one year her friend, Gertrude Mendenhall, to the State Normal and Industrial School in Greensboro. Here she joined the Science Department under the leadership of Dixie Lee Bryant, recent honor graduate of the Massachusetts Institute of Technology. As head of the Department of Chemistry, Miss Petty found herself in congenial company. This young teacher whom the president of Guilford College had described as "a young woman of rare distinction in scholarship and character," for more than forty years made a tremendous contribution toward raising the standards of the institution, as it gradually

152

developed from Normal School to the Woman's College of the University of North Carolina.

Miss Petty, her brilliant intellect never satisfied with meager knowledge, was delighted to receive a year's leave of absence in 1895-96 to work under a fellowship in Chemistry at Bryn Mawr. Throughout the years she took advantage of summer vacations to pursue advanced study at Harvard, Columbia University, Cornell University, and the University of California.

On the faculty Miss Petty was celebrated for her keen intellect, broad vision, great common sense, genial personality, and ready wit. As a member of the faculty, of the faculty council, and of the smaller policy-making body, the faculty cabinet, Miss Petty did yeoman service on many influential committees.

From the beginning the students counted Miss Petty as their friend. An excellent teacher, holding high but not unattainable standards, she was friendly and approachable. The students were "her girls."

In the forty years she was head of the Chemistry Department, Miss Petty saw the small room in the basement of Administration Building expand into laboratories, classrooms and lecture theatre in the now old McIver Building, and she was still on the faculty when the ground was broken for the spacious Science Building which now furnishes ample room and facilities for all the sciences.

After Miss Petty's partial retirement in 1934, she became social chairman of the faculty, turning her office into a pleasant place where tea was served afternoons, and comfortable chairs invited faculty members to sit and chat. Not only at faculty gatherings but at alumnae meetings Miss Petty has been and is now quite likely to be found pouring tea with her accustomed genial friendliness.

The Miss Petty whom faculty, students and alumnae love is quite aptly portrayed in the "Family Album" message to the Alumnae in October, 1935:

"What should a retired member of the faculty say to the children? Perhaps you did not know that I have retired somewhat and am only doing only part-time service. Letters of congratulation or condolence from you have been lacking, so I judge you did not know of my demotion or promotion. Which shall it be? I am having a good time either way. I am retired but not on the shelf.

"I am still in possession of my natural and acquired faculties. I still come to the College five days a week . . . I am very much in the advising business. Besides advising freshmen and sophomores, I can take on any alumnae who care to come to see me. Advice freely given on anything from marriage to make-up.

"Strange to say, the Chemistry Department is flourishing without my guiding hand. I am in the laboratories part of the time to keep

153

my nose accustomed to the aromas and for the satisfaction of seeing the pupils of my pupils at work. Sometimes I run across a granddaughter and find pleasure in hearing firsthand from the mothers, my first loves."

From early young womanhood Miss Petty has been prominent in the work of the Society of Friends. She was an important member of the Advisory Committee of Guilford College from 1901 until it was disbanded in 1935, and its chairman for the last twelve years. In 1936 she made the first woman member of Guilford's Board of Trustees.

In 1920 she was a delegate to the world Conference of Friends in England, and in 1937 to a similar conference in this country.

Miss Annie Petty, reared in the same family atmosphere, naturally followed her sister to New Garden Boarding School, then on into Guilford College, where she was graduated in 1894. After teaching one year at Red Springs, in 1895, Miss Petty joined the faculty of the State Normal and Industrial School, as librarian.

While she was called the librarian she actually was a general utility person, receiving and sorting the mail, signing for express packages, and ringing the bell for classes every forty minutes. The library was a small room in the Administration Building with six tables for reading, and shelves around the side walls. There were very few books except textbooks, which it was her duty to check out to students.

However, Miss Petty saw the vision of what a library could mean to a college, and sought further training. Taking a year's leave of absence she matriculated at the Library School of Drexel Institute, Philadelphia, completing her course in Library Science in 1899. Returning to the college, she had the distinction of being the only one of her class going straight into a position and of being the first trained librarian in North Carolina.

In true Petty tradition, Miss Annie went about her job quietly, earnestly, unostentatiously, and efficiently, building up the library as she envisioned it should be, the heart of the institution.

Miss Petty's appreciation of books and her enthusiasm for the establishment of libraries were contagious. In 1904 she organized on the Normal College campus the first library association in North Carolina, with five members.

In 1906 the Carnegie Foundation gave twenty-five thousand dollars for the erection of a library, the first such grant ever made to a college. At the same time it made a similar grant to the City of Greensboro, this city becoming the first in the country to have two Carnegie libraries.

Under the leadership of Miss Annie Petty and her fellow enthusiasts, North Carolina was becoming library conscious. In 1909, by legislative enactment, the North Carolina Library Commission was established.

154

In 1921 Miss Petty severed her connection with the College and went to Raleigh as Assistant Secretary of the State Library Commission. While in this position she had the pleasure of using the first bookmobile in North Carolina. The report of the Library Commission for the biennium of 1922-24 contains the story of the purchase of this truck by the Kiwanis Club of Durham and its presentation to the public schools of Durham County. It was in this truck, loaned to the State Library Commission, that Miss Petty, with her nephew at the wheel, had the joy of taking books into the countryside of her own Randolph County, among her old neighbors and friends, her own kith and kin.

Retiring, in 1933, Miss Annie returned to the big old Petty home in Greensboro to devote her time to homemaking in her modernized kitchen, and to the peace and contentment of a family life of culture, faith, and good works. Her interest in books and libraries remains as keen as ever.

In February, 1952, the Woman's College Alumnae Journal carried a beautiful article in appreciation of the wonderful women, the Petty sisters. Accompanying the article was an unusually true likeness of the two, in their home just off the college campus. A former student and long - time friend of both, remarked to the sisters: "Those are the most beautiful faces I ever saw!" To which Miss Mary quipped, "You must be blind!" But undaunted, the friend replied, "Miss Petty, love always is blind!"

MRS. HATTIE F. PLUMMER
1871-

ONE of the great pioneer women of the state of North Carolina sits today in a wheelchair, wracked with pain, but smiling as she recalls for numerous visitors her memories of a long and full life. She is seventy-nine year old Mrs. Hattie Frances Plummer, who thirty-six years ago became Vance County's first home demonstration agent.

Mrs. Plummer was born on October 19, 1871, in Granville County, North Carolina, to Joseph Benjamin Parham and his wife, Emma Jane Hunt Parham. She was next to the oldest in a family of eight children and was christened Hattie Frances Parham. Her early education was received in private schools of Granville County taught by Miss Rosa Hicks, Miss Sarah Hunt, and Miss Tazzie Parham. She later attended the Granvile Institute in Oxford where Miss Bettie Clark was Lady Principal. In 1889, Mrs. Plummer was graduated from Greensboro Female College. For three years she taught in Granville County under Superintendent W. H. P. Jenkins. Her teaching career was interrupted at this point, however, by Thomas Van L. Rowland who married her on November 17, 1892, and took her to live in Middleburg, North Carolina. Then followed eight busy years for Hattie Frances as Mrs. Rowland. During that time three children were born to the couple: Garland Thomas, Janie Hawkins (Mrs. Rob Crews), and Harry Tatum.

On July 11, 1901, Mr. Rowland died. Mrs. Rowland again became a teacher, this time in the Middleburg school. She held this position until after her marriage to James Kemp Plummer, of Middleburg, in 1909.

In 1914, Mrs. Plummer became the first home demonstration agent in Vance County and one of the first in North Carolina. She was continuously active in the work until she retired at the end of June, 1946, because of ill health.

The *Durham Morning Herald* for July 28, 1946, has the following to say of Mrs. Plummer:

"The history of home demonstration work in Vance County is largely the story of the life and labors of Mrs. Hattie F. Plummer among the farm women of this area of north central North Carolina in the last 32 years. Mrs. Plummer pioneered in the field when demonstration work was something new in the state . . .

"During this period of more than three decades, Mrs. Plummer saw rural home life transformed in Vance County from a dull, drab existence to that of a happy and contented citizenship, with much of the drudgery removed, with many homes almost self-contained and with many of the modern conveniences and luxuries of urban residents. And what is more, she was responsible for a large part of this rather remarkable transformation and improvement.

"Extension work in Vance County was already well advanced when the Smith-Lever Act was passed by Congress on May 8, 1914. Mrs. Plummer had already heard of work being done among the rural people, in a few other counties, and became interested in seeing home demonstration activities started here. She enlisted the sympathy and support of the county commissioners and the county board of education early in 1914. Because of the efforts she had made, and the enthusiasm of a small group of farm women, the North Carolina Extension Service appoined Mrs. Plummer home demonstration agent in the county in February, 1914, and she served continuously and with marked results as the county's only agent during the more than 32 years until her retirement.

"At the first appointment was on a part-time basis for only two months of the year, but the demand for her services became so great that she actually worked full time without pay for the other ten months.

"The first work undertaken was as corn and tomato clubs among farm boys and girls. Soon three clubs of girls were organized at

Williamsboro, Middleburg, and Cokesbury. These were followed by the formation of betterment societies in schools.

At the time of her retirement, in 1946, there were more than 500 rural women in Vance County who belonged to the home demonstration clubs. Through two wars, two booms, and a major depression, Mrs. Plummer carried on for a generation in developing homelife in the rural sections of Vance County. Her only rival in tenure is Mrs. Rosa Redfern of Anson County, and the two will be known in the history of the work in North Carolina as pioneers in behalf of better rural living."

Many organizations in Vance County and elsewhere in North Carolina have numbered Mrs. Plummer among their active and enthusiastic members. Those which she cherishes most, perhaps, are: Old Bute Chapter, Daughters of the American Revolution; the United Daughters of the Confederacy; and the Middleburg Methodist Church. In this church, she served as a steward for many years.

On October 11, 1949, the Business and Professional Women's Club of Henderson, North Carolina, announced the selection of Mrs. Plummer as the first person whose name was to be inscribed in the Club's *Book of Golden Deeds*. Mrs. Plummer's selection was unanimous as: "an individual in the community who had rendered the greatest civic service 'beyond the line of duty' in his own work or profession."

Today and throughout the decades, Vance County remembers and will remember the work of Mrs. Hattie Plummer, whose efforts have placed home demonstration work on a firm foundation in the community.

LINA PORTER

1832-1897

"SHE taught O. Henry everything he ever knew except the vast knowledge he acquired in the school of life," said a former pupil of Lina Porter.

To O. Henry, or Will Porter, Lina Porter was "Aunt Lina," while to others she was "Miss Lina." Will Porter's mother died when he was three years old, and his Aunt Lina, maiden sister of his father, Dr. Algernon Sidney Porter, was both mother and teacher to him through the years of his childhood and youth. Practically all the schooling O Henry ever had was that which he received from Lina Porter in a one-room, one-teacher schoolhouse which she built in her side-yard on West Market Street in Greensboro. Here she taught her nephews, Will Porter and his older brother, Shirley Worth Porter, and other children of the neighborhood.

Lina Porter was an unusual person. She was educated at Edgeworth Seminary, in Greensboro, which, in its time, was considered a highly superior girls' school. Miss Lina possessed a strong mind—what might be called a masculine mind—and she was masculine in appearance. There was nothing of the clinging vine about her. She stood on her own feet and was the personification of independence in act, speech, and thought. She was a spinster from choice, as well as from the exigencies of a situation which left her responsible for two orphaned nephews at a time just following the War between the States when living was a matter of extraordinary difficulty. She fought her battle alone; and to do this successfully called for unusual courage and ability. She had a keen sense of humor, as well as a high sense of duty; she was a strict disciplinarian, but always fair and just.

Lina Porter's teaching technique was a combination of the strict methods of the little red schoolhouse and its three R's and cultural excursions into the realms of the spirit which were prompted by her old Edgeworth training. Thoroughness was the crowning glory of her teaching, her conviction being that there was no knowing anything unless you knew it thoroughly. Those were the days when floggings were considered a necessity, and Lina Porter kept visible a plentiful supply of switches which she used freely when such treatment was deemed necessary. Mr. John W. Dillard, a former pupil, once paid Lina Porter this high tribute:

"One of the greatest, if not the greatest teacher I have ever known . . . Her fine sense of right and wrong, her scorn for shame and pretense and for anything but the clean, white truth. And her love for the beautiful and the good . . . she was an inspiration to everyone who was fortunate enough to have been her pupil."

On rainy days, at the recess hour, the children sat close around her and were entranced and uplifted by her reading of beautiful stories: poetry and prose from the best literature. It was here that O. Henry got his taste for good books and his devotion to the diamond-chiseled word and sentence.

Then, on Friday nights, the school children were the guests of this gifted teacher in her home. Here they made merry with games and corn-popping and chestnut roasting, winding up the evening with the story hour. This story hour was a highly important influence in the education of O. Henry and in the fashioning of his short-story technique. It was a sort of game, with the children seated in a circle around the room. The one at the head of the line would begin a story, the next one would take it up and add an episode, the next—and on around the circle to the last one who brought the story to a close. The thing that made it interesting and even exciting was the unexpected excursions which the story took in telling and the unexpectedness with which it was likely to end. O. Henry had his first practice in the art of story-telling and particularly in the art of jerking the reader

158

up in a complete surprise at an un-looked for ending, in these story hours conducted by Miss Lina Porter.

When we honor and extol O. Henry's skill and versatility as a story teller, let us honor his devoted "Aunt Lina," also. It was she who taught him to like stories and even how to tell them.

EMMA LYDIA RANKIN
1838-1908

EMMA Lydia Rankin is numbered among those pioneer teachers who helped to keep the schools of North Carolina open during the War between the States. While she taught in several school systems in the State, Miss Rankin is best known for her work in the Kirkwood Schools for Girls which she and her sister founded in the town of Lenoir.

Her father, the Reverend Jesse Rankin, was a scholarly man who combined teaching with preaching. He was the first pastor of the Presbyterian Church of Lenoir. Her mother, Ann Delight Salmon Rankin, was a teacher, also. Thus Emma came from a family of teachers and received a thorough education for her day. Later, she made her mark as a learned and accomplished person, an expert mathematician, and a skilful teacher.

Miss Rankin taught for sometime in the Salisbury schools, in Shelby, and near Fayetteville. She was at one time employed as a private teacher at Pleasant Gardens in McDowell County. During the War between the States, she and her father taught in the Finley High School in Lenoir, thus helping to keep that school open after the male teachers had gone to war.

In the years following the War, before the public schools had been reestablished, Miss Rankin and her sister, Sarah Rankin, founded the Kirkwood School for Girls in Lenoir. Miss Emma served as principal and taught most of the academic subjects while Miss Sarah taught Art. They continued in this school until 1906.

In 1875, "The Vesper Reading Club of Lenoir" appointed a committee of three from its members to investigate the possibility of establishing a circulating library for the town. This committee, of which Miss Rankin was a member, reported favorably and the movement resulted in the opening of the Pioneer Library. This library grew with the years and up to the era of the Carnegie libraries was perhaps the largest town library in the State. Miss Rankin was a moving spirit in it for many years, and during the last years of her life she served as purchasing agent and librarian.

Miss Rankin lived to be seventy years old. She died in Lenoir on February 28, 1908.

Among the tributes paid the memory of this useful woman are the following:

From *The Charlotte Observer:*

"She taught daughters and, in some cases, granddaughters of her pupils, and enjoyed the respect and love of her girls, who "rise up and call her blessed." Few women have exerted an equal influence for good in any community. She was held in highest esteem for her consistent Christian life, her noble work, and her wide influence."

And J. C. Wharton said in *The Presbyterian Standard:*

"She was a woman of strong character and endowed with a strong intellect which had been highly cultivated and used for the highest good of others. Her life was given to the work of teaching in which she was abundantly successful in training both intellects and hearts."

MRS. J. M. ROBERTS
1867-1946

M RS. J. M. Roberts has the distinction of being the "literary," or, as he calls her, the "spiritual mother" of Thomas Wolfe, the noted novelist of Asheville. In a letter written to Mrs. Roberts from New York City, May 30, 1927, and later published in the *Atlantic Monthly* of December, 1946, Wolfe pays the following tribute to her:

"My book is full of ugliness and terrible pain—and I think moments of a great and soaring beauty. In it . . . I have told the story of one of the most beautiful people I have ever known as it touched my own life. I am calling that person Margaret Leonard. I was without a home—a vagabond since I was seven, with two roofs and no home . . . my overloaded heart was bursting with its packed weight of loneliness and terror; I was strangling without speech, without articulation, in my own secretions—groping like a blind sea-thing with no eyes and a thousand feelers toward light, toward life, toward beauty and order, out of that hell of chaos, greed, and cheap ugliness—and then I found you, when else I should have died, you mother of my spirit who fed me with light. Do you think I have forgotten? Do you think that I ever will? You are entombed in my flesh, you are in the pulses of my blood, the thought of you makes a great music in me—and before I come to death, I shall use the last thrust of my talent—whatever it is—to put your beauty into words."

Mrs. Roberts, formerly Margaret Elizabeth Hines, was born on September 8, 1876, in Chillicothe, Ohio. As a student at Valparaiso University in Indiana and at East End College and Vanderbilt University in Nashville, Tennessee, her high records showed special aptitude for English literature and composition.

After leaving college, Mrs. Roberts taught for awhile in the Tennessee School for the Blind at Colorado Springs. In 1900, she was married to John Munsey Roberts, a teacher and a scholar of Greek and Latin. They taught together for several years in the Vanderbilt Training School in Elkton, Kentucky, and in several other schools.

Mr. and Mrs. Roberts with their two children, John Munsey, Jr., and Margaret Rose, moved to Asheville in 1911 where Mr. Roberts became principal of the Orange Street Elementary School. Here the eleven-year old Thomas Wolfe was enrolled in the sixth grade. During that school term, Mr. Roberts kept hearing from his teachers reports of the unusual work of this precocious youngster. One day Mr. Roberts read to all of his pupils above the fourth grade a selection which he asked them to reproduce as a composition. Later, when he was correcting the papers at home, he asked Mrs. Roberts to read some of them. She called the attention of Mr. Roberts to the best one, the reproduction by the above mentioned sixth grader. Through this incident Mrs. Roberts became aware of her later world famous pupil.

In the fall of 1912, Mr. Roberts began conducting his own private school which was finally discontinued in 1920. Then the next year he was made principal of Grace High School where Mrs. Roberts was also a member of the faculty. Here they taught together until their retirement in 1926. For awhile they lived in Chunn's Cove, then in Beverly Hills; and finally they built a home on Dogwood Road on a mountainside above Beaver Lake. At their home the elderly couple enjoyed reading, gardening, and having their former students visit them frequently.

Until her last illness, Mrs. Roberts, who died on May 9, 1946, was an active member of the Asheville Research Club and the American Association of University Women. Those who knew her in these clubs were stimulated by her keen and continued interest in social and economic problems, inspired by her determined devotion to ideals, and delighted with her perennially youthful and happy outlook on life.

Thomas Wolfe's greatest tribute to Mrs. Roberts, a paean in her honor, comes at the end of Chapter Sixteen of *Look Homeward Angel*:

"One by one the merciless years reaped down his gods and captains. What had lived up to hope? What had withstood the scourge of growth and memory? Why had the gold become so dim? All his life, it seemed, his blazing loyalties began with men and ended with images; the life he leaned on melted below his own weight, and looking down, he saw he clasped a statue; but enduring, a victorious reality amid his shadow-haunted heart, she remained, who first had touched his blinded eyes with light, who nested his hooded houseless soul. She remained."

161

Thus Wolfe's first book gives us in shining blue and silver the immortal portrait of one who "looked directly into the beauty and mystery and the tragedy in the hearts of men." His nostalgic recollections have preserved in literature the teacher for whom "teaching was its own exceeding great reward—her lyric music, her life. The world in which plastically she built to beauty what was good."

LUCY H. OWEN ROBERTSON
1850-1930

IN 1902, by unanimous vote of the Board of Greensboro college, Mrs. Lucy H. Owen Robertson was elected President of Greensboro College. Her election and administration were unique. Not only was she the first woman to be elected President of Greensboro College, but she was also the first woman to be elected President of any college in the South. In addition, it is noteworthy that her association with Greensboro College, extended over an extraordinary period of time—almost a half-century.

Mrs. Robertson began teaching in Greensboro Female College, as the school was then called, in 1875. Beginning as an assistant in the Literary Department, by 1890 she was head of the English Language and Literure Department. The long period of teaching—from 1875 to 1900—was broken by a period of seven years: 1893-1900, when Mrs. Robertson left Greensboro College and taught History in the State Normal and Industrial School for Girls (now Woman's College of the University of North Carolina). When she returned to Greensboro College in 1900, a new officer was needed, a Lady Principal, and Mrs. Robertson was chosen for this responsibility, while also teaching History.

It was in 1902, at the close of two years service as Lady Principal, that the Board elected her President of the College. For eleven years she served with honor and distinction in this important office; then, at her own request, became President Emeritus, yet did not sever all ties with the college. She was happy to return to teaching—Bible and Religious Education—and served thus until a few days before her death, May 28, 1930.

Mrs. Robertson was Lucy Henderson Owen, born in Warrenton, North Carolina, September 15, 1850. Two years later, the family moved to Chapel Hill, and in a few more years to Hillsboro where she grew up. During several years, she attended the school of Misses Nash and Kolloch in Hillsboro; and, in 1868, she was graduated from Chowan Baptist Institute in Murfreesboro. The next year she married Dr. D. A. Robertson of Hillsboro; and in 1872 they moved to Greensboro. Her husband died in 1883, and she faced the world alone.

After the election of Mrs. Robertson to the Presidency of Greensboro College, the announcement brought various comments. Among these, the College Catalog said:

"It seems eminently fitting that the College which was the pioneer in the State in higher education for women should thus be the first to confer upon a woman the highest honor within the gift of the institution, and thereby evincing the highest confidence possible in woman's ability as well as truest interest in the promotion of her welfare; and at the same time giving an earnest, continued labor and devotion to the cause of woman's education."

Annie M. Pegram, who taught with Mrs. Robertson on the Greensboro faculty, described her thus:

"A tall and graceful person, much beloved by those she taught, and admired by others who knew her less well . . . Well, educated, well traveled, well read, vitally interested in people. No wonder she was the center of attraction for faculty members and friends after meals, or when time was found for a social hour, or for informal discussions over the tea cups . . . Always winning the love and confidence of those around her, there was never a more lovely sight than the devotion and thoughtfulness shown by students for her in her later years."

In her long years of work in Greensboro College, Mrs. Robertson came in contact with more than 2500 girls, leaving a lasting influence on each life. Dr. Samuel B. Turrentine, who followed Mrs. Robertson as President of Greensboro College, said of her:

"Amiable in disposition she was easily approached; and frank in spirit she was easily understood . . . She combined modesty with courage, culture with simplicity, and frankness with gentleness and kindness . . . Endowed with fine judgment, she rendered clear decisions, and gave wise counsel. Recognizing that true education consists of more than the products of text books, she sought to promote the college spirit and life adapted to develop true character and conduct."

Then Dr. Turrentine finally added:

"As one looks into the years we behold the portrait of a noble life that began aright. Inheriting the blessings of a worthy ancestry, reared and trained amid the environments and under the influence of Christian culture, she was destined to render the service that during these many years has contributed to make earth more like heaven and the children of men more like Christ."

MRS. JAMES A. ROBINSON

1865-1947

FORTY-EIGHT years of active service in the city schools of Durham, eighteen of which were spent as classroom teacher and thirty-four as supervisor, and a lifetime of service in its civic, historical, and religious organizations, is the record of Mrs. James A. Robinson. No one has stood higher in the esteem and appreciation of the citizens of Durham. She was the wife of a leading citizen, but in her right was one of the illustrious who helped make Durham what it is today. Durham honored her by choosing her once as its "woman of the year."

She was Alice Page, the daughter of Captain and Mrs. W. M. Page. She was born on August 11, 1865, in Davie County. The family soon moved to Morrisville, Wake County, and her early education was in private schools there. She was a student in Oxford Female Seminary for two years, 1880-1882, and after that attended Hollins Institute, Roanoke, Virginia, graduating in 1884. In 1887, she married James A. Robinson, founder and editor of one of Durham's oldest newspapers, the *Durham Daily Sun*. Mrs. Robinson's teaching career in the Durham city schools began in 1895. She first taught for four years in Morehead School in the intermediate grades. Her love for little children soon led her to accept a position in the Fuller School as first grade teacher and she remained there from 1899 to 1913, when she was made Supervisor of Elementary Work in the Durham city schools. She held this position until her retirement in 1943. She continued her residence in the city at the home of a friend and was active in the civic and church life of the city. Shortly before her death she moved to Greensboro to live with her sisters. Although she had been in declining health for some time, she died suddenly, on June 10, 1947.

Throughout her career, Mrs. Robinson spent few idle summers. Her educational work usually continued throughout the year as she was either attending summer schools as a student or was teaching. She continued her study in the University of North Carolina, Trinity College-Duke University, Columbia University and the University of Tennessee. She frequently visited schools in other cities for bringing back ideas into the Durham schools, as in Washington, D. C., New York, and cities of Massachusetts and California.

She was in demand as a teacher and leader in North Carolina Teachers Institutes and work shops. She taught in the University of North Carolina, Trinity College and Duke University, Ohio Northern University and the University of Arkansas and other summer schools.

For years she served on the State Textbook Commission and wrote a number of articles for educational magazines, such as the *Normal Instructor*. She also did a great deal of writing in connection with her husband's newspaper, the *Durham Sun*. One of the valuable contributions Mrs. Robinson made to Durham was the organization of the night schools.

Mrs. Robinson was a valuable member of several city, state, and national organizations and held positions of honor and trust in them. Among these were the Delta Kappa Gamma Society, the Julian S. Carr Chapter of the Daughters of the Confederacy, and the Tourists Club of Durham, of which she was a charter member.

Perhaps the work closest to her heart outside of her daily work in the classroom was in the Primary Department of St. Phillips Episcopal Church Sunday School where she was superintendent for a long period. She took part in many phases of church work. During World War II she was an active hostess in her church work and in the neighborhood U.S.O. Mrs. Robinson never grew old except in years. She had the spirit of eternal youth and her work with youth nurtured that spirit and kept it most active.

She knew how in the classroom to imbue her pupils with her spirit and so interest them in their work that they developed study habits and character traits that were meaningful throughout life. She always gave her best thought and efforts to the work in hand and was unwilling for those with whom she worked to do less. Many a Durham man and woman will say with pride, when asked who their teachers in early life were, "Mrs. Robinson taught me in the first grade at Fuller School and how we loved her."

When Mrs. Robinson left classroom teaching for supervision, she did not lose her touch with children. She had the rare gift of being able to impart her understanding of children to others so that the teachers under her supervision caught her spirit and became successful teachers.

The teachers who worked with her could go to her with their problems and she always lent a helping hand. They loved and honored her not only for the help she gave in her ability and training but because of her noble Christian character for she was truly an example of a cultured Christian with a deep and abiding love for people, especially children. That love never grew cold.

Mrs. Robinson's life was truly a career of service and she will live in the memories of her former pupils many of whom are prominent business men and women in the city of Durham. She has a living memorial in the quality of Citizenship that she engendered in literally hundreds of her pupils. She was one of North Carolina's outstanding teachers and citizens and her life was a noble example of love for human kind.

WINIFRED BLOUNT ROWLAND
1875-1950

HAVING lived her entire life in Lumberton, "Miss Bunch" (as Miss Winifred Blount Rowland was affectionately called), taught as many as three generations of pupils. To evaluate her happy influence on the children of this town would be an impossible undertaking. Lumberton, in recognition and appreciation of her life's work with its children, has attempted to honor her, her sister (Miss Penelope Rowland), and another primary grade teacher (Miss Emma Norment) by naming its new school building "The Rowland-Norment School."

Miss Rowland was born on May 3, 1875. She was the daughter of Colonel Alfred Rowland (who was at one time Congressman from the Lumberton district) and his wife, Sue Blount Rowland.

During her childhood, she was taught by private tutors or she attended private schools. Later, as a young girl, she was a student at the Durham Conservatory of Music.

Miss Rowland pioneered in education in the Lumberton community by organizing and operating with her sister, Miss Penelope Rowland, a private school known as the Rowland School. After five years of work here, she taught for two years elsewhere. Next, she entered the new public school system in Lumberton where she taught for a period of thirty-eight years, or until her retirement in 1946. During the latter years of this tenure, she served as Principal of the Primary School.

When a child, Miss Rowland joined the Presbyterian Church in Lumberton and was a loyal, constructive member until her death. She held the position of organist for a number of years, taught a Sunday School class for fifteen years, was Superintendent of the Primary Department for thirty-one years, and for twelve years served as Bible teacher for the Business Women's Circle of the Women's Auxiliary. In 1947, she was presented an honorary life membership in the Auxiliary.

Miss Rowland passed away on August 14, 1950, at the age of seventy-five.

CORNELIA REBEKAH SHAW
1869-1937

FOR more than thirty years, Cornelia Rebekah Shaw was an outstanding figure on the campus of Davidson College. She was the first woman connected with the college in any official capacity and for a long time remained the only one.

Miss Shaw went to Davidson in 1905 as secretary to President

Henry Louis Smith, then one year later was made librarian and registrar. In 1921, she became head librarian and served as such until 1936 when she retired as librarian emeritus. Her presence on the campus in those early days meant much to the college. She reflected order and beauty and a feminine touch that was felt and appreciated. Annuals were dedicated to her; commencement speakers thanked her for the many and varied services that she rendered to the college; and the boys showed their love and gratefulness by giving her beautiful presents. She was an institution in the college and in the community.

Miss Shaw was born at Mt. Gilead on February 3, 1869. She was a member of a distinguished North Carolina family. One brother was Judge Thomas J. Shaw of Greensboro while another brother was Dr. A. R. Shaw of Charlotte, a promonent Presbyterian minister.

She was the author of *The History of Davidson College,* a book of nearly three hundred pages, representing many years of historical research. This book will remain as one of the monuments of her life. From this work one can see her humor and her appreciation of others as well as her painstaking efforts to give facts.

Miss Shaw was a leader in various kinds of civic and religious work. For years she ararnged the flowers in the Davidson Presbyterian Church. She had no garden of her own and no car in which to carry the flowers given her, yet Sunday after Sunday she never failed to provide the ararngements of flowers for the services. It was only after her death, when this service was shared by many, that others realized how much work she had done and what her faithfulness in this one particular meant.

One friend wrote of her: "During the early years of her connection with Davidson, she knew personally every boy on the campus, as the student body at that time was not nearly as large as it is now." Hundreds of Alumni, scattered all over this country in various positions of life, have testified to her valuable and unfailing friendship and eager assistance at all times. She was always faithful to duty. She was always where she felt she ought to be. It was her work that she considered, rather than herself. One of her fellow workers, when asked the question, "What would you say was Miss Shaw's outstanding characteristic?" replied: "It was the great amount of work she could do and do well. She had all the qualities of a good librarian—accuracy, efficiency, punctuality." Then the fellow worker added: "She was so understanding."

Miss Shaw traveled widely during her vacations and from these travels brought back much of interest to give to others in her Book Clubs, her Civic Clubs, and also to her individual friends.

In Aberdeen, on December 28, 1937 she passed away.

CLARA MAUNEY SHERRILL
1855-1952

MRS. Clara Mauney Sherill began teaching at the age of sixteen and when she retired at the age of seventy she had fifty-five years of teaching to her credit. These years were spent in the rural schools of Graham and Cherokee counties. She says in her autobiographical notes, written at the age of ninety-four: "I taught in about eighteen different schools."

Clara was one of eleven children born to Ambrose H. Mauney and his wife, Catherine Brittain Mauney, of Cherokee County, North Carolina. She grew up during the turbulent days of the War between the States and the Reconstruction days when there were few educational opportunities. She attended high school one year in Murphy and began teaching at Robbinsville the next year as assistant to her brother, Lycurgus Mauney. In her eagerness to advance in scholarship, she studied under him each evening throughout that year. Then she later continued her studies at summer schools.

She was a conscientious teacher and made an immeasurable contribution to her mountain region. In her previously mentioned autobiographical notes, she mentions former pupils:

"Lowney Axley is teaching in Savannah, Georgia; he wrote me a few months ago that I taught him his A B C's . . . Mrs. Lilly Mae Cover of Andrews, a cousin of mine, whom I taught, has represented Cherokee County in the Legislature . . . I have two pupils now living in Texas who write to me. One is an outstanding teacher and the other owns four farms."

Mrs. Sherrill lived to enjoy a number of years after her retirement. She died in December, 1952, at the age of ninety-seven.

CATHERINE CAMERON SHIPP
1859-1932

WHILE Miss "Kate" Shipp was connected with the public schools of Raleigh and Charlotte, also with the faculty of St. Mary's and the institution now called Queens College, her name is synonymous in North Carolina with the noted Fassifern School. She was a co-founder of this school and served as its head mistress for seventeen years. Her name was prominent in educational circles and it was interwoven into the reputation which Fassifern acquired and maintained, thus drawing girls from many of the best families of North Carolina as well as from other states.

Miss Shipp was the daughter of Judge William M. Shipp of Lincoln County and his wife, Catherine Cameron Shipp. She was born in Hendersonville on March 18, 1859. Here she attended the preparatory school conducted by Mary Wood Alexander and was graduated from St. Mary's in Raleigh about 1878.

After graduation at St. Mary's, Miss Shipp taught in the city schools of Raleigh and Charlotte, at St. Mary's, and the Presbyterian College, now Queen College, Charlotte. In 1900, she opened a private school in Lincolnton which she named the Mary Wood School in honor of her former teacher.

With about four years' experience in this school, Miss Shipp decided that she needed further study for the work of preparing girls for college. Accordingly, in 1904, she closed her private school and went to Cambridge University, England. After two years of study, she was granted a degree. When she returned to North Carolina, she taught at St. Mary's for one year. Then, in 1907, she and her sister, Mrs. Annie McBee, opened the Fassifern School in Lincolnton as a preparatory school for girls. The school soon became outstanding for the high character of its work. Its graduates were received at Smith, Vassar, Bryn Mawr, and other colleges for women.

About 1914, a group of business men of Hendersonville made such an attractive financial offer that Fassifern was moved to Hendersonville. The school flourished in its new environment for ten years. In addition to its excellent academic standing, Miss Shipp's delightful personality, culture, and ability as a teacher attracted girls from a wide area to the school.

Miss Shipp was a tall, handsome woman, the epitome of culture, and always well dressed. Her standards for manners and culture were comparable to the academic standards of the school. Among her remarks which have been frequently quoted are: "Fassifern girls do not chew gum" and "Girls get journey proud just before holidays." Her humor is illustrated by the following instance: In the fall of 1920, during the meeting of the North Carolina Education Association in Asheville, Miss Shipp was the speaker at a banquet of the group, Women in Administration. In the course of her address, she referred to the difficulties of teaching girls by saying, "My biggest job is to keep clothes on and powder off." Then, later, describing her busy life, she remarked: "I suppose when I die, I'll no more than get settled for a rest than someone will come along and say, 'Get up, Kate, it's time to ha'nt!'"

A quotation from a student at Fassifern during Miss Shipp's rigime reflects the standards she held for her students: "Miss Shipp selected her pupils very carefully; family meant more to her than money. She expected her girls to be 'ladies' at all times. They were

169

never to cross their legs, but were required to keep their feet on the floor at all times. She was a true type of her day."

A teacher who was a contemporary of Miss Shipp's characterizes her thus: "Miss Shipp was a person of high standards, compelling personality, forceful, with a keen sense of humor."

In 1924, Mrs. McBee died. Miss Shipp, unwilling to continue the school alone, sold her share to the Reverend J. A. Sherrill and returned to the home of her childhood in Lincolnton. In October, 1931, she suffered an accident which caused her to suffer considerable pain and hastened her death.

She died on November 12, 1932, in Lincolnton and was buried in the Shipp plot at St. Luke's Episcopal Church in that town.

"BOBBIE" SPEIGHT
1845-1929

ROBERT Ann Rhoads, "Bobbie" as she was called, was born in Keyburg, Kentucky, May 7, 1845, the third of seven children. Her father was John Wesley Rhoads, of Buncombe County, North Carolina, a Methodist minister. Her mother was Laurinda McLary Davis of Kentucky, whose father and grandfather were Presbyterian ministers.

Due to the fact that her itinerant minister father was moved from place to place, her early educational experience was quite varied, ranging from one teacher country schools to exclusive female boarding schools in three states, Kentucky, Georgia and Florida.

Her teaching began as assistant in her mother's private school after the death of her father. She began teaching at the early age of sixteen and continued at intervals until her death at the age of eighty-four, covering a span of sixty-eight years. Due to the War between the States there was no opportunity to go to college so she continued as a private teacher in the home of Dr. Hines, a physician in Montecello, Florida. Then, after teaching in Lock Logan and Madison, Florida, and Brunswick, Georgia, she was married and after a few years came to North Carolina with her husband and children.

She married at the age of twenty-one, in 1866, to William Hayward Speight, who was born in Greene County, North Carolina. From this union three daughters were born, Alma, Laurie and Daisy. After graduation, as they finished school, all three daughters taught school until they were married. Alma married E. Carl Duncan, a prominent business man, and lived in Raleigh. Laurie married John B. Hooks of Fremont and later of Goldsboro, where he was Clerk of the Superior Court for many years. They had three children, Laurinda, John B. Jr.,

170

and Wiliam Borden.   Daisy married Albert S. Barnes, a Methodist minister and for over thirty years Superintendent of the Methodist Orphanage in Raleigh.   They also had three children, Albert S. Jr., Speight and Maude.

When Mrs. Speight's husband died in 1899, she moved to Beaufort and started a private school.   Her influence was far-reaching because she was a teacher of ability, a good manager, an organizer, a spiritual guide and leader.   Much of her teaching experience was gained in her own private schools which she organized and managed.   She gave employment as well as personal guidance to many young ladies who became teachers and leaders in their communities.   Her dynamic personality and high standards of living were so revered by all who knew her that even when she taught in public school, many friends and relatives sent their daughters to board in the town in which she taught that they might come under her influence.   She enjoyed her private schools but was much sought after as a public school teacher and principal.   She says in her *Memoirs:*

"The Chairman of the Board called me up and said, 'We need you for this place.   We will pay you whatever you demand.   You can spend all the weekends with your daughter, and we shall do everything to make it easy and pleasant for you.'"

Among the towns in North Carolina where she taught or was principal were Goldsboro, Beaufort, La Grange, Whiteville, Black Creek, Sunburg, and Fremont.

In her late years her hearing was impaired and her daughters urged her to give up teaching and live with them.   She was not allowed to do so, however, because of the many calls for teaching that she received.   Yet she did divide her time, whenever possible, between her daughters and figured greatly in the training of her grandchildren.

Many of her students occupy places of prominence in North Carolina and in other states. Among these is Bishop Costin J. Harrell, author and outstanding minister in Southern Methodism.

Bobbie Rhoads Speight loved people and people loved her.   Her brilliant mind, her understanding heart, and her high sense of moral duty account for the profound influence that she had on all who came in contact with her—both young and old, small and great.

171

CELESTE HINKLE SMITH
1885-1935

CELESTE Henkle is numbered among the few women who have held the office of County Superintendent of Schools in North Carolina. She was the oldest daughter of Mr. and Mrs. L. P. Henkle and was reared in Lenoir. About 1920, the family moved to Statesville.

She attended Davenport College but graduated from Salem College. Later she received a degree from Columbia University.

Miss Henkle taught home economics at Mitchell College, then worked in the capacity of Home Demonstration Agent in Iredell County for a few years. About 1925, she was elected County Superintendent of Schools of Iredell County, a position which she held for three terms.

There was a decided improvement in the schools of the county under her progressive administration. She advocated better equipment such as maps, globes, charts, and the like. She stemulated the teachers to do better teaching. The high esteem in which she was held by the people of the county was shown by the fact that one of the new schools was named the Celeste Henkle High School.

Miss Henkle served on the State Textbook Commission. She was a member of the Board of Trustees of Appalachian State Teachers College. And she was a member of the North Carolina Democratic Executive Committee.

In 1933, Miss Henkle was married to Dr. Charles Lee Smith of Raleigh. After her mariage she traveled abroad and entertained her friends by her interesting reports of her travels. She had started to New York to sail for Europe in 1935 when she became very ill and was taken to a hospital in Baltimore. Here she passed away on September 30, 1935.

LENA H. SMITH
1854-1943

TO LENA H. Smith, teaching was an opportunity for service to her community and to her fellow man. At her feet the young people of Scotland Neck for three generations learned not only the three R's, but found guiding inspiration and appreciation for the best things in life.

Miss Smith was graduated from St. Mary's School at the age of eighteen. Immediately upon her return to her home in 1871, she began teaching her younger sisters in her bedroom at Sunnyside, their country home. It was not long until relatives requested that she teach their children, also. Therefore, with seven pupils, she moved into larger quarters. Here the little family grew. Boys and girls came from the whole community, and she continued the school for seven years. It seems that Miss Smith was beginning to fulfill her destiny as Dr. Smedes, head of St. Mary's, advised her to make teaching her career. One pupil of that period wrote:

"Miss Lena was deaf at that time, but gave her boys and girls good training and cultural background . . . On Friday she had a class in mental Arithmetic, for instance—she would say as fast as she could rattle off: "If 4 dogs are running 6 rabbits, they jump 9 ditches and scare up 12 birds that flew 115 yards, how many dogs, rabbits, ditches, birds, and yards.?" She gave about a tenth of a second to answer; and if no answer, or the wrong one, down you would go. That class in mental Arithmetic did learn to calcuate quickly."

This alert teacher had a remarkable gift for helping each pupil regardless of whether the appeal was directly connected with the school. Her own deafness, which began when she was a young girl and which became total in her maturity, she did not allow to be a handicap. Instead, it seemed to give her a more sympathetic understanding of the disabilities of others. For instance: one little girl in her school had an arm useless from infantile paralysis. With infinite patience Miss Smith gave the child special calisthenics. Finally, after long months of tedious cooperative work, the afflicted arm became normal.

In 1878, Miss Smith became assistant principal of Vine Hill Female Academy, the forerunner of the public schools in Scotland Neck; and in 1893 she was made principal. In the late nineties, she established Cottage Home School as a private institution. She continued this school until 1903 when the local Graded School opened and her school was no longer needed. At this time she retired from active teaching except to instruct private pupils in art and history—two subjects for which she was exceptionally equipped—until the year of her death, in 1943.

With indomitable courage and high enthusiasm she gave generously of her great gifts of mind, heart, and spirit. Hundreds of young people of Scotland Neck received their entire education in Miss Smith's schools. She followed with keen interest the careers of her pupils who went to college. Among these were a Governor of the State, a College President, Congressman, Senators, Missionaries, College Professors, and Clergymen.

MARY NELSON SMITH
1825-1907

MORE than a century ago, Mary Nelson Smith started in her plantation home in Pitt County, near Ayden, a primary school. Later, when the demand for instruction became more acute, she set about preparing herself to teach more advanced subjects. After this, she and her husband built a new and larger school where she taught such courses as Latin and algebra to both local and boarding students. This was true pioneering.

Mary Nelson, the daughter of Edward Nelson, Jr., and Sarah Roach Nelson, was born in Craven County, October 2, 1825. She married William Henry Smith of Pitt County on March 15, 1846. Before her marriage she had taught for a few months, and she continued teaching at her home in Pitt County until the size of her family forced her to stop for a certain period. In the meantime her husband employed someone to teach their children and the neighborhood children in the schoolhouse on the Smith plantation.

At the close of the War between the States, Mr. Smith was too poor to pay a teacher's salary, and the schoolhouse remained closed. Mrs. Smith was, however, so determined not to let her children grow up in ignorance that she began teaching them daily in a large room on the second floor of her home. Desks and benches were placed on one side of the room and her spinning wheel and carding combs on the other. Each morning, after doing her household work, Mrs. Smith would have a three-hour school, carding and spinning when not "hearing lessons." Again in the early afternoon, when the noonday meal was over, she would begin another three hours of school.

When the neighbors on the nearby plantations heard that she was teaching, they asked that their children be admitted to the school. The result was that she had to move into the old school house on the farm. On the first day of school she had over forty pupils, and later she had to have the schoolhouse enlarged to take care of the increased demand for schooling. Then she gave her entire attention to teaching.

For awhile she taught only children of elementary school age. Although she longed to take her more advanced pupils on to higher grades, she feared that she was not prepared to do so. However, a timely visitor opened the way for carrying on her work. A retired educator, John G. Elliott, a graduate of the University of North Carolina, was invited to visit, then later to make his home with the Smiths in order to qualify Mrs. Smith for teaching advanced classes. Although she was then over fifty years of age, she studied Latin, algebra, geometry, and surveying. Her courses in these subjects prepared her unmarried daughters for college.

Because the urge for more knowledge continued to grow stronger in the county, Mrs. Smith and her husband built a new two-story schoolhouse which was opened in 1882. At this time, they also opened their home for boarding pupils who came from other communities to study with her and Mr. Elliott.

Her grandson, the Reverend William E. Cox, an Episcopal minister, who had his first schooling under her, tells the following in his book, *Southern Sidelights:*

"So thoroughly did she ground us in elementary things as the Additive, Subtraction, Multiplication, and Division tables; also the various tables of weights and measures, that to this date I can recite them as I did to her sixty years ago. She was especially intersted in thoroughness in Spelling and Writing. My own experience has made me grateful to her for laying the foundation simply but solidly."

Mrs. Smith has been called "a pioneer Pitt County educator" because she pioneered in putting into the public schools subjects of high school level. It is impossible to say how many lives she influenced during that period when the education of children in the South depended upon such indomitable individuals as Mrs. Mary Nelson Smith. Because of her contribution, she has been called "an emergency school teacher" as well as "a pioneer Pitt County educator."

ETHEL M. SOLLOWAY
1878-1944

ETHEL M. Solloway gave twenty-seven years of excellent service to the Durham city schools. She was a member of and an officer in many professional organizations, both local and national, and a leader among commercial teachers of the State. Durham appreciated her loyalty and her work to such an extent that the city gave the Civic Honor Award of 1939 jointly to her and another teacher.

Miss Solloway was a native of Kent County, Maryland. She was the daughter of John J. and Mary C. Solloway. She received her education in the schools of Maryland and Delaware and began her teaching career in a grammar school in Maryland.

After some experience in grammar grade work, she decided to go into the field of commerical education which offered many advantages to a person of Miss Solloway's characteristics. Accordingly, she entered Philadelphia Business College where she made such an excellent record that she was given a position to teach in that institution. Later, Miss Solloway taught at Churchill and at Snow Hill, Maryland, and then went to Georgetown, Delaware.

Her work at Georgetown was so outstanding that Superintendent

E. D. Pusey of Durham, North Carolina, heard of her reputation and asked her to meet him in Philadelphia for an interview. This resulted in her coming to Durham in 1914 as commerical teacher in the Durham High School. In 1917, she was made Director of Commerical Education for the Durham city schools. She served in this capacity the remaining years of her life.

One secret of Miss Solloway's success was her eagerness to give to her work the best training she could obtain; therefore, she studied during many summers in leading universities. She took courses at Temple University, Philadelphia; Johns Hopkins University; and the Universities of Pennsylvania and California, Harvard and Duke. She read and studied extensively, ever on the alert for new improvement in her department which was soon recognized as one of the finest in the South.

A keen interest in her pupils while they were on their jobs and in their homes was another reason for Miss Solloway's success. She was happy in their business successes and in their home joys. The homes of many of her pupils were often graced by the presence of their beloved teacher, adviser, and friend. A group of her first graduates in in Commerical Education entertained Miss Solloway each year on her birthday, and many a happy home was opened to her on that occasion.

Miss Solloway had her sorrows and disappointments, but she bore these with great courage. One of her greatest sorrows was the loss of her fiance, an appointee in the counsular service to China, who died suddenly about two months before they expected to marry and go to China to make their home. She came out of this tragedy with a firm determination to give her life to her profession. She lived a life of great service not only to her relatives and friends but to her school and city. She never seemed too tired nor too busy to help anyone who needed her aid. She emphasized thoroughness, accuracy, and proficiency; yet she was gentle and unobtrusive in her manners.

Miss Solloway passed away on November 3, 1944; and, according to a request she had made, she was buried in Durham.

CORNELIA PHILLIPS SPENCER
1825-1908

ALTHOUGH Cornelia Phillips Spencer never occupied an official position with the University of North Carolina—woman's place in education having not yet been established—she was one of the strongest intellectual, spiritual, and moral forces on the campus during the period of about 1860-1890. The campus intellects centered about her; and Governor Zebulon B. Vance said of her in the 1870's: "She's not only the smartest woman in North Carolina, but the smartest man too."

Cornelia Phillips, born in Harlem, New York, March 20, 1825, was the daughter of James Phillips who moved to Chapel Hill about 1826 to fill the chair f mathematics at the State University. This Cornelia was about one year old when she came to Chapel Hill, and here she grew up.

In the early days of the University, there was no village school in Chapel Hill therefore Dr. and Mrs. Phillips taught their three children, Charles, Samuel, and Cornelia in the home. Certain parents, learning of these private lessons, began to urge that their children, particularly the girls, be included. This led to the opening of the Phillips Female Academy in the Phillips home. According to the advertising of the day, this school offered "English, Latin, Greek, and French languages, Arithmetic, Algebra, Geometry, Natural History, Natural Philosophy, Drawing, and Needlework."

It was in this school that Cornelia received her education. When she was eleven years old, she was reading Xenophon in Greek under William Hooper in a class that included her brothers and the two daughters of Elisha Mitchell.

In 1855, Cornelia Phillips was married to James Munroe Spencer of Alabama, an honor graduate of the University of North Carolina, and went to Alabama to live. Four years later a daughter, Julia Spencer, was born to her. In 1861, her husband died and she returned to Chapel Hill to live.

In the two decades following her return to the village of her youth, Mrs. Spencer made her influence felt in the State through her writings.

The main objective of her first period of writing was to help boycott the administration of Solomon Pool as president of the University. Pool was an appointee of the radical governor of the period, W. W. Holden. A second objective was to aid in the reopening of the University when it was closed during the Carpetbagger regime. She published numerous articles on these two causes in the *North Carolina Presbyterian*, the *Raleigh Sentinel*, *The Watchman*, and other journals. The second period of her writing resulted in the reopening of the University. When Mrs. Spencer received on March 20, 1875, a message from the committee in Raleigh that the University would be opened again, she climbed the stairs to the belfry in old South Building and with her own hands rang the bell which had been silent for five years.

In 1866, her first book, *The Last Ninety Days of the War*, was published; and in 1889 she published *First Steps in North Carolina History*.

As the years passed, Mrs. Spencer realized more and more the need of facilities for the education of women. Soon after the University was reopened in 1875, she wrote Ellen Mitchell Summerell:

"I think North Carolina ought to give the girls of the state some attention as well as the boys. Co-education will never do in these latitudes, but don't you think the state ought to make some provision for the girls? When I think of what mere crumbs they have to pick up, I get angry. [Quoted from: Russell Phillips, *The Woman Who Rang the Bell.* p. 161. Chapel Hill, University of North Carolina Press, 1949.] "

To Mrs. Spencer belongs the credit for first obtaining the permission of the University authorities to attend a series of class room lectures in the regular term. The subject was Botany, given by Professor W. H. Smith. Mrs. Spencer, her daughter June, and her niece Lucy Phillips were admitted to the lectures under the agreement that they were to occupy the rear seats and that they were to keep very quiet.

Later, Mrs. Spencer heartily supported the establishment of the State Normal and Industrial College for Women at Greensboro.

Until she was seventy years old, Mrs. Spencer continued to live in Chapel Hill. Then, in the summer of 1895, she reluctantly went to live with her daughter, Mrs. James Lee Love, in Cambridge, Massachusetts. Here she died on March 11, 1908, at the age of eighty-three. Her remains were brought back and laid away in the Chapel Hill cemetery.

That North Carolina recognized Mrs. Spencer's ability and her contribution to the State has been attested by the honors bestowed upon her. The University awarded her the first honorary degree it ever conferred upon a woman; a dormitory on the campus of Womans College of the University of North Carolina bears her name; a dormitory on the University campus at Chapel Hill is named for her; and, in 1943, thirty-five years after her death, a merchant ship named in her honor was launched at Wilmington, North Carolina.

ETTA RIDER SPIER
1876-1938

A BOU Ben Adhem's angel would certainly have written the name of Etta Rider Spier in his book of gold. Undoubtedly she loved her God and her fellowman; home, family, friends; school, community, synagogue. This may sound pontifical, which Miss Spier was not, being a joyous soul ready for laughter.

Born in Tarboro, North Carolina, November 21, 1876, daughter of Samuel and Amelia Rider Spier, she early in life moved with her family to Goldsboro. Having graduated from the Goldsboro schools, Miss Spier, in the fall of 1892 became a member of the first student body of the State Normal and Industrial School in Greensboro, where she graduated with the class of 1895.

Returning to her home in Goldsboro she there taught the first grade for twelve years. So successful was she that in 1907 she was invited to become supervisor of the first grade in the demonstration and practice school of her Alma Mater, where, with brief periods of absence for study, she remained, serving in various capacities in the college, for the remainder of her life, a period of thirty-one years.

Always ambitious for self-improvement, Miss Spier, at various times studied at Columbia University, receiving the B. S. degree in 1917 and the M.A. degree in 1921. In line with her advanced study and her own capabilities and interests, from 1915 on, Miss Spier's teaching was confined chiefly to college classes in both winter and summer sessions. Her major teaching fields centered around the growth and development of young children and the needs of rural teachers. In later years she taught all of the major courses for primary teachers.

Miss Spier made every effort to keep up-to-date in her theory and in her first-hand knowledge of actual classroom conditions. From time to time she borrowed a small section of a primary grade, making herself responsible for teaching this group for one hour daily.

In cooperation with the Guilford County Schools, she sought the privilege of being helping-teacher in certain underprivileged communities, seeking to imbue the teachers with her enthusiasm for teaching and her love for and understanding of boys and girls, while helping them locate suitable instructional materials. She focussed their attention upon community resources, especially in nature study, and brought to their attention the best in children's literature of the ages. Health and social living were emphasized.

Enthusiasm, unstinted labor, and selfless devotion characterized all of Miss Spier's work for the college Her extra-curricular activities on campus reflected her sincere interest in the students. For many years she was faculty adviser to transfer students, a position for which her kindness and understanding made her eminently fitted. Deeply interested in student welfare she gave to many her counsel, encouragement, and even financial aid, setting up, with her sister, Mrs. Hattie S. Weinberg, a student loan fund. Students of her own religious faith found in her a wise friend and mentor. Her majors remember her helpful conferences, punctuated with laughter, over a cup of tea in her office. In her home she dispensed gracious hospitality especially to faculty and students away from home at Christmas and Easter.

One of Miss Spier's major interests was the Alumnae Association of which she was secretary 1912-1914, visiting alumnae groups all over the State in the interest of the McIver Loan Fund. No alumnae meeting on the campus was complete without her.

Miss Spier's education was a continuous process throughout her career. She was in frequent attendance at numerous educational conventions and conferences. She was an early member of the Progressive Education Association, and a devoted supporter of the Association for

Childhood Education, being a charter member and leader of the Greensboro group. On the national level her chief contributions were to Rural Education and College Teachers of Education.

Miss Spier possessed a broad social outlook, contributing time and valuable counsel in matters embracing not only local but national and world problems, especially inter-racial questions and world peace. She worked through many civic and religious organizations, including the League of Women Voters, American Association of University Women, the Inter-Faith Council, and the Council of Jewish Women. She was a founder of Temple Emanuel, a member of its board of directors, and was a potent force in its spiritual and educational activities.

Honors and honorable positions were Miss Spier's in her life time. In 1920, when the faculty of the Woman's College was reorganized, Miss Spier was one of a small number to be raised to full professorship.

In 1936, she was elected a charter member of Alpha Chapter of Delta Kappa Gamma, and at the time of her death was serving as its first president. She had recently been elected vice-president of the Northwestern District of the North Carolina Education Association.

Upon her death on October 29, 1938, in accordance with her wishes, friends, instead of sending flowers, contributed to a student loan fund.

On November 22, 1938, a memorial service was held for Miss Spier in the college auditorium, to which the members of the class of 1895 received special invitations from the college. Tributes were paid her by her Dean of Administration, her Rabbi, and a friend and co-worker of many years.

Two tributes summarize her life of service. A student group wrote: "The services of Miss Spier to the college and to all who knew her were so long, so varied, so effective, and so valuable that she earned our respect, and won our admiration."

A colleague paid this tribute: "Throughout the years Miss Spier had evolved a satisfying philosophy of life built upon ethical principles involving perspective, love, and tolerance. Her favorite admonition was, 'Don't waste time on trivialities'; her most frequently used word, 'share.'"

BESSIE STEEDMAN
1880-1941

BESSIE Steedman is listed among the women who have served as school principals in western North Carolina. A search for health brought her from her native state of South Carolina to the mountains of North Carolina. Miss Steedman's father, James B.

Steedman, a cotton broker, was living in Charleston, South Carolina, at the time of Bessie's birth. But, soon after, he moved to Camden where she spent her childhood.

Miss Steedman's education began with a private tutor, then continued in the public schools of Camden and Valley Seminary in Virginia. During her early childhood and until she reached womanhood, she was the victim of asthma. However, this affliction was finally overcome.

In 1902, Miss Steedman began her career as a teacher in the Hendersonville High School. A few years later, she was elected to a position in the Asheville High School. Then, because of the illness of Mrs. McDowell, the aunt with whom she had lived when in Hendersonville, she gave up her work in Asheville, returned to Hendersonville and resumed her position in the high school. In 1920, she was elected principal of the East Flat Rock School in Henderson County. She thus served until her death, January 19, 1941, at the age of sixty-one years. During these years the school grew from one of small enrolment, housed in an old wooden building, to an accredited school with sixteen teachers, established in a modern brick building.

While engaged in the development of this school, Miss Steedman found time to give to extra-curricular activities. Coaching dramatics was one of her specialities. Many of her pupils who have since gained prominence as attorneys, legislators, and ministers of the Gospel began public speaking under "Miss Bessie's" tutelage.

Miss Steedman served as president of the Western District of the North Carolina Education Association during the term of 1927-28.

Her love for poetry was testified to by the collection of works of poetry found in her library. Nature study, also, was close to her heart. She once told a class that she could not bear to see a flower crushed or carelessly thrown aside to die. "Everything has a purpose in this world and should be permitted to serve that purpose," she said.

FLORENCE STEPHENSON
1857-1930

IN ALL periods of history and in all places there have been forceful personalities not known to the world at large yet who have impressed those near them that their influence persists with undiminished strength long after they themselves have left the earth. Such a personality was Florence Stephenson.

In the year 1887, she came to Asheville, North Carolina, as a quiet, unassuming young woman, to become principal of a boarding school just started under the auspices of the Presbyterian Board of Missions for the education of girls from the Southern Mountain area. She remained in that position for thirty-one years. When she laid down the responsibility for younger hands to carry on, she was made principal emeritus of the school.

Miss Stephenson's name betokens her Scotch ancestry. She was a descendant of Scotch pioneers who came to Pennsylvania in the early days and built their cabins in the mountains. She was born in Butler, Pennsylvania, in 1867, the daughter of a Presbyterian elder.

In childhood, she was taught by her father to consecrate her talents; and, when she had finished her college preparatory course at Witherspoon Institute, she realized that her teaching ability was a gift to be consecrated. Therefore she entered the State Normal School, Indiana, Pennsylvania, for professional training. Here she granduated as valedictorian of her class in 1882. Certain members of the State Board of Examiners asked the principal, Miss Leonard, as to whether a young woman who looked so frail could ever teach throughout the two years necessary to obtain a permanent certificate. Miss Leonard's reply was prompt and emphatic: "Miss Stephenson is the pine knot of the class." Forty years of subsequent service proved this estimate to be correct.

Her first four years after graduation were spent as assistant principal of a public school in Pittsburg. At the end of that period, Miss Stephenson decided to enter home mission work as a teacher. She would not go, however, without special training therefore a year was spent in the New York City Mission Training School. This was at that time under the care of Mrs. R. A. Brown, a woman of remarkable gifts. Among these was the power of imparting what she had learned by experience of the then little known science of Social Service. Miss Stephenson was an apt scholar and learned from this course much that fitted her for her future work. It was from this mission school that she was called to the principalship of the Asheville Home School.

One of her first pupils, a girl of fourteen, who delighted in Miss Stephenson's neatness and the appropriateness of her dress on every occasion writes:

"I can see her now as I saw her first—black hair carefully ararnged in a coil on top of her head, with skillfully curled "bangs" in front, an immaculate white apron over her dark blue dress which fitted without a flaw and was trimmed with rich blue velvet."

From the first day, her influence molded the school. She made of the Home Industrial School a place where individuality was not all ironed out and where one could indeed feel at home. To achieve this and still keep order and routine so essential in an institution was no small triumph.

From the beginning, Miss Stephenson won respect and regard throughout the city of Asheville. Upon her arrival, this was yet a small place. The enterprises for social welfare were either non existant or in their infancy. Cordially welcomed as a helper by the women of the city, she gladly gave to them the benefit of her experience and her practical wisdom.

In her buggy, driving "Old Jerry," over the mile and a half between the school and town or on errands into the country, she soon became a familiar sight and a most welcome one.

In 1892, under the auspices of the Home Mission Board of the Presbyterian Church of the United States of America, Dr. Thomas Lawrence established the Normal School on the campus already occupied by the Home Industrial School. Miss Stephenson was vitally interested in the new teacher training project and gave it her loyal support. She was instrumental in interesting the Board in establishing the Pease Memorial House in 1908. This was used by the girls below the age of twelve and provided a practice school for the Normal seniors.

For a number of years, Miss Stephenson was the Sunday School teacher of the senior classes of the Normal. The writer, a member of that class, recalls vividly how the teacher challenged the girls to think and how she used practical ilustrations to clarify the meaning of the material studied.

In 1923 the original building occupied by the Home Industrial School was torn down and replaced by a modern brick structure. The new building was given the name Florence Stephenson Hall. Miss Stephenson made the address at the dedication of this new building.

Soon after reaching the age of sixty years, Miss Stephenson resigned the charge of the Home Industrial School. At this time the Board made her principal emeritus and comissioned her to teach Social Hygiene in their boarding schools where girls were being educated. She was to stay about two months at a school.. She worked in this capacity for three years traveling widely over the United States, Alaska, and Hawaii. In September, 1922, she was called to the principalship of New Jersey Academy at Logan, Utah, where she remained for three years.

Three years later, Miss Stephenson retired and went to live with her sister in Pennsylvania. Here she passed away on February 19, 1930.

HESTER COX STRUTHERS
1872-1941

To GIVE and not count the cost; to labour and not ask for any reward save that of knowing she had taught youth to be strong and show itself a man—" so spoke the Student Body of New Hanover High School in 1942 when they placed a bronze plaque in the hall of New Hanover High School, their tribute to Miss Hester Cox Struthers, beloved teacher and friend. This testimony of the third generation of her students in New Hanover County confirms the fact that her life was devoted to the developing of mental and physical powers, to the teaching of moral and spiritual truths, and to the molding of boys and girls into responsible citizens.

Born in Bridgeport, New Jersey, on July 10, 1872, Hester Cox Struthers moved to Columbus County in North Carolina with her parents, William Struthers and Hester Giverson Cox Struthers, when she was eight years old. Her education, begun in Brigeport, was continued under private tutelage until she entered the Wilmington schools. Graduating from Miss Amy Bradley's school in Wilmington, she entered the State Normal and Industrial School in Greensboro. The Normal did not confer degrees then, but she later received her A. B. degree from the University of North Carolina. She did graduate work in summer sessions at Harvard and Columbia Universities. Although she traveled in Europe and the States, she often said her real vacations were those summers between 1915 and 1938 when she went to Chapel Hill to study at the University. She completed sufficient courses in mathematics and English to receive a master's degree, having taken nearly every course the University offered in these two curriculums.

Her summers at the University were not entirely devoted to study, for she taught in the practice school there. And as hostess in one of the dormitories, she made an enviable record.

Miss Hettie's long, varied professional career began in a country school near Holly Ridge in 1891. The following fall she came to New Hanover County, but she stayed less than a decade before returning to Columbus County. There she served as teacher and as principal of the Cerro Gordo School and as rural supervisor, one of the first in the country. Driving her horse from place to place, she encouraged young and old alike to attend the Moonlight School, organized for adult education, in which she taught. During the fourteen years she was in Columbus County she made valuable contributions to the summer institutes held for teachers in that area who were unable to go to college.

Returning to New Hanover County in 1915, Miss Hettie resumed her former place in the teaching personnel of the county. For the next twenty-six years she set such an example of integrity of character and of devotion to her profession that her fellow-teachers paid sincere and honest tribute to her after her death in November, 1941, in the resolutions adopted by the New Hanover Unit of the North Carolina Education Association:

For her ability as a teacher;
For her interest in the accomplishment of her students;
For her leadership in educational work;
For her examples of Christian womanhood;
We thank God.

Every movement for the promotion of sound educational principles

Miss Hettie enthusiastically supported. The local Parent Teacher Association recognized its indebtedness to Miss Struthers for her help in its organization and growth by presenting her with a life membership. Her superintendent, Mr. H. M. Roland, and her principal, Mr. T. T. Hamilton, Jr., regarded her as a great teacher, one of God's noblewomen. Her counsel was sought by the students, the teachers, and the administrative personnel.

Miss Hettie's first thought was teaching, but she gave valuable service to civic, religous, and professional organizations. For thirty-five years a member of the North Carolina Sorosis, she added "to the dignity and loftiness of its purposes, ideals, and activities." An ardent member of the Baptist church, she served it with loyalty and devotion as a member and a leader. She was active in the affairs of the North Carolina Education Association both local and state, and in the Classroom Teacher Association. In 1938 she was elected to the membership of Eta State of The Delta Kappa Gamma Society and in 1939 assisted in forming Theta Chapter in New Hanover and Columbus Counties. Theta Chapter made steady progress during those years 1939-1941 as Miss Hettie guided and nurtured the young organization. It has been the rich heritage which she left to Theta that has stimulated succeeding presiding officers to direct the chapter. Grateful for her guidance, Theta Chapter added its tribute to its beloved first president: "...Theta will honor her by cherishing and upholding those ideals of genuine Christian living which Miss Hester Cox Struthers, the teacher, exemplified in her civic, professional, and religious life."

ALICE GASKINS THURSTON
1846-1910

ALICE Gaskings Thurston and her husband, the Reverend Thomas G. Thurston, were pioneers in the early educational development of Hickory and its vicinity. Both were natives of the state of New York.

Alice Gaskings was born in Rhinebeck, New York, on June 7, 1846. She received her early education in the public schools of her native state, then later graduated from the New York State Normal. In 1870 she went to California where she remained for four years. When she returned to New York, she married Thomas G. Thurston, a Presbyterian minister, on May 13, 1875.

Soon after her marriage she came to Taylorsville, North Carolina, with her husband who had accepted a call to the Presbyterian Church in that town. Here they taught for three years in the boys' Academy, Mrs. Thurston serving as primary teacher.

In 1883 they moved to Hickory where Mr. Thurston became pastor of the First Presbyterian Church and head of the Highland Academy for boys. This school later became the present Lenoir Rhyne College. He held this position until his death in 1884. After the death of her husband, Mrs. Thurston organized a private school in her own home, but the next year she went to Claremont Female College to teach.

It was while she was teaching at Claremont in 1896 that the Traveler's Club was organized in North Carolina and she became a member of that group. In the second year of its existence, the Club decided to devote its program to the cause of public education. Mrs. Thurston was instrumental in interesting the leading men of Hickory in the improvement of the schools of their town. Accordingly, an educational rally with a three days' program was planned for the town. On this program appeared the leading educators of the State: Charles B. Aycock, Charles D. McIver, J. Y. Joyner, P. P. Claxton, and other noted men of that period. This rally marked the beginning of a progressive public school system for Hickory.

In 1893 Mrs. Thurston was married to E. M. Stevenson of Taylorsville. She died November 4, 1910, and is buried in Taylorsville.

ANNIE ELIZABETH TILLETT
1887-1920

ANNIE Elizabeth Tillett, who for twelve years was an outstanding teacher in the Durham High School, came from a family of teachers and educators. Her father, James Wyche Tillett, was for a number of years Superintendent of Person County Schools. Her sister, Miss Laura Tillett, was one of the early kindergarten teachers in Rockingham County. And her brother, Dr. Wilbur Fiske Tillett, was for a number of years a member of the faculty of Vanderbilt University and is also the author of several books.

Annie Elizabeth was born in Roxboro, Person County, April 24, 1887, while her father was superintendent of schools. When his health compelled him to resign that office, Mr. Tillett moved to Burlington in order that the children might attend Burlington Academy. There Annie completed the greater part of her elementary schooling. Then, in 1898, the family moved to Durham where she finished high school, graduating in 1903. In the fall of that year, she entered Trinity College, now Duke University. Here she pursued the classic course and in 1907 was graduated *Magna cum Laude* with highest honors in Greek and Latin.

The year after her graduation from college, Miss Tillett taught in Ward Seminary in Nashville and in connection with her teaching began graduate work at Vanderbilt University. At the close of the year, she returned to Durham and taught one year in the Edgemont Grammar School.

The following year she was transferred to the Department of English in the Durham High School and soon became head of the department. It was during this period that she took part in the organization of the English Council of North Carolina. In 1908, she became Dean of Girls in the Durham High School, one of the first women to hold such a position in a North Carolina high school. This work she launched with her usual understanding and sound judgment, and with great success.

Miss Tillett was a loyal member of the Alumnae of Trinity College and worked zealously for its welfare, her efforts being directed particularly toward elevating the status of women in the college. She was one of the two Alumnae who secured from Mr. James H. Southgate, Chairman of the Board of Trustees, the first contribution for a modern dormitory for women at Trinity College. The building is now called Southgate Memorial Hall. She even helped to organize the Alumnae Association and served as one of the early presidents. She worked in the Association the remainder of her life. Finally, the College, recognizing her high scholastic attainments and her professional achievements, elected her an Alumna member of Phi Beta Kappa when a chapter was installed there. However, the letter of notification of her selection for this well-merited honor came at the very time of her death therefore she never learned of it.

In the fall of 1919, her health became so impaired that she could no longer overcome it with her strong will power and personal courage as she had been doing for some time. Therefore, she was forced to accept the leave of absence which an appreciative Superintendent and City School Board urged. She went to Jefferson Hospital, Philadelphia, for treatment. There, when she seemed to be improving, she contracted influenza-pneumonia, and, after a brief ilness, passed away on Januray 30, 1920.

The Messenger, a publication of the Durham High School, in paying tribute to Miss Tillett said:

"These maxims were found jotted down in a little book which Miss Tillett used daily. We are printing them because we think they express her attitude toward life and because we feel they will help us in our daily living.

1. The best way to 'get even' is to forget.
2. The world looks brighter from behind a smile.
3. Remember the kindness of others; forget your own.
4. Flattery is like cologne water—to be smelt of, not swallowed.
5. The only people who really enjoy hearing your troubles are lawyers. They get paid for it.

6. If a man cannot smile, he is built wrong. If he can smile and wont, keep away from him.

7. When you trip up, fall forward and get up farther along.

8. You will never be sorry for thinking before speaking, for forgiving and forgetting, for being generous to the poor and needy, for looking before leaping, for living a square and fair life, for doing your level best—for all these things you will never be sorry.

EULA TODD

1869-

A PIONEER in Delta Kappa Gamma, a pioneer in education, is still living in Jefferson, North Carolina. Although she is retired from teaching, Miss Eula Todd, affectionately known by former students and friends alike as "Miss Billie," possesses a keen mind, a sense of humor almost unequaled, and a wit so clever that wherever she is, preachers, politicians, and people of all classes gather to her side to hear her tell stories that her fertile mind keeps ever ready. Only "Uncle Remus" can compare with her in the telling of Negro floklore, and her imitative style holds her audience spellbound.

"Miss Billie" was a student at Woman's College of the University of North Carolina — then the State Normal — during a fire. She escaped with only a few dresses. Yet she was not distressed as, according to her philosophy, clothes mattered little. Though she was always well dressed, her charm, manner, and brain clothed her so completely that what she wore was of small importance.

Throughout 1909-1923, Miss Todd was principal in one of the schools of Greensboro when the town was small and the schools were few. Here she taught and exemplified the principles of Democracy and gracious living which have guided many a boy and girl to outstanding citizenship. She blazed the trail for many a teacher and pupil. Indeed, she "left her footprints on the sands of time." Her favorite poem is "The Bridge Builder." This is not surprising as she has made the way easier for others to travel.

Then, for twenty-two years, Miss Todd was critic teacher in the Demonstration School of Appalachian State Teachers College at Boone. Here her rich background, her thorough preparation, and her genuine iove for children and understanding of their needs made her a teacher never to be forgotten. The fortunate student-teachers under her supervision received an inspiration from her ideals which they later carried into their own class rooms. They felt that they had a "Mark Hopkins" as a teacher. When some one commented to a certain young physician

188

concerning his excellent educational foundation, he replied: "You would have been educated, too, if you had had Miss Billie Todd for a teacher." And a young college girl said: "I never could have passed this English course if I had not studied grammar in Miss Billie Todd's seventh grade."

Miss Todd's cheerful attitude and her wonderful humor are constantly evident. Her faith stands forth in a remark she made to the doctors who were about to operate upon her for a serious ailment. One of these said, "Don't be afraid." To this she replied: "Of course, I won't; with you doctors, I feel as if I were in God's lap."

Her father was Jo Todd, a widely known lawyer and a Captain in the Southern Confederacy. Perhaps she inherited some of his brilliant wit and logical thinking. However, much of her success has been achieved because of her practical integrity, her philosophy of life, and her high ideals.

LINDA RUMPLE VARDELL
1864-1948

L INDA Rumple Vardell was one of North Carolina's leading cultivators in the field of music. She broke the ground, tilled the soil, and sent forth others to do likewise.

Her training began far back as she came of sturdy, intelligent stock. Her parents were the Reverend Jethro Rumple, D. D., and Elizabeth Wharton Rumple of Salisbury. In this home of refinement and intellectuality, her early years were imbued with the strength, piety, knowledge, and fervor that go into the making of a great character.

Linda was graduated from Peace College when she was in her late teens. So talented was she that upon graduation she was asked to remain as an assistant professor of music. Here she taught for two years, and then she entered the New England Conservatory. After her graduation, she served for a while as director of the Statesville College Music Department. Following this, she went back to Boston for further study and substitute teaching. Upon her return to North Carolina, she organized the Salisbury Institute of Music.

In 1891 Linda Rumple was married to Charles Graves Vardell, then pastor of the Newberg Presbyterian Church. In 1896 they went to Red Springs, Dr. Vardell as the first president of Flora MacDonald College and Mrs. Vardell as dean of the music department.

Even as a young woman, Linda Rumple was considered one of the most outstanding musicians of the State. This honor, however, did not once cause her to become vain nor to stop growing. When she went to Flora Macdonald, she determined to make the music department the equal of the best conservatories in the country. As a result, the Music School of Flora Macdonald College is one of the best known throughout the South.

She resigned her post to another only when, in 1926, she was no longer physically able to carry the load. Even after her resignation, she served as the chief consultant of the department.

Not only was Mrs. Vardell a brilliant musician, an expert teacher, and an unparalleled organizer, she was a homemaker as well. To her and Dr. Vardell were born six children, one son and five daughters, all of whom are living. The son, Dr. Charles Graves Vardell, is at present Dean of Music at Salem College in Winston-Salem, North Carolina.

Mrs. Vardell died March 7, 1948. She left an ever-living, ever-expanding musical and otherwise great inheritance not to be measured.

CORINNA BRUCH WARREN
1856-1942

BEHIND the fact that Mrs. Corinna Burch Warren, or "Miss Betty Warren" as she was lovingly called, taught primary subjects for a half century lies a colorful and interesting story. Since this has been so beautifully told in the March, 1951 issue of *North Carolina Education,* by her son, Jule B. Warren who for more than twenty-five years served as Executive Secretary of the North Carolina Education Association, it is here reproduced in its entirety:

WITH HER SHOES ON
By Jule B. Warren

She wanted to be buried with her shoes on—this veteran of fifty years of teaching experience in North Carolina classrooms.

It was not out of character with her life and teaching career that Corinna Burch Warren (Mrs. C. C.) wanted to wear shoes on her final journey into eternity. Her life was one of boundless and varied activity—not slippered ease. To meet the exacting demands of tireless energy, which scorned reliance on others; to keep interested in helping thousands of elementary children learn and understand the fundamentals of arithmetic, in which she specialized; to match mental alertness with physical fitness, this veteran of fifty years teaching had to keep her shoes on.

And, so will any other good teacher.

Though there can be no higher tribute, I think it is not a violation of good taste for her son to say that Corinna Burch Warren was a good teacher. My own evaluation, both as one of her pupils and as an observer of hundreds of other teachers, is supported by the mature judgment of men and women whom she taught as children—three generations of them. Before she left the classroom, her first pupils had grandchildren in her school.

A fusing of courage, will-power, realism, honesty, and mental alertness produced an undefinable character trait which prompted the request that she be buried with her shoes on, which made her a good teacher. It kept her on the job when the annual salary was not as much as a teacher gets now in one month. It enabled her to teach all day, run a household in off hours, educate a family, and acquire and maintain a home on an income that would not buy today's non-essential trifles.

These things she did by keeping her shoes on, literally as well as figuratively. It enabled her to do the impossible. It changed a scrawly, hen-scratchy handwriting into almost perfect penmanship. It enabled this five foot, one hundred pound woman to thrash a 200 pound impudent bully when she was the only teacher in a one room school. It kept her everlastingly at the task of correcting papers at night, devising projects to stimulate children's interests, supervising her own children's study, prodding them into doing household chores, and providing a home for the family 61 years after her husband's death.

Corinna Burch Warren was not an educator.

She was just a teacher.

She could string no alphabetical appendages after her name. This worried her, at times, but she made up for this lack of formal accreditment from colleges and universities by keeping her shoes on and wading into the fight against ignorance. Neither was she an educational philosopher. Her only pedagogical theory was that there was no easy road to learning. Thus she believed that work—hard work by both pupil and teacher—was the only way. She spent a lifetime teaching children the basic tool subjects they must master to become educated.

For fifty years she did the commonplace things that all good teachers do in elementary schools, little jobs unmentioned in method courses. Most of them were spent in one community, the northern section of the city of Durham. She taught country schools before the city's corporate limits were extended and her schools became a part of the city system. She was one of the corps of teachers who worked with Dr. Henry Highsmith when he bgan his teaching experience as principal of the newly erected North Durham School. She remained in this school until her eightieth year. She retired about ten years before she was buried with her shoes on.

Corinna Burch Warren died with her shoes on. The last act of a long life was the preparation of her noon meal on December 17, 1950. Before she ate she lay down on a couch and slipped into eternity to join her children's father who had died nearly 61 years before.

I am thankful that my mother wanted to be buried with her shoes on. I am thankful that she wanted her final resting place on this earth to be the family burying ground, among the rolling hills of Caswell County, on the very land to which her father had carried his bride nearly a hundred years ago. In a time when too many consider marriage a transitory arrangement, I am comforted that she wanted to be buried at the side of a husband, whose memory was as fresh in her ninety-year-old mind as it was when he died in 1889.

And I am happy over one other final request. She wanted to be buried in the light blue—perhaps it was sky blue—dress, which North Durham teachers, her former colleagues, had given her a few Christmasses before she died, a token of appreciation for a long life of service.

My prayer is that her children, her grandchildren, her great-grandchildren, the thousands of boys and girls she taught, and all teachers everywhere, may somehow be imbued with the spirit that made Corinna Burch Warren meet life's challenging problems with her shoes on. I believe they will be so imbued.

MARTHA BURTON WATKINS
1858-1930

MARTHA Burton Watkins did most of her teaching in colleges and twenty years of her work was done in Flora Macdonald College.

She came from a long line of ancestors who were engaged in educational activities. It was in the home of her great-great-grandfather Nathaniel Venable that Hampden-Sydney College was born. Another great-grandfather Francis Watkins was on its first Board of Visitors. Since that time her grandfather, father, and brother have been members of the Board at Hampden-Sydney College. Her grandfather Henry E. Watkins was appointed by the legislature on the committee headed by Thomas Jefferson to select the site for the University of Virginia. Her father, Judge Frank Nat Watkins, was a member of the Board of Visitors of Hampden-Sydney Collge, Hampden Institute for Negroes, and was on the first Board of Visitors for State Teachers College for Women at Farmville, Virginia. He was also for many years treasurer for the Union Theological Seminary at Hampden-Sydney.

It can readily be understood why "Miss Patty" was inherently interested in education and why she dedicated her life to it.

"Miss Patty" was born November 3, 1858, at "Ingleside," Prince Edward County, Virginia, the home of her father, Judge Frank Nat Watkins, and his wife, Martha Ann Scott Watkins. Patty was the tenth child of a family of twelve children.

Her early education was received in the home under her older sisters, then in 1881 she entered Wellesley College.

In 1885, she began her teaching career at Stuart Hall in Staunton, Virginia, where she remained until 1891. Here she was head of the departments of English and History. From 1891 to 1897, she was head of the Mathematics Department of Agnes Scott College in Decatur, Georgia. Because of her mother's ill health she returned to Farmville, Virginia, in 1897.

Through helping her father in home mission work among Negroes when she was young, Patty acquired an interest in the education of Negroes. Therefore while teaching at Farmville, aided by friends, she organized and carried on a Sunday School for Negro children and on Saturday she taught young Negro girls cooking and sewing.

After her mother's death, Patty did Social Service work in Richmond, Virginia, for a few years. Then, in the fall of 1904, she went to Flora Macdonald College, Red Springs, North Carolina, as head of the Mathematics Department. She was made Dean of the Faculty in 1911 and continued herein until her retirement in 1925.

At Flora Macdonald, as in all other places where she had taught, "Miss Patty" had her Sunday School class. Her pupils still remember the forcefulness with which she explained and fastened certain truths of the Bible in their young minds. After teaching this class in the morning, she would then go to the Colored Church in the afternoon and teach again. Her influence cannot be measured, and the whole community felt keenly the loss of her presence when after twenty-one years of teaching she retired.

The last few years of her life were spent in quiet and peace with a brother and his family in her old home town, Farmville, Virginia. Here "Miss Patty" passed away on January 29, 1930.

ELIZABETH McIVER WEATHERSPOON
1870-1939

MRS. Elizabeth McIver Weatherspoon, a pioneer in Art education in North Carolina and the South, had no need of her brother's prestige and fame to make a place for herself on the campus of the North Carolina State Normal and Industrial School, which Charles Duncan McIver founded. In her thirty-three years of splendid service to the college, to the State, and to art education in general, her dignity, her integrity, her loyalty to her family and friends, her generosity, her kindness and sweetness of nature were as marked as her devotion to beauty in all its forms.

Elizabeth McIver, daughter of Henry and Sarah Harrington McIver, was born November 24, 1870, at Sanford, North Carolina, of a long line of sturdy Scotch ancestry. After receiving her early education at a private school taught by a relative for the neighborhood children, she attended Peace Institute, Raleigh, for the years 1888-1890 and studied at the State Normal and Industrial School in Greensboro 1892-1893.

The following years she taught in the primary grades of the Greensboro city schools, until her marriage on June 12, 1900, to James R. Weatherspoon of Sanford. Upon the death of her husband in 1906, she became a member of the faculty of the Practice and Demonstration School of the State Normal and Industrial College, where for three years she supervised the first grade.

From earliest childhood Mrs. Weatherspoon had shown talent and interest in Art. Realizing a long cherished ambition, she was in 1909-1910 granted a leave of absence to study Art under Professor Arthur Dow at Columbia University.

Returning to the college in the fall of 1910, Mrs. Weatherspoon became Supervisor of Art in the Demonstration and Practice School and taught classes in Art education for elementary school teachers, both in the regular year and in summer sessions, for the remainder of her life.

Ever a dreamer of dreams where the college and the study of Art were concerned, she realized her longest and dearest dream when in 1935 the college established a Department of Art. She proudly accepted an associate professorship in the new department and loyally supported the young and talented artist, Gregory Ivy, who became its head.

In her professional life Mrs. Weatherspoon was indeed a pioneer. She was a charter member and first president of the Division of Art in the North Carolina Education Association. She was also a charter member and an enthusiastic worker in the Southeastern Arts Association and frequenty contributed to its programs. She held membership in the American Federation of Arts, and was a member of the Reviewers Club, the oldest study club in Greensboro.

For a generation Mrs. Weatherspoon was an important figure in the educational, social, and civic life of the State. In consideration of her many fine contributions, she was in 1936 elected a charter member of North Carolina's Alpha Chapter of Delta Kappa Gamma.

Mrs. Weatherspoon was a person of rare taste and great artistic skill. There was beauty and perfection of detail in everything she touched, from the tiny child's cap to be worn in the pageant to the gracious setting of her own hospitable table, and the works of art produced by her students.

Mrs. Weatherspoon and her students were friends. They enjoyed the hospitality of her home and her delightful cuisine; for she was an excellent cook.   (And, of course, Nannie, old Johnson's wife, was there to help.)

Faculty members coveted her friendship.   "She never gossiped," said one friend.   "She could write the kindest, most beautiful little notes," said another.   "She was a tower of strength when you were in trouble," said a third.

Mrs. Weatherspoon was indeed a "woman nobly planned." She possessed a keen intellect and a ready wit. Her name became synonymous with determination, strength of character, high personal and professional integrity.   Buffeted by the storms of life, she always stood four-square to the world. Courage dominated her life. She was a great soldier.

Her devotion to family and personal friends was exceptional. A loved one could do no wrong, or, if he did, her love made him whole again.

When Mrs. Weatherspoon died on May 25, 1939, the taxi driver who had driven her to school many years, said: "She was a fine lady. I'll miss her."

No more fitting memorial to Elizabeth McIver Weatherspoon could have been chosen than the establishment, after her death, of the Weatherspoon Art Gallery at the Woman's College.

Her best tribute is in the words of her colleagues: "Because Mrs. Weatherspoon lived among us, it will be easier at the college to stand for genuineness as opposed to sham; and for accurate as opposed to slip-shod work; to cultivate the beautiful as opposed to the crude; to further what is generous and highminded as opposed to what is petty and cheap. We believe she would ask no higher memorial."

ANNIE W. WILEY
1870-1947

THE splendid characteristics—high idealism, courage, and steadfastness in carrying on in the face of seemingly insurmountable difficulties—of Calvin H. Wiley, first Superintendent of Schools of North Carolina and sometimes called the Horace Mann of the South, were inspirational factors in the career of his daughter, Annie W. Wiley, whose work appeared in four separate fields of educational endeavor of a foundational nature. These fields were as follows: as grammar grade teacher at West End School during the formative beginning years of the Winston public schools; as supervising teacher in the Training School (Curry) of the State Normal College (the Womans College of the University of North Carolina) at Greensboro; as grammar grade sup-

195

ervisor in the city schools of her home town; and as organizer and first principal of Central Park School, also in Winston-Salem.

The fruitful years of her teaching have a parallel in the words of Daniel Webster: "If we work upon marble, it will perish . . . if we work upon immortal minds, we engrave on those tablets something which will brighten to all eternity." This task of engraving upon the tablets of human personality lofty ideals seems to have been the high purpose of Annie Wiley's teaching years. "Even the *faces* of the children change after she has taught them," her superintendent, John J. Blair, said of her work.

This ability to bring out the best in a pupil, to get response even from the dullest or the seemingly unteachable boy or girl was characteristic of her teaching throughout the years. And another rare gift she possessed was that of winning the lasting love and loyalty of those she taught. This holding quality upon the thought and love of her pupils was strikingly shown one Sunday afternoon when a stranger called upon her. He was a physician of note from South Africa, a scientist with degrees from two continents. Yet in all the years he had been absent from Winston-Salem, the memory of his fourth grade teacher lingered in his heart and he had sought her out upon his first visit back to his old home.

At the age of seventeen, on the death of her father, Annie Wiley left her studies at Statesville College (Mitchell) and began her life work as a teacher. Through private study and reading of professional journals and books, through attendance upon lecture courses and institutes, and through association with people of culture, she fed her thirst for self improvement and kept abreast with educational thought and practice.

Inspirational in her teaching, yet thorough and holding her pupils to a high sense of personal conduct, she early gained a reputation in her home town. A quotation from an article in *The Twin City Daily Sentinel* in regard to the severing of her relations with the city schools shows the esteem in which she was held:

"This offer (to become practice teacher in the State Normal College comes to Miss Wiley unsought by her and is a great compliment. She is without doubt one of the best teachers in North Carolina . . . While we regret exceedingly to see her leave Winston, yet we rejoice that promotion has come to one so richly deserving it. Such offers do not come to teachers every day, and Miss Wiley has done such faithful service for the schools in this city that everybody will be pleased at her promotion."

Geography was the subject she especially delighted to teach, and so well known did she become as a teacher of this subject that other teachers often visited her classroom to observe her work. Dr. Edwin A. Alderman, afterwards President of the University of North Carolina,

196

spoke highly of her teaching of Geography as he had observed it, and Dr. Charles D. McIver, founder of the State Normal College for Women (Womans College of the University of North Carolina) made Miss Wiley a flattering offer to inaugurate a course in the teaching of Geography in his institution and at the same time she could work toward her college diploma.

A high sense of responsibility for her family prevented her accepting Dr. McIver's offer, but when some years later he came with another offer, that of being practice teacher in the newly established training school of the College (now Curry Training School) she reluctantly resigned her position in her home town and undertook the work, new in the State, of preparing college seniors through observation of her teaching and practice teaching under her direction to become better grammar grade teachers.

Of this phase of her work, one of the college seniors whom she thus trained, Jane Summerell, now of the English Department, Womans College, University of North Carolina, writes:

"Teaching is like playing an instrument," Miss Wiley said to her group of fledgling student teachers. "You must know what notes to touch." We did not know the notes, and Miss Wiley did. Gradually, however, we began to discover something of how she made the harmony.

"Miss Wiley had the ability to enter imaginatively into the mind of each pupil. She knew the purposes, the inner workings of every boy and girl in the room . . . She knew the problems in the homes . . . the puzzled religious strivings of youth. Al these things she treasured in her heart and used—instinctively, I think—for achieving an intelligent mastery of the matter in hand. So there appeared in that youthful group a certain dignity, maturity, integrity, and independence that augured well for the achievement of the full grown citizens.

"Miss Wiley was as thorough in her discipline as she was in her instruction. There really was not very much discipline as such. But she would not overlook slovenliness and disorder of any sort."

The third phase of Miss Wiley's life work, that of supervising the grammar grades of Winston-Salem City Schools, was under conditions requiring tact, sympathetic understanding of teacher and pupils, patience and courage and poise. Here she did a notable work in coordinating the work of the various grades and teachers, in establishing standards, in working out courses of study, in improving methods of classroom procedure, and in inspiring teachers-in-service to greater effort in self-improvement.

When staid old Salem and bustling Winston were united as one municipality and the first city school—Central Grade—was opened in Salem, Miss Wiley was elected principal. Again her work was foundational: the pupils of Central—from various private schools, unaccustomed to the ways of tax-supported schools—had to be classified, mold-

197

ed into composite groups working in harmony, and inspired with school loyalty and unity. During this time, Superintendent R. H. Latham of the City Schools said of her work:

"It was once said of a valued teacher that she made ladies of girls and gentlemen of boys. No finer tribute could be paid to any teacher and this can truthfully be said of Miss Wiley . . . In her work she was conscientious to the Nth degree, being willing always to go the last mile to see that the job was properly done . . . Her influence was always thrown on the side of right, both in her contact with teachers who served under her and with the pupils in her school.

"When after twenty-three years as Principal she gave up her active duties, her Central teachers paid her this beautiful tribute:

"We feel that the growth of Central School is due to her thorough understanding of elementary school work and her untiring efforts.

"Those of us who have worked beside her each day know the valuable guidance and influence she exerted in her unassuming way.

"Her Christ-like life and teaching of the Word has influenced all who have come in contact with her. Living as she has taught others, the under-privileged children as well as the more fortunate found her their comrade and good friend.

"Miss Wiley embodies the highest ideals of educational effort and Christian aspiration."

At her retirement the student body of Central School, in loving appreciation of her services, had her portrait made, and this was placed in the main hall of the school.

While in Greensboro, she was a member of the Presbyterian Church of the Covenant. The Reverend Murphy Williams, her pastor, writes thus of her work and influence in Greensboro:

"Devotion marked her every act as a teacher in Curry School and as a member of the Church of the Covenant. At the time she came, ours was a weak church, struggling to make its way. No member we ever had was more of an inspiration and showed more interest. Every one who knew her loved her, and her influence will live far beyond the lifetime of those she instructed because it will be transmitted to others of another generation. So her influence will live on and on in this way."

Miss Wiley passed away at her home in Winston-Salem in 1947.

MARY CALLUM WILEY
Retired

ALTHOUGH most of her life has been spent in North Carolina, Mary Callum Wiley, affectionately known to Winston-Salem as "Miss Mary," is by no means provincial, for she has traveled much in the "realms of gold," not only through literature, but through the minds and hearts of thousands of students with whom she came in closest contact through approximately fifty years of public school teaching.

Born in Winston-Salem, the daughter of Calvin H. and Mittie Towles Wiley, she was graduated from the city schools and from the State Normal (now Woman's College), to which she later returned at the personal invitation of President McIver and became a member of that college's first class to receive degrees. All of her teaching career, except for two years, has been devoted to her native town, where, in 1910, she became head of the English Department of the city high school.

To her influence and to her ability to impart knowledge come constant tributes from ex-pupils and from fellow-teachers. Such words as these from a college professor of English speak for themselves: "This is a letter which for years I have intended to write. Though you do not know me at all, I want to tell you how much I have come to admire your work. During my twenty-five years at————————— College, it has been a joy to teach the students you have prepared. From no other one teacher do I have year in and year out students whose preparation is so consistently excellent. You have set an example I hope to follow all through my years of teaching." Those who have been in her unforgettable classes, those who have taught with her through the years and who have respected and loved her know that her individuality is based on fundamental consistency, on a firmness of character that does not shift with each fad or turn of thought.

When, upon her retirement, the seniors presented Reynolds High School with a portrait of Miss Mary, the Reverend Gordon Spaugh, representing her former pupils, thus voiced the thought of the large audience gathered to pay her homage: "Our hearts' appreciation of loving service freely given makes us want to honor one who has honored us throughout the years with her presence, her faithfulness, her loyalty, and her gifts." And her principal, Mr. C. R. Joyner, stated: "I have learned from her that the highest degree of strength of character can bring joy to everyone."

Versatile in other fields beside teaching, "Miss Mary" has spoken before clubs of various kinds; she has taken an active part in the work of her church, the First Presbyterian, for a number of years serving as superintendent of the Beginners' Department of the Sunday School;

199

at the request of the session, she wrote the history of the first seventy-five years of the church.

Throughout the years she has contributed widely to historical, and religious periodicals. For some years she edited the woman's page of the *Christian Observer* of Louisville, Kentucky While teaching *Hill's History of North Carolina*, she prepared a Manual for the use of instructors; she also revised her father's *North Carolina Reader*. For the centennial celebration of Forsyth County, she served as co-author of*Forsyth on the March.*

She is an honorary member of Delta Kappa Gamma, to which she was also eligible for active membership; upon retirement, she was awarded a life membership in the N. C. Parent-Teacher Association. She is a member of the N. C. State Literary and Historical Assocviation, the Wachovia Historical Society, and the N. C. Society of Colonial Dames of America.

The Greensboro Daily selected her as the subject of one of its *Tar Heel Biographies,* quoting selections from the dedication in the Reynolds High School Annual: "Her home room the joy of every senior's heart . . . classes never have a dull moment . . . known for classroom dramatizations."

When conferring upon her the honorary degree of Doctor of Education from the University of North Carolina, Dr. Frank Graham said: "By reason of strength and of personality and the art of devoted teaching, she brought to the open mind and spirit of youth the fellowship of the greatest minds and spirits of all ages and all nations in an age in need of the perspective of time and the valuations of the spirit . . . It is inspiring to this college to honor her for her own most worthy self and as a living link of present North Carolina with the heroic age and service of her great father, Calvin H. Wiley, son of this University."

But, although she is now Dr. Wiley, it is as "Miss Mary" that she lives in the hearts of hosts of students and that she will continue to live for many generations to come; for, to use one of her favorite maxims, it was by "line upon line, precept upon precept" that she became a part of the thoughts, the ideals, and the lives of her students.

When she retired from teaching, the editor of a local paper thus expressed the true sentiments of all of Winston-Salem:

"Versatile in her teaching talents, thoroughly grounded in academic knowledge and in those techniques which enable the good teacher to impart her knowledge to students in the most effective manner, Miss Wiley added to these invaluable assets an inspiring personality imbued with high ideals in character and service, and enduring faith in things divine and an abiding love for young people and unflagging interest in their welfare."

BARBARA L. SUMEY WILFONG

1809-1888

M RS. Wilfong is best remembered for her work in the founding of Claremont College.

She was the daughter of George Summey and his wife, Elizabeth Corpening Summey. Her maternal grandfather was Albert Corpening, a French Huguenot who settled in Burke County.

In the "old field" schools of her day, she received her education. She was married in 1826 to John Wilfong, Jr., son of a prominent Lincoln County pioneer. She became the mother of twelve children, ten boys and two girls. Yet despite the care of a large family she never lost interest in the cause of education. She was never too busy nor tired to discuss the subject that was dearest to her heart: "Equal Education for Girls."

Six of her sons fought in the Confederate Army. One of these was killed on a battlefield in Virginia. And this brave mother made a trip to the battlefield, going through the dangerous line to Richmond, to nurse another sick son.

For a number of years Mrs. Wilfong lived in Newton. Here her home was "second home" to the boys of Catawba College.

Then after the family moved to Hickory, a group of friends met at her home on August 8, 1880, and at this meeting the foundation was made for the organizing of Claremont Female College. The first classes of this institution were held in the old Reformed Church on Ninth Avenue.

In 1885, Mrs. Wilfong donated a bell to be placed in the new Claremont Female College. Here it was rung regularly until the school was closed on May 24, 1915. This bell, stored for a number of years, was finally placed in the Claremont High School which was built on the site of the former college.

Mrs. Wilfong died in 1888 and was buried in Newton.

CLEE WINSTEAD

1875-

" T O LEARN, to teach, to serve, and to enjoy" well expresses the aim of life as exemplified by Miss Clee Winstead. Also, she once wrote in a letter: "To be entrusted with another's most precious possession, his child, to teach and guide during the most impressionable period of his physical, mental, and moral life is a compliment which implies the utmost faith and confidence and carries with it a challenge to all that is worthwhile in a teacher." With such a philosophy, Miss Clee never lost sight of the sacredness of her trust as a teacher; and in carrying on this high task she found her own happiness and won for herself love and admiration from those who knew the worth of her endeavors.

Miss Clee was born in Wilson county in 1875, and here she has spent her entire life.

She graduated in 1898 from the State Normal and Industrial College, Greensboro—now the Womans College of the University of North Carolina. As a college student, she was vice-president of the Senior class, a member of the Mandolin and Guitar Club, and an active participant in dramatics and sports. These talents she developed throughout her career; and her versatility together with her originality, keen sense of humor, and quick repartee have made her a popular figure in many circles.

For sixteen years after her graduation, Miss Clee was a primary teacher. In her classroom it was fascinating to see her enter into her work, the games, the dramatics, and the music enjoyed by her little pupils. In spite of her seriousness of purpose, her heart was light and gay. In her classroom there was never a dull momen.t Referring to this living and learning with little children, she says: "In no other way could I have enjoyed real life and known so many phases of it."

For the last twenty years of her career, she was principal of an elementary school which in 1922 was named in her honor, the Winstead School. Here her enthusiasm spread to both teachers and pupils to such an extent that the school was considered outstanding in school spirit and morale. The cooperation given to the teachers and children by the patrons and friends in the community is a matter worthy of note.

Realizing the value of the cooperation of parents in building up a school, Miss Winstead organized the first Parent-Teacher Association in Wilson. This was valuable pioneer work and a cause that has always been close to Miss Clee's heart. Since her retirement in 1935, she has continued to teach the class in Parent-Education and has kept alive the enthusiasm and interest.

In the field of religious education, Miss Clee has rendered valuable service as head of the Children's Department of the Church School and as Chairman of Christian Education in the Wilson Methodist Church. In the Woman's Society for Christian Service, she holds a life membership presented to her by the women of the church.

In civic work, she has served as a member of the County Board of Public Welfare and as president of the Business and Professional Women's Club. She is also an active member of the United Daughters of the Confederacy and has served as Recording Secretary and Chaplain of the local chapter.

After teaching thirty-six years, Miss Clee retired to live with her sister on their farm two miles from Wilson. She still finds time for outside activities; and her love for the schools, her church, and community has not lessened.

RHODA MACY WORTH
1837-1915

RHODA Macy Worth, "Miss Rhoda" to all who knew her, gave a lifetime of service to the children and youth of Greensboro and Guilford College. She was born in 1837, into a Quaker family of English ancestry. Her parents, Hiram and Phobe Worth, were living on a farm near the small village of Greensborough in North Carolina, when Rhoda was born. Their home was a log house, built in 1829. This log house, many years later converted into a frame house, was one of the oldest houses in the village. When the small town spread to and beyond the Worth home, the street was named for her family—Worth Street—and is still—100 years later—Worth Street.

Here Rhoda grew up. And here she made her home throughout most of the seventy-eight years of her life. In preparation for teaching, she attended Greensboro Female College (now Greensboro College) for two years—1850-1852—then later graduated from New Garden Boarding School (now Guilford College).

A log house in Greensboro became her first schoolroom. Here she established a private school where she taught many boys and girls from the leading families of the little town. Once, she left her home school to teach in a school near Kinston, but after two years she returned to Greensboro. The last private school in which she taught was known as the Little Brick School. It was located just around the corner from the lot on which the Church of the Covenant was later built; and the small brick building remained a landmark as "Miss Rhoda's School" for many years.

"Miss Rhoda" was known and loved by everyone in the vicinity of the town of Greensboro. Her happy, vital personality; her sincere interest in people; and her kindness and helpfulness to everyone who needed assistance made her a choice friend and citizen. A familiar sight on the streets of the little town was Miss Rhoda, smiling and nodding to her many friends and especially to the children, as she rode along in her buggy, driving a mule named Peter.

Rhoda Worth was a devoted and faithful Quaker who sought out pupils for a Sunday School which she taught in her home. From this project developed the Friends' Monthly Meeting in Greensboro. In 1886, she was appointed to the Advisory Committee of Guilford College, a committee that gave strong support and guidance to the development of the College, especially during the years that it evolved from being New Garden Boarding School to become Guilford College. This development was completed in 1888, and the legal Act was ratified by the State Legislature in January 1889.

In that same year, 1889, Mary Mendenhall Hobbs, determined to assist worthy girls who did not have enough money to pay their College expenses persuaded the Trustees of the College to try a cottage plan where these girls, by self-help, would earn much of their expenses. Rhoda Worth was asked to take charge of this experiment as Matron of Cottages, and she served in this new and untried situation efficiently and graciously. After several years of the cottage system with results that it did not prove as satisfactory as expected, the College built a large dormitory for girls where some self-help was stil possible through co-operative living. This was named New Garden Hall, and Rhoda Worth was asked to assume charge. She managed the Hall during its first year, then resigned as she felt no longer able to carry the great responsibility.

This concluded Rhoda Worth's contribution to education, but she was now seventy years of age and had taught nearly fifty years.

Rhoda Macy Worth passed away March 22, 1915. Her last years were happy, peaceful years in the old home on Worth Street with the companionship of her brother, William, and the loving devotion of friends.

MRS. BETTIE W. WRIGHT
1843-1921

MRS. Bettie Wright, pioneer teacher and educational leader in eastern North Carolina in the latter part of the nineteenth century, when "school days were few and worth little," filled the gap between the old academy and the standardized public school by opening her home, in the Coharie neighborhood of Sampson County, as a home-boarding school where both sexes were given the same training as her own children and were prepared for college.

"Mrs. Wright's School" was one of the great educational influences in the years 1888-1906 in that section and it was felt throughout the State.

This energetic woman's whole life had been a preparation as she was always a teacher. Sent off to school when she was quite young, she said, "I was told I would have to get all the knowledge I could as I would have to teach my five younger brothers and sisters." The

204

twenty-two years spent in rearing a family of nine did not interrupt the preparation. Determined that her children should not grow up in ignorance because there were no educational facilities at hand, she opened school for them. "My object in teaching," she said, "was to teach my own children for I saw they would never be educated unless I did."

Born November 19, 1843, Bettie Vaden Herring, the fourth of nine children of Bryan Whitfield Herring and Penelope Simms Herring, was reared in a home of culture and hospitality on a big plantation in Duplin County, North Carolina. Frail but eager, she early came under the influence of teachers of high quality and was inspired with zeal for learning. At fourteen, under a schoolmaster, in a class of one, she studied Latin, Mental Arithmetic, and Algebra. At eighteen, she was sent to Edgeworth Female Seminary in Greensboro, a school named for Marie Edgeworth and advertised as "a home for gentle women desiring to do literary work." Here she acquired good habits of scholarship and high standards of work.

After graduation, she fulfilled her obligation to teach the home school. At twenty-three, she married John Cromartie Wright and moved into the home in Sampson County in which she was to spend the remainder of her life. She took with her two of the five brothers and sisters, and they continued their studies.

Undaunted by the confusion and improverization of the times, the young couple, with faith and energy, began to build up their home, bring up a family, and raise standards in a community greatly battered by the War. After twenty years, they had managed to send three of the eldest children off to college or school. Struggling with the risk of frequent changing of teachers and the expense of a subscription school, and realizing no help could come from a short-term free school, with six more children to be prepared for college, Mr. and Mrs. Wright decided it was wise for Mrs. Wright to open her own school.

When others applied for admission for their childrn, her reply was, "Let me have them, and don't you interfere." There were no day pupils and no combination with the local "free schools." Every child lived in the home, fitting into the family life, each having household duties, the girls such as bed-making and darning, and the boys such as bringing the wood and picking the peas. Duties were part of the teaching process, and work was supervised and inspected, rewards meted out or privileges withheld. Character training was part of all she did ,and religious training not omitted. Bible reading and prayer opened the school each day. " I tried to mould men and women more than I tried to make them scholars," she would say. But she did both.

The call "Books" meant getting down to the task of learning, each individual according to his capacity. She did not try to fit each one into a grade or require a set amount, but would guide hime to master thoroughly whatever he undertook. A teacher's part, she claimed, was to help himself. Tasks had to be finished yet she never pushed or nagged or scolded. She could be firm, but never hard. She taught children, not textbooks; she would explain and she caught the child's point of view. Sometimes the class would meet under the trees or study Nature out of doors. She was quick to discover the shirker; and, in the battle of wits, she came out the winner. Common sense was the whole of her psychology. Methods and theory had no place in her program, but her practice was in line with the progressive education of a later day. When playtime came, all entered into the games and sports with zest because it was rewarded for work well done. Mrs. Wright's sense of humor, love of fun, and the belief that "all work and no play made Jack a dull boy" are qualities that her former pupils often recall.

Mrs. Wright drew her teaching staff from her family. The eldest daughter, recently graduated from Mount Holyoke, was her first assistant. Then, as each of the older three daughters returned from college, she began teaching. Whenever instruction in some special subject was needed a daughter was sent where she could master that subject. Thus, after graduation from the Woman's College in Greensboro, one daughter later went to Sophia Newcombe to prepare herself adequately in French. Another daughter who had finished at Salem Academy later went to Boston for further training in Music and Kindergarten work. Occasionally another teacher was brought in; but never was the policy of the school changed. The sons were encouraged to go on with their chosen professions.

As numbers increased, the house was enlarged and a schoolhouse was built. Finally the limit of pupils was set at fifty, and many were turned away. Then the day came when Mrs. Wright, though still vigorous, realized that her objectives had been reached. All her own sons and daughters were educated and established in life. Good schools were in sight and the standards of the community had been raised. Therefore she closed her school. For eighteen years it had been a factor synonymous with high standards.

All nine of Mrs. Wright's children went to college. Four boys attended the University of North Carolina. One of these returned home to carry on the work of the farm and to become a leading citizen in his community. One became a teacher and went to a distant state but was recalled to North Carolina as president of a teachers college. One became a lawyer. And another is a prominent physician in the capital city. The fifth son who graduated from the State A. and M. College is a civil engineer in another state. All nine have reflected honor upon their teacher-mother whereas hundreds of foster children, far and wide, have exemplified the same qualities as proof that Mrs. Wright accomplished what she tried to do: "mould men and women."

Erect, with head and shoulders raised high; her naturally wavy hair, at first dark then a soft gray, always parted in the middle; her dresses with long, outspread skirts of heavy black taffeta with touches

206

of trimming on her best ones and a soft ruche of white lace at the neck; sleeves according to the style of the time; and the ever present "breast-pin"—thus Mrs. Wright always looked well dressed and never out of style. All who knew her or even saw her were impressed by her air of poise, culture, and grace.

FEMALE ACADEMIES, SEMINARIES, INSTITUTES, COLLEGES, AND OTHER SCHOOLS IN NORTH CAROLINA WITH FEMALE DEPARTMENTS

	DATES	PLACE	COUNTY
Fayetteville Academy	1800-1814		Cumberland
Raleigh Female Academy	1800		Wake
Belvidere Academy (co-ed?)	1801		Perquimans
Falkener's School for Young Ladies	1802-1819		Warren
Franklin Female Academy	1802 (authorized)		Franklin
Louisburg Female Academy	1802		Franklin
Salem College (1772 girls school) Salem Academy	1803		Forsyth
Williamston Male and Female Academy	1806		Martin
Gault's English Seminary	1807		Wake
Milligans' Female School	1807		Mecklenburg
Salisbury Female Academy	1807-1839		Rowan
Gault's Female Seminary	1807		Orange
Gregory's Boarding School	1808		Orange
Mordecai Female Seminary	1809	Warrenton	Warren
Williamsburg Female Academy	1811-1838		Vance
Vine Hill Academy	1811-1900	Scotland Neck	Halifax
Mrs. Bevens' School for Girls	1812	Mecklenburg	
Oxford Female Academy	1814		
Jamestown Female Seminary	1815		Guilford
Miltons Female Academy	1815	Charlotte	Caswell
Munford's Female School	1815		Granville
Prendergast's School for Girls	1818		Caswell
Union Female Academy Male and Female	1818		Orange
Wake Forest Female Academy	1818		Wake
Graves' Female Boarding School	1819	Chapel Hill	Orange
Warrenton Female Academy	1819-1830		Warren
Mrs. Harriett J. Allen's School	1820-1834	Warrenton	Warren
Anson Male and Female Academy or Wadesboro Academy	1820		Anson
Mrs. Robert Edmonds' Female Boarding School	1820		Anson
Greensboro Female Academy	1820		Guilford
Midway Female Academy	1820	Pactolus	Pitt
Lawrenceville Female Academy	1821		Montgomery
Lincolnton Male Academy	1821		Lincoln
Andrews and Jones Female Academy	1822		Granville

	DATES	PLACE	COUNTY
Charlotte Female Academy	1822		Mecklenburg
Littleton Select School	1822		Halifax
Shocco Academy (male department added)	1822		Warren
Shady Grove Male and Female Academy	1822		Warren
New Bern Academy— Female Dept.	1823		Craven
North Carolina Academy	1823	Oxford and Williamsborough	Granville
Morganton Female Academy	1824		Burke
Ballantine's Seminary	1825		Caswell
Hillsborough Female Seminary	1825-1836		Orange
Sunnyside Female Seminary	1825	Mocksville	Davie
Pittsboro Female Academy	1825		Chatham
William Greene Female Seminary	1825	Hillsboro	Orange
Mrs. Stith's Female Seminary	1826		Caswell
Rychman's School for Girls	1826	Wilmington	New Hanover
Smithfield Female Academy	1827		Johnston
Mount Pleasant Female Academy	1827		Cherokee
Nelson's Female School	1827	Graham	Alamance
Chapman's Select School for Young Ladies	1828		Iredell
Cushman's School for Girls	1828		Mecklenburg
The Kelvin School	1828		Chatham
McPheeter's School for Girls	1828	Raleigh	Wake
Rock Rest Academy	1828		Alamance
Tarboro Collegiate Institute	1828		Edgecombe
Lumsden Private School	1828-1839	Raleigh	Wake
Anderson's Female Academy or Boarding School	1830		Orange
Asheville Female Academy	1830-1842		Buncombe
Mrs. Bobbitt's School 8 miles from Louisburg	1830		Franklin
Greenville Female Academy	1830		Pitt
Sparta Academy Male and Female	1830	Tarboro	Edgecomb
Asheville Female College	1830-1901		Buncombe
Forest Hill Academy	1831		Wake
Kerr's Male and Female School	1831		Wake
Pitt Female Academy	1831		Pitt
Berkeley's Literary Scientific Institute for Young Ladies	1831		Wake
Pleasant Grove Academy Female Dept.	1832		Granville or Wake

	DATES	PLACE	COUNTY
Rolesville Female Academy	1832	Wil-mington	New Hanover
Mrs. Bingham's School	1834		New Hanover
Northampton Academy Female Dept.	1835		
Corbin's —Miss Sarah Jane School	1836-1838		New Hanover
Lochiel Boarding School 1 mile from Hillsboro	1836		Orange
Phillips Female Academy	1836		Halifax
Phillips School for Girls	1836-1839	Chapel Hill	Orange
Phillips Female Seminary	1836	Chapel Hill	Orange
Burwell's Female Academy	1837-39		Orange
Hannah Moore Academy	1837		Duplin
Edgeworth Female Seminary	1837-1871	Greensboro	Guilford
Grant's Female Boarding School	1837	Near Enfield	Halifax
La Vallee Female Seminary	1837		Wayne
Scotland Neck Female Seminary	1837		Halifax
Wilkesboro Female Seminary	1837		Wilkes
Tarboro Male and Female Academy	1838		Edgecombe
Trenton's Female Academy	1838		Jones
Wood's Female Academy	1838		Northampton
Greensboro Female College	1838 (opened 1846)		Guilford
Asheborough Female Academy	1839		Randolph
Cobia's Select Boarding School	1839		Chatham
Oaky Mount Academy 9 miles east of Raleigh	1839		Wake
Randolph Female Academy	1839		Randolph
Miss Bessie Simpson's School for Girls	1839		New Hanover
Goldsboro Female Academy	1840		Wayne
Grant's Female Boarding School	1840		Halifax
Lloyd and Bailey (Misses) School	1840	Wil-mington	New Hanover
Floral College (Female)	1841-1878	Shoe Heel	Robeson
Warrenton Female College	1841		Warren
Clemmonsville High School (co-ed)	1842		Randolph
Asheboro Female College	1842		Randolph
Saint Mary's School for Girls	1842	Raleigh	Wake
Black Creek Female Institution	1846		Wake
Miss Sophie Partridge Boarding School for Girls	1846		Wake

	DATES	PLACE	COUNTY
Mitchell Female College Statesville F. College (First Concordia)	1846		Iredell
Warrenton Collegiate Institute	1846		Warren
Clio Academy	1847		Iredell
Leasburg Classical School	1847-1860		Caswell
Somerville Female Seminary	1847-1892	Leaksville	Caswell
Chowan Female Institute Later College (Baptist)	1849-1942 1849	Murfrees- boro	Hertford
Sylva Grove Seminary Glen Anna and Thomasville F. College	1849		Davidson
Lexington Academy (Female Dept.)	1850		Davidson
St. Katherine's Hall (Jackson)	1850		Northampton
Carolina Female College	1850-1858	Ansonville	Anson
Wilson Female Academy	1853		Wilson
Murfreesboro Female College	1853-1893	Wesleyan F. Col.	Hertford
Wilson Female College	1853		Wilson
Goldsboro Female College Same as Wayne F. Col.	1854		Wayne
Clinton Female College	1855		Sampson
Louisburg Female College	1857 (as "college")		Franklin
Oakdale Female Seminary	1857		
Presbyterian College (Queen's)	1857	Char- lotte	Mecklenburg
Mt. Pleasant Female Seminary Evangelical Lutheran	1858		Cabarrus
Nash and Kollock's School for Young Ladies	1858	Hillsboro	Orange
Clay Hill Seminary	1858	Mocksville	Davie
Concordia College	1858	Statesville	Iredell
Davenport Female College	1858	Lenoir	Caldwell
Hendersonville Female College Same as Judson and Western	1858		Henderson
Smith Wood Female College	1859		Guilford
Methodist Female College	1859	Jamestown	Guilford
Wesleyan Female College	1859	Murfrees- borough	Hertford
Greenlee Male and Female Academy	1867		McDowell
Shelby Female College Davenport moved there for 2 years	1867		Cleveland
Mount Amoena Female Seminary	1868	Mt. Pleasant	

	DATES	PLACE	COUNTY
Twitty and Jones School for Girls Mrs. Pendleton's School	1869		Warren
Fayetteville Female Seminary	1871		Cumberland
Wilson Collegiate Institutes for boys and girls	1871-1874		Wilson
Peace Institute	1872	Raleigh	Wake
Claremont Female College	1880	Hickory	Catawba
Oxford Female Seminary (college later)	1880		Granville
Chapman's Select School for Young Ladies	1881		Wayne
Graham Normal College (co-ed)	1881		Alamance
Littleton Female College	1883		Halifax
Kinsey Female Seminary	1886		Lenoir
Asheville Normal School	1887		Buncombe
Henderson Female College "Rhoees'" School Littleton Moved for short time.	1890		Vance
Normal and Industrial School for Girls (Woman's College UNC)	1892	Greensboro	Guilford
Flora Macdonald College (Red Springs successor to)	1896		Scotland
Elizabeth College	1897	Charlotte	Mecklenburg
Meredith College (Baptist Female University)	1898		Wake
Fassifern-Lincolnton, Hendersonville	1906		Lincolnton

For The Following The Dates Are Unknown To The Author:

School	Location	County
Miss Margaret Eastwood's Boarding School		Wake
Katherine Hall School		Northhampton
Leaksville Female Academy		Rockingham
Liberty Hall Female Academy	Salisbury	Rowan
Mt. Almaena		
Mt. Bernon School		Chatham
Raleigh Female Benevolent Society		Wake
Mrs. Ransom's Female Academy		New Hanover
Scotland Neck Female Academy (same as Hine Hall later)		Halifax
Wiley's Select School		Rowan
Miss Williams' Select School for Girls		New Hanover
Wilmington Female Benevolent Society		New Hanover
Baptist Female College	Raleigh	Wake
Charlotte Female Institutes		Mecklenburg
Charlotte Methodist College		Mecklenburg
Greenvile Female Seminary		
Highland College	1 year	
Linwood College		Gaston
Southern Female Classical Seminary	Williamsboro & Oxford	Granville
Wiley's Select School for Young Ladies	Salisbury	Rowan
Willamsborough Young Ladies' and Gentlemen's	Granville	Vance
Wilson College and Female Seminary		Wilson